The
Good-for-Your-Health
All-Asian Cookbook

*Low-Sodium, Low-Fat, Low-Cholesterol,
and Low-Calorie Gourmet Recipes from
China, India, Indonesia, Japan, Korea,
Malaysia, the Philippines, Singapore,
Thailand, and Vietnam*

Low-Sodium, Low-Fat, Low-Cholesterol, and Low-Calorie Gourmet Recipes from China, India, Indonesia, Japan, Korea, Malaysia, the Philippines, Singapore, Thailand, and Vietnam

The
Good-for-Your-Health
All-Asian Cookbook

by
Marie Wilson

CHARLES E. TUTTLE COMPANY
Rutland, Vermont & Tokyo, Japan

Published by the Charles E. Tuttle Company, Inc.
of Rutland, Vermont & Tokyo, Japan
with editorial offices at
2-6 Suido 1-chome, Bunkyo-ku, Tokyo 112

LCC Card No. 89-50955
ISBN 0-8048-1559-3

First edition, 1989

Printed in Japan

To
My mother

Contents

Desserts   319

Appendixes   329

Preface

When I wrote *Siamese Cookery* more than twenty years ago, I was blissfully ignorant of the hazards of too much fat, cholesterol, and sodium in the diet. Having spent many years in Thailand, I was addicted to all the mouth-watering foods of the area, especially the salty sauces and the deep-fried dishes. Monosodium glutamate had a niche next to my salt shaker, and I used soy sauce, fish sauces, and Chinese condiments liberally. I also loved eggs, steak, butter, cream-rich desserts, and especially French cheeses. I had the best of both worlds, and, insofar as good health is concerned, the worst.

I fear this may be happening to affluent Japanese in Japan today. To their salty diet they are adding the West's penchant for beef, cream, butter, and eggs. The trend is noteworthy enough to make news in the American press. An article from the *New York Times* describes exquisite French-inspired pastries by Yukio Sakase available at a Japanese pastry shop in Tokyo. His green-tea genoise contained four whole eggs and one egg yolk and his green-tea mousse, one cup of heavy cream. They were described as "maintaining the incomparable softness of the genoise and the silken airiness of mousse and Bavarian cream." I'm sure that if I were in Japan today I would have a difficult time resisting such tantalizing temptations.

My purpose in writing this book was to prove that it is possible to prepare conspicuously delicious Asian dishes without the use of salt. It proved to be an enormous challenge, but the variety of seasonings and exotic flavorings that these countries have to offer can not only substitute for the taste for salt but also overcome the need for it. What follows is a collection of recipes for lovers of Asian foods who are seeking better health without sacrificing the pleasures of good eating. I hope also to appeal to those who are not familiar with Asian foods but who watch their diets and wish to enlarge their repertory of good-tasting recipes that are

xi

low in fat, sodium, and cholesterol. My concern is lowering the risk for heart disease, high blood pressure, and cancer—to the extent that such a diet can do so—by eating good-tasting and attractive foods.

I go on the assumption that if the food doesn't taste good, the chances are excellent that the diet, and the good intentions behind it, will disappear within a short time. The principles and guidelines I have followed are recommended by the American Heart Association, the National Academy of Sciences, and other leading medical authorities.

I have selected only those dishes that could be satisfactorily adapted to remain as good tasting as the originals. Very little fat is used in their preparation, and salt and monosodium glutamate have been wholly forsaken. In their place stand those miracles of flavor and aroma: garlic, fresh ginger root, spices, and herbs to add zest and pungency; pepper, chilies, horseradish, and mustard powder for those who like food hot; and wine, lemon juice, vinegar, and sugar for a sweet-and-sour touch. All these ingredients can spark foods to new taste pleasures without the need for salt. Keep in mind that it took a lifetime to acquire this taste for salt and salty condiments, so you cannot expect to change it overnight. If you cut back a little at a time, your taste buds will gradually become so used to savoring other flavors that some foods and seasonings that were once craved and found palatable will seem intolerably salty and wholly inedible.

—Marie Wilson

Acknowledgments

I would like to acknowledge my indebtedness to the many writers and cooks who brought me closer to the cultures and cooking of Asia, and to those in the fields of health and medicine whose writings helped me to understand more fully the connection between diet and health. Reading their works started me on long and pleasurable journeys of experimentation, and without their help this book would not have been possible. Their names and works are listed in the bibliography.

I am also grateful to the University of California East Asiatic Library and the South/Southeast Asia Library in Berkeley, from whose collections the drawings for this book have been derived.

My special thanks also go to those who helped with the following chapters: China: Zhang Yaqi, an exchange teacher from Hunan Teachers University, who demonstrated to me that large quantities of soy sauce are not necessary to prepare good-tasting Chinese food; India: Amrita Sengupta; Indonesia: Tati Gonomondo and Krishni Simanjuntak; Japan: Masayo Watanabe Wilson, my very dear daughter-in-law and friend; Korea: Clare You, who introduced me to Korean food and who gave so generously of her time; Pakistan: Naheed Aftab; and Vietnam: Chanh Nguyen. For professional advice about the nutrient analysis of foods, thanks to Carol Lynn Carr, R.D., Helen Black, R.D., Nan Moon, R.D., and to Teresa Chew, R.D., for the use of her work on Chinese condiments in sodium-restricted diets. Her article is also listed in the bibliography. Thanks are also due to Jack and Mary Murchio for advice on weights and measures and for the use of their art library, to Barbara Phillips for her editing skills, and to Stephen Comee for his. My thanks to him also for six of the recipes. I could not have been luckier. I am deeply grateful to all, but I alone am responsible for any mistakes.

Acknowledgment is also due to The Centre, a meeting place for families from all over the world who are visiting the United States as students and scholars at the University of California at Berkeley. They came together and generously shared their customs and foods.

My biggest debt is to my children, Elizabeth and Stephen, who spent a significant part of their formative years in Thailand and Japan, for their professional advice, gentle encouragement, and unflagging support. No words of thanks will ever be enough. As medical practitioners, talented cooks, and loving children, they both sustained me to a degree that only I can appreciate.

Introduction

You've heard the warnings loud and clear: cut back on meats, salt, eggs, butter, cream—all those rich, zesty, fatty, flavorful foods—or risk developing heart disease, high blood pressure, and cancer. You wonder what to do. Must you give up all the foods you love and face a lifetime of thin soup and boiled mush? Happily not! At least not if you take advantage of the variety of exciting flavors that Asian cooking has to offer. You can still eat delicious food, and lots of it, while automatically protecting your health and maintaining your ideal weight. Whether you have a family history of disease, or have no health problems at all and want to stay that way, the recipes in this book are for you.

Asian cookery is remarkable for its variety of delectable taste sensations and health-promoting benefits. The dishes I've selected and modified for this book retain the tantalizing flavors—the redolence of ginger and garlic, the zing of sweet and sour—while further increasing the nutritional advantages. The main health benefits of Asian cooking come from its emphasis on plant foods: vegetables, legumes, and starches. Meats play only a supporting role: in a meat recipe, just two or three ounces per portion, but it is appetizingly cooked with lots of vegetables that contain no cholesterol.

"Two or three ounces!" (I hear you protest), "What about protein?" If you're a Westerner, you were probably brought up with the idea that if your dinner plate wasn't dominated by a big slab of meat you'd suffer a dire protein deficiency. Science has proven that to be wrong. You were probably told that to be healthy and slim you'd have to cut out carbohydrates, including starches such as bread, rice, potatoes, and noodles, in favor of protein foods, such as meat, cheese, and eggs. Wrong again. In fact, red meat is loaded largely with fat, not protein, and that fat is packed with heart-threatening cholesterol. It may also lead to certain types of cancer, and ounce for ounce it contributes twice the number of calories that starches and other carbohydrates do. While droves of Western dieters following the protein myth have succeeded only in gaining weight and endangering their health, millions of people in the Far East have stayed fit and slim on little or no meat but large amounts of vegetables, legumes, and rice. So, by substituting chicken and fish for red meat and by emphasizing vegetables, legumes, and starches, the recipes in this book will help you to lower your risk of heart disease and cancer and to reduce automatically the number of calories you consume.

The high-fiber content of vegetables earns another plus for Asian cooking. Science now shows that a high-fiber diet reduces the risk of certain forms of cancer and helps to lower cholesterol levels. It also combats constipation and other intestinal disorders. And for weight watchers, fiber provides a very low-calorie way to satisfy the appetite.

Even some of the Asian cooking techniques deliver health benefits. Most notably, there's steaming and stir-frying, which not only seal in the flavor and original color of foods but also ensure a maximum retention of vitamins.

"Come on now," (the skeptics among you say), "aren't there any health shortcomings to Asian cookery?" Yes, there are three serious ones, but they are corrected in this book. In fact, that's what this book is all about. Asian cooking normally tends to rely on (1) salty condiments (bad news for people with high blood pressure), (2) monosodium glutamate (MSG, also sold as *Aji-no-moto,* a high-sodium taste enhancer to which many people are allergic), and (3) large quantities of fat for deep frying (inviting heart disease, cancer, and obesity).

The challenge I faced in developing the book was to choose the healthiest of Asian recipes and then to modify them to remain as delicious as the originals while containing no salt, no MSG, and very little fat. I believe I have succeeded. Very few of my recipes contain beef, pork, and lamb, because red meat is highest in cholesterol. Instead they contain chicken and fish. In place of salt, MSG, and large quantities of salty condiments, they achieve zest and pungency with ginger, chilies, garlic, and a range of other herbs and spices.

But before going on to the recipes, you may want to read a bit about the scientific findings concerning your health and what you eat. The sources from which I took these findings are listed in the back of the book.

Salt and High Blood Pressure

A high salt intake can lead to high blood pressure and its potentially fatal consequences, cardiovascular disease and stroke. The incidence of heart disease is practically nonexistent in pre-industrialized cultures where little or no salt is added to foods.

In the Solomon Islands of the South Pacific, scientists observed two tribes, one living in the hills and one on a lagoon. Each was similar to the other except for the high incidence of hypertension in one tribe and the low incidence in the other. The hill people ate almost no salt at all because they boiled their food in rain or well water. They had a low incidence of hypertension. The lagoon people cooked their food in salty sea water, thus taking in 15 to 20 grams of salt a day. They had a high incidence of hypertension.

In Japan, where hypertension is the leading cause of death, the disease is more frequent in the north than in the south. This is not surprising, since salt consumption is highest in the north.

Your body needs salt, of course, or rather the sodium contained in it. But the amount of sodium required—about 230 milligrams per day—is miniscule compared with the 4,000 to 8,000 milligrams that Americans now consume. The 230 milligrams are easily supplied by the food you would eat daily in its natural state. So where do the other thousands of milligrams come from? Well, one teaspoon of salt contains about 2,000 milligrams. Hundreds and thousands of more milligrams come from processed foods bought at the supermarket, restaurant, and fast-food counter. One ounce of cornflakes, for example, contains about 350 milligrams; two slices of bread, about 260; one cup of canned chicken noodle soup prepared with water, 1,100 milligrams; a fast-food hamburger, about 990; and a fast-food chicken dinner, about 2,200. So cutting back on salt may be harder than it sounds if processed foods with hidden amounts of sodium are consumed regularly.

Heart Disease and Cholesterol, Fats, and Fish Oil

Cholesterol Is the way to a man's heart still through his stomach? It most certainly is. But the old saying has now taken on a second meaning. Give him a regular diet high in cholesterol and saturated fat and you will increase his risk of a heart attack.

Cholesterol—a soft waxlike substance found among the fats in the bloodstream—may build up on the inner lining of blood vessels and, over time, obstruct them. This narrowing of the blood vessels, called atherosclerosis, keeps oxygen-carrying blood from getting to the heart. The result can be severe chest pain and eventually heart attack.

Our bodies need some cholesterol to maintain health and we get it in two ways. Our livers manufacture it naturally no matter what we eat, and we ingest it by eating foods of animal origin such as egg yolks, meats, poultry, fish, and dairy products. No plant-derived foods, whether fruits, vegetables, grains, or nuts, contain cholesterol.

Studies have shown what can happen when people from a country with a low-fat diet move to a country with a high one. Japanese living in Japan, where fat consumption is low, have low blood cholesterol levels and a low rate of heart disease. Japanese who have migrated to Hawaii, where fat consumption is higher, suffer significantly more heart attacks than their stay-at-home cousins. Those who have settled in California, where fat intake is even higher, suffer more heart attacks still.

The evidence mounts daily that most people, even those with an inherited tendency to heart disease, can substantially reduce their risk of heart disease by following a low-cholesterol diet. Some studies even show that cholesterol reduction helps reverse cholesterol deposits that have already formed. But cholesterol is not the whole story.

Fats—Saturated, Polyunsaturated, and Monounsaturated   Perhaps equal in importance to the actual amount of cholesterol in the diet may be the amount of saturated fats that are consumed. They tend to raise the cholesterol level in your blood no matter how little cholesterol you ingest.

Saturated fats are the fats that become hard at room temperature. They're found primarily in animal products such as meats, cheese, butter, cream, whole milk, and egg yolks. They're also found in some vegetable products such as coconut oil, palm oil, and cocoa butter.

But now the fat story brightens. Two types of fat may actually be beneficial for cholesterol control. Polyunsaturated fats, such as safflower, corn, and sesame oils, and monounsaturated fats such as olive oil and peanut oil, may help to lower blood cholesterol levels. Of course our bodies need some fat to maintain health, but you shouldn't eat too much of these beneficial fats either, since all fats may pose a cancer risk.

Fish Oil   Rapidly mounting evidence shows that eating certain ocean fish at least twice a week, in place of meat or eggs and butter fats, may diminish your risk of coronary heart disease. This new research from the University of Leiden in the Netherlands, the Oregon Health Sciences University, and Harvard Medical School[*] has shown that fatty fish, with their high levels of omega-3 fatty acids, may be even more useful than polyunsaturated vegetable oils when it comes to lowering blood cholesterol levels. In fact, fish oils may also affect another aspect of body chemistry beneficially: by reducing the stickiness of certain cells important in blood clotting, they may help prevent blood clots from forming and blocking your arteries, thereby reducing your risk of heart attack and stroke.

The discovery of the beneficial value of fish oils grew out of observations by Danish researchers in the 1970s that had long seemed contradictory to cardiologists. Why did Eskimos, who eat huge amounts of animal fats, have such a low rate of coronary heart disease? Similarly, in coastal regions of Japan where despite rampant high blood pressure caused by high salt intake, heart attacks are not a frequent cause of death. One logical explanation put forward was that Eskimos are genetically resistant to heart attacks. But it turned out that it was not their genes that protect

---

[*]   Articles about the benefits of fish olls are listed in the bibliography under Dr. Daan Kromhart of the University of Leiden, Dr. Tak H. Lee of the Harverd Medical School, and Dr. Beverley E. Phillipson of the Oregon Health Sclences University.

them, because the few who move to Denmark and switch to the local diet are just as prone to heart disease as Danes.

The studies applied only to salt-water fish. It is unknown whether fresh-water fish would produce the same results. Fish richest in these protective oils are those that live in deep, cold waters. Examples include salmon, tuna, and Atlantic mackerel. Shellfish, such as shrimp and lobster, though higher in cholesterol than fish, also have this protective fish oil and are now considered desirable alternatives to red meat once or twice a week.

Fats, Fiber, and Cancer

Eating too much fat (both saturated and unsaturated) not only increases the risk of heart disease but may also lead to cancer of the colon, breast, prostate, and lining of the uterus. Consider colon cancer, prominent in nearly all the countries where heart disease is a major killer. The scientific evidence suggests that a diet low in fat and high in fiber (especially from whole grains, fruits, and vegetables) can help prevent this cancer. In Japan, for example, with its traditionally low-fat, high-fiber diet, colon cancer is rare. But when Japanese migrate to the United States and ultimately adopt a largely Western diet, their rates of the disease approach the high U.S. rate.

Of course there are other risk factors that play a role in heart disease, high blood pressure, and cancer, such as heredity, overweight, inactivity, and smoking. With regard to heredity, there is some evidence to support the theory that though your genes may place you at high risk, it may be possible through changes in diet to minimize the consequences of genetic factors. Insofar as weight is concerned, cutting back on fats and meats in the diet reduces calories considerably, so weight control becomes much easier.

What Medical Experts Tell Us to Do

According to the American Medical Association dietary guidelines, your cholesterol intake should be kept to less than 100 milligrams per 1,000 calories and never more than 300 milligrams per day. Saturated fat should comprise less than 10% of calories, and total fat intake should account for less than 30% of total caloric intake. They also recommend that you reduce your sodium intake to about 1 gram per 1,000 calories, not to exceed 3 grams per day. For the average person eating about 2,000 calories a day, these guidelines mean a daily intake of no more than 200 milligrams of cholesterol and 2,000 milligrams of sodium.

The Heart Association also advises you to keep total calories low enough just to maintain your ideal body weight and to get your carbohydrates primarily from grains, fruits, and vegetables. The following is a summary of the dietary guidelines issued by the American Heart Association:

- Saturated fat intake should be less than 10% of calories.
- Total fat intake should be less than 30% of calories.
- Cholesterol intake should be less than 100 mg per 1,000 calories, not to exceed 300 mg per day.
- Sodium intake should be reduced to approximately 1 gram per 1,000 calories, not to exceed 3 grams per day.

Other specific dietary guidelines issued at the same time by the American Heart Association were:

- Protein intake should be approximately 15% of calories.
- Carbohydrate intake should make up 50–55% or more of calories with emphasis on increasing sources of complex carbohydrates.

If alcoholic beverages are consumed, the limit should be 15% of total calories, not to exceed 50 cc of ethanol per day.

- Total calories should be sufficient to maintain the individual's best weight.
- A wide variety of foods should be consumed.

An example for an average person consuming 2,000 calories per day:

200 milligrams of cholesterol
2,000 milligrams of sodium
22 grams of saturated fat
66 grams of total fat (1 gram of fat yields 9 calories.)

Therefore:

$$(2,000 \times 10\%) \div \text{by } 9 = 22.$$
$$(2,000 \times 30\%) \div \text{by } 9 = 66.$$

To reduce the risk of cancer, the National Academy of Sciences in its report *Diet, Nutrition and Cancer*, recommends that fat comprise no more than 30% of your total calories and preferably less. The Academy also urges the consumption of more vegetables, fruits, and whole grains, and less salt-cured, smoked, and charcoal-broiled food (these are carcinogenic). It further recommends that you moderate your consumption of alcoholic beverages, get some exercise on a regular basis and stop smoking.

How to Apply These Recommendations to Everyday Life

Developing a healthy diet means following two basic rules: moderation and variety. In other words, cut down on the things that put you at risk and eat a wide range of other foods that are rich in specific nutrients. These rules are right for everyone, not just people with already established health problems. They hold particularly exciting promise for children, who can benefit by forming tastes for the right foods early in life that may protect them when they reach adulthood.

Moderation   If your favorite foods today are high in sodium, fat, or cholesterol, you don't have to give them up entirely. Just eat less of them, and eat them less often. Don't expect to change your eating habits overnight. Do it gradually and steadily. For example, if you abruptly stop cooking with salt, you're likely to find your foods unpalatable. But if you gradually cut down on the amount you use, you'll hardly notice the difference.

The guidelines are simple and should guide you the rest of your life. Go easy on fatty meats, on animal products such as eggs, butter, and cream, and on rich desserts, processed foods, and salty snacks. Increase your intake of fresh vegetables, fruits, poultry, fish, whole grains, dried beans, and low- or nonfat milk products.

Often it is a matter of trading off. For example, if you start the day with cholesterol-rich eggs and then have a high-sodium fast-food hamburger for lunch, just eat mostly vegetables for dinner. A stir-fry of broccoli, carrots, and onions (with perhaps an ounce or two of fat-free chicken) flavored with plenty of garlic and fresh ginger root will do very nicely.

Variety   The need for a balanced diet cannot be overstressed. Eat a variety of foods with at least two servings of ocean fish per week. Include fresh fruits, vegetables, and whole-grain bread and cereals in your diet every day. For protection against certain forms of cancer, look to vegetables in the cabbage family (such as broccoli, cauliflower, cabbage, and turnips) and to fruits and vegetables that are rich in vitamins A and C (dark green vegetables and all yellow-orange fruits and vegetables such as carrots, sweet potatoes, pumpkins, squashes, cantaloupes, apricots, and citrus fruits).

In sum, good nutrition doesn't mean you have to become an extremist or food faddist. Nor does it mean you have to eat bland foods or miniscule amounts. As the recipes in this book prove, you can enjoy all the pleasures of good eating and still protect your health.

Ingredients and Cooking Tips

In the pages immediately following are notes about nutrition, ingredients, substitutions, and some cooking tips that apply to many of the recipes contained in this book.

Meat, Poultry, Seafood, Fats and Oils, and Eggs

Meats   Allow ¼ pound of uncooked, very lean meat, poultry, or fish per person. This will yield approximately 3 ounces of cooked meat (not including bone or fat).

Eat beef, lamb, and pork less frequently than poultry and fish. Pork is the preferred meat in Chinese, Thai, and Vietnamese cooking, and insofar as fat is concerned there are no very lean cuts of pork. Fortunately, chicken substitutes satisfactorily for pork in most Asian dishes. Avoid duck, goose, fatty meats, bacon, sausages, luncheon meats, and organ meats such as liver and kidney. Choose lean cuts. Half the battle is won if you take care to trim visible fat, discard poultry skin, use as little oil as possible in cooking, and skim off and discard the fat that results from the cooking process.

Chicken   Chicken provides high-quality, low-fat protein. Most of the fat is in and under the skin. Removing the skin and fat after cooking will cut your fat intake and calories considerably; removing the skin and fat *before* cooking will cut them even more. White meat has less fat and cholesterol than dark meat. Keep in mind that small young chickens are leaner than large older ones, so if you are planning a meal for a party, it's better to buy two small chickens than one big one. To estimate servings of uncooked chicken, on the average, half a medium chicken breast will yield approximately 3 ounces of cooked meat, as will a chicken leg (drumstick plus thigh).

Chicken and Beef Stock or Bouillon   Stocks and bouillon can add large amounts of salt and fat to a soup. When unsalted chicken stock is called for in a dish, the recipe on page 10 in the Japanese section is recommended. There is also a recipe for beef stock on page 69 in the Korean chapter. Be sure to make the broth a day before you plan to use it to allow for defatting after refrigeration.

If desired, canned or powdered low-sodium chicken and beef stock or bouillon may be substituted. Canned stock should be refrigerated before the can is opened so that visible fat may be removed before using. To season canned stock, heat it with a slice or two of fresh ginger root.

Fish and Seafood   Fish and seafood provide high-quality, low-fat protein with fewer calories than meat. Actually, up until recently it was widely believed that fatty fish and shellfish should be avoided, and the best choices were thus thought to be lean fish like sole and flounder. However, recent research reported in the *New England Journal of Medicine* has shown that these fatty fish, with their high levels of polyunsaturated fatty acids, known as omega-3s, may be useful in lowering blood cholesterol levels and are therefore recommended as desirable substitutes for red meat once or twice a week. Moreover, shellfish, especially shrimp, are no longer prohibited from diets designed to lower blood cholesterol, because improved laboratory techniques have shown that they are not as high in cholesterol as was thought in the past. An important point to be made in comparing fatty fish with red meat is that the fat content of fish ranges from less than 1 percent to 13 percent. This is very different from the fat content of red meat, which ranges from 10 percent to over 30 percent. Thus, the fish with the highest percentage of fat is almost as lean as the red meat with the lowest.

The benefits of omega-3s notwithstanding, health practitioners warn against taking cod-liver oil or fish-oil supplements and derivatives. Their safety and efficacy have not been established, and some of these supplements may even have serious toxic effects. It is always more beneficial and more enjoyable to use the foods themselves rather than supplements.

Some seafoods that are high in omega-3 fatty acids include Atlantic mackerel, herring and sardines, blue fish, four varieties of salmon—pink, chinook, red or sockeye, and coho—rainbow trout, lake whitefish, sablefish, American eel, European anchovy, Pacific oysters, New Zealand green mussels, squid, and striped mullet'albacore and blue fin tuna. Many of these, such as squid and fresh tuna, are more appreciated in other cultures than they are in the United States.

The cardinal rule to follow when preparing fish is that it must be very fresh and it must not be overcooked. A simple way to estimate cooking time is to measure the fish at its thickest point and cook it no longer than 10 minutes per inch. Keep in mind that fatty fish is more perishable than lean fish and should be cooked on the day it is purchased. If you are unable to cook any oily fish immediately, marinating is a good way to keep it for a day or two.

Squid   Squid is widely appreciated in Asian and Mediterranean countries. It is caught along the southern Californian coast, but most of it is canned for export. Recently, it has begun to win favor in the United States, earning the affectionate title of the "poor man's abalone." It is an inexpensive protein food whose fat content is only about 1 percent and it is very low in calories. But its cholesterol content is high and varies dramatically depending on the season. On the average, after cleaning, it contains approximately 250 milligrams in 3½ ounces. To stay within the recommended allowances for cholesterol, it is suggested that squid be eaten only in small amounts.

If it is fresh, squid will be sweet-smelling and ivory colored (not yellow) beneath its spotted skin. Also, the transparent quill or center bone should detach easily. The tentacles are a substantial portion of the squid's edible meat and should not be discarded. The ink from the squid was an important source for Europe's ink, called sepia, until about half a century ago, when other dyes were invented.

In some countries, notably Spain and Italy, this ink is used as an ingredient in cooking. Arroz negro (black rice) is rice cooked with squid, tomato, peppers, onions, and squid ink mixed with wine. It is served with a potent garlic-olive oil sauce. Spaghetti nero is al-dente cooked pasta that is served with a sauce made by sauteing minced garlic in olive oil and adding the squid ink and small pieces of chopped squid.

The maximum cooking time for stir-fried squid is three minutes. For moist cooking, baking, or stewing, at least 20 minutes are required to tenderize it. Do not marinate squid any more than 30 minutes, or the meat may soften too much; and be warned that it will taste bitter if vinegar or lemon juice is used.

Cooking Fats and Oils   Safflower oil is preferable to other vegetable oils because it is lighter and has more polyunsaturated fat and less saturated fat than other oils. In this book, it is substituted for pork fat and lard, and for coconut oil, which is highly saturated. *Ghee* used in Indian cooking is similar to clarified butter, which is pure butter fat with all the milk solids removed. Safflower oil or polyunsaturated margarine takes its place. Avoid solid vegetable shortenings and substitute polyunsaturated vegetable oils and margarines. The total fat and calorie content may be the same, but the saturated fat content is much lower and there is no cholesterol in pure vegetable fats. Ideally, the oil or margarine should contain at least twice as much polyunsaturated (P) as saturated (S) fatty acids.

If the label shows a P/S ratio, it should be 2 to 1 or higher. Also, do not buy margarines that list "partially hydrogenated" or "hardened" oil as the first ingredient. The label should list *liquid* vegetable oil as the main ingredient. Avoid any product that contains coconut or palm oil. (*See* Fat-Cholesterol-Sodium Tables on pages 332–34.)

To cut down on the quantity of fat needed in cooking, Teflon- or SilverStone-coated nonstick pans are recommended because foods brown nicely in them without sticking, even when the smallest amount of grease is used. Do not heat fat to the smoking point. Fat that begins to smoke releases undesirable chemicals and should be discarded.

Eggs Eat no more than 3 egg yolks a week, including eggs used in cooking and baking. A single egg yolk has 265 to 275 milligrams of cholesterol, nearly the maximum amount recommended for an entire day. More than half the protein in eggs is in the white, which is free of fat and cholesterol and can therefore be eaten in unrestricted amounts. The yolk is nearly twice as rich in fat as it is in protein and has more than three times the number of calories found in the white. These facts should not be cause for giving up omelets. A very good one can be made with 1 egg yolk and 3 whites. Feed the unused yolks to your pets. They do not get atherosclerosis because unlike humans they excrete cholesterol.

Another alternative is to use an egg substitute. Commercial egg substitutes that are made from egg whites are available in the dairy section of the supermarket. Read the labels carefully, however, and do not buy any that contain coconut oil, palm oil, or other saturated fat. A recipe for an egg substitute based on one from an American Heart Association cookbook will be found in the Korean section under Fish Fillets and Vegetables Wrapped in Egg Batter on pages 75–76. Still another American Heart Association cookbook recommends an even simpler substitute: for each egg in a recipe, substitute 1 egg white and 2 teaspoons vegetable oil. For recipes that require a lot of eggs, such as a sponge cake or a souffle, these substitutions will not work, though they will work for other cake and cookie recipes. Some experimenting may be required.

About Some Essential Ingredients Used in These Recipes

Black Pepper A native of India and Indonesia, black pepper is the berry of a tropical vine. It is green when immature and red and yellow when ripe. The berries are gathered before they are ripe and allowed to dry in the sun. The result is black peppercorns. Black pepper is lower down on the heat scale than chilies, but when sprinkled generously on food it wakes up the tongue and enhances the flavor of the food itself rather than overpowering it. Black pepper is used extensively in Asian cooking and is one of the main spices in the *garam masalas* of India. Perhaps larger amounts are added to these dishes than you are used to. If you wish, use a smaller quantity but keep your peppermill (not your salt shaker) on the table to add more if you need it.

Chili Peppers   The chili pepper is an indispensable ingredient in Asian cooking. It was once thought to have been brought to Asia from the New World by way of Spain and Portugal, but some botanists believe that the plant, like corn, was carried by pre-Columbian voyagers across the Pacific from the Americas. As a general rule, the smaller the size of a chili, the hotter it is. For example, the tiny, pea-sized chilies used in Thai and Indonesian dishes can be so excruciatingly hot that they will jolt the palate like an electric shock, bringing tears to the eyes and a searing blast to the nasal passages. Devotees of this chili swear that when the discomfort subsides, only pleasure remains. The amount used in a dish is a matter of taste. Not all palates can tolerate chilies. For me, too much chili is a palate-searing assault that overpowers all other tastes in the dish. There are many varieties of chilies with differing flavors and uses, but I have not specified which to use in these recipes, although fresh ones are preferable to dried ones. Serrano chilies are the choice of many cooks, though I prefer the Anaheim chili because it is milder. But chilies are notoriously unpredictable.

Even chilies of the same variety can vary drastically in heat and flavor depending on the soil they were grown in. When I do not have fresh chilies on hand, I resort to my supply of small dried red ones and usually use one or two at the most. Dried chili flakes are also very convenient and have a nice flavor. Both fresh and dried chilies are no longer difficult to find and are available in almost every supermarket.

A word of caution about handling fresh chilies. More heat is concentrated in the white ribs and seeds than in the flesh itself. So if the ribs are large enough they should be scraped away and discarded. You may want to wear a pair of gloves when cutting chilies as the chili oils may be irritating to your hands. Do not rub your face or eyes after handling them, as these oils will cause painful irritation. Dried chilies will provide almost as much heat and flavor as fresh chilies, but their effect on the skin is less irritating.

Coconut Milk   An essential ingredient in the cooking of nearly all coconut-growing countries, coconut milk is used in soups, curries, and meat and fish dishes, as well as in sweets. It is not the delicious clear fluid found inside of a young coconut. Rather, it is the milky liquid extracted from grated fresh coconut or from dried (desiccated) shredded coconut. It has a unique flavor and richness that no other ingredient can duplicate exactly.

Twenty years ago it was almost impossible to find coconut in the United States except for the very sweet packaged variety used for desserts or the occasional wizened coconuts found in some markets. Today desiccated coconut is easy to find in many markets and health food stores. However, some visitors from Southeast Asia have commented that no dried shredded coconut they have bought in the United States is really satisfactory, because it has an unpleasant after-taste, which is a sign that the coconut is too old or rancid.

In the countries where it grows, they say, a coconut at this stage of life is called copra and is turned into coconut oil, the main cooking fat for many of the region's people, especially Muslims, who do not use pork fat. It is also used in the manufacture of soap, perfume, and face and hair creams. For the freshest taste and ease of preparation, unsweetened canned coconut milk, both fresh and frozen, is by far the best tasting. The brand that comes from Thailand, called *Cheokoh*, is superior, although one other, a frozen brand from the Philippines, is also good. It must be kept in mind that though it contains no cholesterol, coconut is high in saturated fat, which medical practitioners warn should be used in limited quantities in a low-fat diet. Keep in mind that there are about 280 calories, 25 grams of saturated fat, and 0.5 grams of polyunsaturated fat in one cup of coconut, an obviously unfavorable P/S ratio.

Substitutes for coconut milk: In these recipes, I have substituted low-fat yogurt wherever possible. However, if more authentic taste is desired, some coconut milk mixed with a similar amount of stock, water, or nonfat milk may be used. You can vary the amount further by changing the proportion of coconut milk to the diluting liquid. I have tried bottled coconut extract as a substitute for coconut milk and put a few drops of the extract in nonfat milk. While the result certainly gives a coconut flavor, it is too artificial for my taste. However, it may be worth trying if you wish to cut down further on fat. Though my preference is for low-fat yogurt, which has so many health-giving properties, buttermilk, which is marvelously tangy, is another good substitute for coconut milk and blends well with spicy sauces. Both yogurt and buttermilk are low in saturated fat and have a lot more flavor than nonfat milk, though they are decidedly different in taste from coconut milk. It is all a matter of individual taste and the choice is yours.

Please note that my book on Thai cooking (*Siamese Cookery*; Tuttle, 1965; p. 36), which recommended the use of sour cream as a substitute for coconut milk, gained the hearty approval of Thai friends living in the States. Though it does not resemble the taste of coconut, it is very delicious and has the rich, thickening effect of coconut milk. Unfortunately, it is too high in saturated animal fat to be considered for use in this book.

Making coconut milk: To make coconut milk from desiccated coconut, the quickest way is to use a blender. Mix 1 cup desiccated coconut with 1 ¼ cups very hot water and blend at least 30 seconds. Strain through a piece of cloth or fine sieve squeezing out all the moisture. This will be the richest coconut milk and will yield approximately 1 cupful. You may repeat the process using the same coconut pulp and 1 ¼ cups more hot water. Then discard the pulp. The yield will be thinner but still flavorful and with less saturated fat.

If you have no blender, combine the desiccated coconut and hot water in a bowl. When it cools, mix and squeeze repeatedly with your hands and then strain.

To make coconut milk from freshly grated coconuts, use warm water instead of hot. Proceed as above to extract the milk. Dishes with coconut milk should be stirred frequently and not allowed to boil. It is also best not to cover the pot, as drops of hot water that fall from the lid into the mixture may cause it to curdle.

Note: For those who wish to cut down drastically on saturated fat, no matter whether the coconut milk is hand extracted or ready made, it is recommended that you let the milk stand in the refrigerator for a few hours to allow the rich layer to rise to the top, so you can skim off the cream, much as cream is skimmed off dairy milk.

Coriander Coriander is an indispensable herb in Asian cooking. All parts of the plant are used. The seed is used in blends of curry powder and the fresh coriander leaf—called Chinese parsley, Mexican parsley or cilantro—is used in soups and garnishes. It has a pungent, spicy taste and aroma that some find too strong. It is available in the produce sections of most supermarkets.

Garlic Almost every dish in this book has garlic in it. It not only imparts a marvelous flavor to foods, but also, as medical studies have shown, may have a wide range of health benefits as well. Related to the onion, leek, and shallot, garlic has been cultivated since ancient times and is believed to be native to southwest Asia. Mentioned over 5,000 years ago in Sanskrit, one of the world's first written languages, garlic was also a staple in the ancient Sumerian diet. Revered by the ancient Egyptians, Romans, and Greeks for its curative powers, it was used in the treatment of a whole range of ailments ranging from headaches to tuberculosis. In ancient China garlic was worn to ward off the evil eye. It was even found entombed with King Tutankhamen. The Romans fed it to soldiers and slaves to give them courage and strength. It was thought to have protected garlic-eating French priests from contracting the Black Death from victims they attended, whereas English priests who reviled garlic caught the plague easily. By World War I, the British and Russians were using it to control infection, and the Germans used it to prevent gangrene. There are even claims made for its pesticidal properties.

In China and Japan it has been used for some time in the treatment of high blood pressure, and the Japanese food and drug administration has approved garlic therapy for this purpose. Garlic is also credited with antibiotic properties that inhibit the growth of certain fungi that cause disease.

I have learned all of this information and more by reading the daily press and several interesting books about garlic. Whether the curative powers of garlic are as all-encompassing as the reports indicate, the fact is that garlic is the one most indispensable ingredient to Asian and Mediterranean cooking. It is also important in Latin American cooking and was probably introduced there by Spanish and Portuguese explorers. Northern European immigrants to the United States disdained it—with the exception of its use by the French—until the nineteenth century, when garlic-loving immigrants from southern Europe, the Middle East, and China changed the culinary climate of the country and began the trend that has given garlic the popularity it now enjoys.

The odor from garlic, which keeps many people from eating it, is the result of a chemical action activated by mincing and pressing the clove. The greater the damage to the cell membrane, the more it will smell. Slicing and bruising will produce less odor than mincing and pressing. Also, blanching or parboiling unpeeled garlic before using will render the garlic almost odorless, as will long cooking. Another way to combat garlic odor is to chew parsley or some other chlorophyll-rich green after eating it. (Perhaps the best way to cope with garlic's aromatic property is to get everybody you know to eat it!) Use at least the amount of garlic called for in the recipes, which specify that the cloves be large.

Ginger Root   This fresh gnarled root, with an aromatic, sweet, spicy, penetrating taste, is another indispensable ingredient in Asian cooking. In the past it was available only in Asian grocery stores but now it is in the produce section of every supermarket. Peel and discard the brown skin and grate or mince the flesh. Powdered ginger cannot be substituted.

Lemon Grass   Fresh or dried, lemon grass is an essential flavor in Southeast Asian cooking. It has a bulbous root and long thin bladelike leaves with a lovely lemony fragrance. It is a hardy plant and can be grown in a pot in almost any climate. A few inches are added whole to flavor a dish. Brewed in boiling water, the leaves make a wonderful herbal tea. Grated lemon rind and lemon juice is suggested as a substitute.

Mushrooms   Only two varieties of dried mushrooms are used in these recipes. Dried Chinese and Japanese black mushrooms (*shiitake*), also known as "fragrant mushrooms," are shaped like an umbrella and have a unique flavor. They must be soaked before using and the soaking liquid is used as a stock in soups as well as in other dishes, in both Japanese and Chinese cooking. Another type of mushroom is shaped like an ear. The most common is variously known as "tree ear," "cloud ear," or "wood ear." (The Japanese name for it, *ki-kurage*, literally means "tree jellyfish.") It is prized not for its taste, which is almost negligible, but for its unique crunchy texture. It also must be soaked before cooking.

Noodles Four varieties of noodles have been used in the recipes in this book. They are available in Asian grocery stores and in some supermarkets. *Cellophane noodles,* or mung-bean threads, are thin translucent noodles made from ground mung beans and dried on looped skeins. The Japanese name for these noodles is *harusame* [spring rain]. *Rice vermicelli,* or "rice sticks," are very thin rice-flour noodles. *Udon* are thick wheat-flour noodles used in Japanese cooking. Spaghetti may be substituted for *udon. Sōmen,* also used in Japanese cooking, are very fine white, wheat-flour noodles. Very fine vermicelli may be substituted for *sōmen.*

Pepper See *black pepper; chili peppers*

Rice Rice is the most important food in the Asian diet and a staple food for more than half the world. Chinese records of rice cultivation go back 4,000 years. There are countless varieties of rice, and, as any Asian cook can tell you, such facts as how old the rice is, where and how it was grown, as well as its color, flavor, aroma, tenderness, and stickiness make a big difference in how much satisfaction is derived from eating it. For example, in Japan, November, the month of harvest, is the time when rice (*gohan*) tastes best. It will take on a special name (*shinmai* [new rice]), and it will require less water for cooking than last year's crop.

Every country of Asia has its own standard of quality. Some like it dry and flaky, others prefer it sticky and glossy. Even the method of boiling rice varies widely from place to place. But besides its importance for centuries as the main sustainer of life, rice has deep religious and psychological associations.

In some Eastern languages, the words for rice and food (meal) are identical. Many ceremonies have arisen in connection with planting and harvesting rice based on the notion that rice has a spirit that must be propitiated. In some farming communities, even the cutting implement that is used to harvest rice may be sacred to the rice goddess and therefore cannot be forsaken for new and more efficient cutting methods. In Thailand, when the rice plants begin to seed, the Thai expression is that the rice becomes pregnant. In China, when one loses a job, it is referred to as "breaking one's rice bowl."

Only three varieties of rice are used in the recipes in this book: long-grain white rice, short or medium-grain Japanese rice, and long-grain brown rice. Basmati rice is suggested in the Indian recipes, but it is expensive and difficult to find. Long-grain rice becomes quite fluffy and the grains tend to remain separate after cooking, whereas short-grain becomes more sticky and the grains tend to cling to one another. Brown rice is gaining favor in the United States because a more health-conscious public is aware that many nutrients are lost in the polishing process. Strange as it may seem, in some Asian countries brown rice is scorned for human consumption and is used to feed livestock. Recently, however, some Chinese restaurants in California have begun offering brown rice on their menus. To wash or not to wash rice, that is the question. The debate goes on. I find it unnecessary and wasteful of nutrients, although Asian cooks will agree on nothing else. The amount of water required to cook rice varies depending on its age. In general, if rice is old and therefore very dry, more water will be needed. For more about rice, please refer to the recipes themselves.

Soybean Curd   Bean curd, also known by its Japanese name, *tofu*, is a high-protain food made from soybeans. It has a delicate, custardy consistency and though quite bland on its own, it readily absorbs the flavors of other foods, making it a useful extender. In the United States it comes packed in water in plastic tubs, in soft, medium-firm, and firm consistencies. When it is labeled "regular" it is medium-firm. Rinse packaged curd after opening. Then cover with cold water and refrigerate for up to a few days, changing water daily.

Soy Sauce and Other Asian Condiments   Asian condiments are loaded with sodium. Use a low-sodium alternative whenever possible, and, to ensure a measure of control over how much sodium you ingest, never pour soy sauce or any other condiment out of a bottle. Consult the Fat-Cholesterol-Sodium Tables (pp. 332–34) for an approximate idea of how much sodium these substances contain, and always use a measuring spoon. But before you add more of a condiment to a particular dish, consider adding instead chili pepper flakes, black pepper, Japanese pepper, seven-spice mixture, vinegar, or lemon juice. It is my contention that it is possible to dine on very appetizing meals and still keep within the American Heart Association guidelines for sodium.

Tamarind   The brown acidic fruit shaped like a large broad bean that grows on the tamarind tree is widely used in Southeast Asian cooking. To make tamarind water, combine 2 to 3 ounces tamarind pulp with 1 cup boiling water in a nonmetallic bowl. Mash with a fork and soak for 10 to 15 minutes. Strain by rubbing through a sieve. Tamarind has such a fine tart flavor that it is worth making some effort to locate it if it is not readily available in your locality. It is possible to substitute the juice and rinds of limes or lemons, or vinegar, but the taste is not the same.

*   *   ·   *

Processed Foods   Choose low-sodium and low-fat processed foods whenever there is an alternative. Read labels carefully. You may need your glasses because the print is usually too fine for the naked eye.

Cooking Tips

Utensils   Most of the dishes in this book can be cooked with available

Western utensils. Though a *steamer* would be handy, especially for cooking a whole fish, it is not essential, since one can be easily improvised. In a large tightly-covered pot or roasting pan, place two small heat-proof bowls or small empty tuna cans. On top of these bowls set the heat-proof food-laden plate. Add water to the pot but keep it at least two inches below the food. There must be enough space around the plate to allow the steam to rise and circulate freely.

Another important piece of equipment in an Asian kitchen is the *mortar* and *pestle* used to reduce chilies and spices to a paste. An electric blender will give the same results in much less time though it may be impossible to pulverize small quantities of food in it without the addition of extra liquid. If you don't have a blender, or just do not want to take the trouble to use it, dishes will be just as good tasting if you simply chop things finely and mix them together before cooking.

Stir-Frying   Some enthusiasts insist on using a *wok*, which is the basic Chinese cooking vessel. It is widely used all over Southeast Asia, its bottom fitting nicely into the open top of a charcoal brazier. Its shape, unchanged for centuries, is ideal for stir-frying, because food is easily turned over along its sloping sides. I find it impossible to use on an electric stove because its rounded bottom barely touches the hot coils, making it impossible to heat it to a high enough temperature. A wok works better on a gas stove, but the fit is still not right. I am partial to nonstick skillets coated with Teflon or SilverStone because they permit stir-frying with a minimum of fat without ingredients sticking to the pan. But you can also produce perfect stir fried dishes in a heavy cast-iron skillet, though more fat will be needed to keep foods from sticking. If you decide to use a nonstick pan, be sure to buy the largest size available to ensure that foods will not be crowded when they are being stir-fried.

In most Chinese cooking, all the pieces of food in a recipe should be cut about the same size and shape to ensure uniform cooking. Meat is sliced across the grain to make it more tender. Stir-frying requires a very hot pan and sizzling oil. When the ingredients are added there should be loud crackling and popping noises as they are briskly tossed and turned to keep them from scorching. The heat must remain high and the cook must resist any temptation to turn it down. Onions and garlic are usually stir-fried first to flavor the oil before introducing other ingredients. Cook the onion before adding the garlic, because garlic tends to burn easily. The basic process is quite simple, and the recipes are clear in stating how long each step should take. Cooking time rarely exceeds 5 minutes.

Much of the success and most of the effort required lie in the preparation. Everything you need to do for a particular dish—cutting meat and vegetables, measuring seasonings, and mixing sauces—should be carefully done ahead of time and the necessary ingredients should be placed in separate bowls within easy reach of the stove, because a delay in the cooking could lead to disappointing results. Foods are usually cooked in a certain order, those which take the longest being cooked first.

A stir-fry cannot be made ahead of time, so you must be prepared to leave your guests for 5 minutes to do the cooking without interruption immediately before you sit down to eat. Each food must be cooked until it is just done and not a moment more. Vegetables must be crisp. Fish and meat must be succulent, never overdone and dry, and, needless to say, all the ingredients you use must be as fresh as possible.

A word of caution is necessary on how to avoid limp, soggy, stir-fried dishes. The smaller the quantity of food stir-fried at any one time, the better the dish will turn out. No more than a recipe for four should be attempted in one batch. If you double a recipe, cook each batch separately.

The stir-frying and steaming process results in many health benefits. The coating of food with hot oil seals in all the juices, flavor, and nutritional value of the ingredients while increasing their fiber content, and steaming removes less soluble fiber than boiling.

Most of the nutrition data in this chapter came from the American Heart Association publications listed in the bibliography. The information in the section on garlic came from journal articles and books on garlic, which are also listed in the bibliography. The articles about the benefits of fish oils have been listed elsewhere.

Weights and Measures

Conversions, Equivalents, and Substitutions

You will find that all of the recipes given in this book are given in the American system of weights and measures, but metric equivalents are also given wherever possible. When doing your own cooking, decide which one of these two systems you are going to use—the U.S. or metric—and stick to it! The reason for this is that the conversions are only equivalent, and that the proportions will only be right within one system. The conversion and equivalent tables are given here to help you sort out the trickiest problems.

Conversions

Solid Measures

Ounces and Pounds to Grams and Kilograms

Ounces	Pounds	Approximate Weight	Convenient Equivalent	Actual Weight
1 oz		30 g	30 g	28.35 g
2 oz		57 g	60 g	56.7 g
3 oz		85 g	85 g	85.05 g
4 oz	¼ lb	113 g	115 g	113.4 g
5 oz		142 g	140 g	141.8 g
6 oz		171 g	170 g	170.1 g
7 oz		198 g	200 g	198.5 g
8 oz	½ lb	227 g	225 g	226.8 g
9 oz		255 g	255 g	255.2 g
12 oz	¾ lb	340 g	340 g	340.2 g
16 oz	1 lb	454 g	450 g	453.6 g
24 oz	1½ lb	680 g	680 g	680.4 g
32 oz	2 lb	907 g	905 g	907.2 g
35.2 oz	2.2	1 Kg	1 Kg	1 Kg

The relationship between volume measures and weight measures varies depending upon the type of ingredient. For example, the weights of 1 cup of sliced fresh mushrooms (70 g), spinach leaves (100 g), chopped almonds (127 g), rice (200 g), low-fat yogurt (227 g), and skimmed milk (245 g) are radically different.

Below is a list of useful conversions of dry measures:

USA	UK (metric)
1 oz	28.35 g (rounded to 28 g)
1 lb	453.6 g (rounded to 454 g)

UK (metric)	USA
1000 mg	.035 oz
1 g	.035 oz
1 Kg	2.21 lb

Liquid Measures

Spoons and Cups (USA)	Fluid Ounces (floz)	Approximate Metric Term (dl/L)	Approximate Centiliters (cl=cc)	Actual Milliliters (ml)
1 tsp (⅓ Tbsp)	⅙ floz	1 tsp	0.5 cl	4.9 ml
3 tsp (1 Tbsp)	½ floz	1 Tbsp	1.5 cl	14.8 ml
2 Tbsp (⅛ cup)	1 floz	2 Tbsp (.3 dl)	3.0 cl	29.6 ml
4 Tbsp (¼ cup)	2 floz	4 Tbsp (.6 dl)	6.0 cl	59.1 ml
5 Tbsp (⅓ cup)	2⅔ floz	5 Tbsp (.75 dl)	7.5 cl	78.9 ml
8 Tbsp (½ cup)	4 floz	1.0 dl	12.0 cl	118.3 ml
⅔ cup (10 Tbsp)	5⅓ floz	1.5 dl	15.0 cl	157.7 ml
¾ cup (12 Tbsp)	6 floz	1.75 dl	18.0 cl	177.4 ml
1 cup (16 Tbsp)	8 floz	0.25 L	24.0 cl	236.6 ml
2 cups (1 pint)	16 floz	0.50 L	47.0 cl	473.2 ml
4 cups	32 floz	1.0 L	95.0 cl	946.4 ml

Note that the British, or metric, cup is larger than the American cup, which makes a difference in the capacities of pints and spoons as well. This is why you cannot cook with metric measures and American measuring spoons—the proportions will be off. The following is a table of some useful equivalents:

	USA	UK (metric)
	1½ tsp	1 tsp
	1½ Tbsp	1 Tbsp
1 tsp	4.9 ml	6.25 ml
1 Tbsp	14.8 ml	20.0 ml
¼ cup	59.1 ml	62.5 ml
½ cup	118.3 ml	125.0 ml
1 cup	236 ml	250.0 ml
1 pint (2 cups)	473 ml	500.0 ml
2 pints	946 ml (1 qt)	1.0 L (1.057 qt)
1 gallon	3.78 L (4 qt)	4.0 L (4.228 qt)

Approximate Temperature Conversions

Temperature	Fahrenheit	Centigrade
Coldest area of freezer	−10	−23
Freezer	0	−17
Water freezes	32	0
Water simmers	115	46
Water scalds	130	54
Water boils (at sea level)	212	100
Soft ball	234	112
Firm ball	244	117
Hard ball	250	121
Very low oven	250–275	121–133
Low oven	300–325	149–163
Moderate (medium) oven	350–375	177–190
Hot oven	400–425	204–218
Very hot oven	450–475	232–246
Extremely hot oven	500–525	260–274

To convert Fahrenheit into Centigrade (Celsius), first subtract 32; then multiply the result by 5, and then divide by 9.

$$Example:\ 212-32=180$$
$$180 \times 5 = 900$$
$$900/9 = 100$$

To convert Centigrade into Fahrenheit, follow the above procedure in reverse. That is, first multiply by 9; then divide the result by 5, and then add 32.

$$Example:\ 100 \times 9 = 900$$
$$900/5 = 180$$
$$180+32 = 212$$

Approximate Conversions of Prepared Foods

1. Canned goods

Can sizes	Contents (oz/g)		Approximate Cups
5-oz	5 oz	(142 g)	⅝
8-oz	8 oz	(227 g)	1
Picnic	10.5–12 oz	(298–340 g)	1¼
12-oz vacuum	12 oz	(340 g)	1½
No. 300	14–16 oz	(397–454 g)	1¾
No. 303	16–17 oz	(454–482 g)	2
No. 2	1 lb 4 oz	(567 g)	2½
or:	1 pt 2 floz	(625 ml)	2½
No. 2½	1 lb 13 oz	(822 g)	3½
No. 3	46 oz	(1.3 Kg)	5¾
Condensed milk	14 floz	(397 ml)	1⅓
Evaporated milk	5⅓ floz	(151 ml)	⅔
or:	13 floz	(369 ml)	1⅔

2. Frozen foods

Product	Contents (oz/g)	
Fruits, boxed	10–16 oz	(284 g)
canned	13½–16 oz	(383–454 g)
Juice concentrates	6 oz	(170 g)
Vegetables	8–16 oz	(227–454 g)

Substitutions

coconut milk	=equal amount of low-fat yogurt or buttermilk
coriander leaves, fresh	=fresh mint leaves (but it gives a different flavor to the dish; mint is an excellent substitute in Indian and Thai dishes)
cornstarch, 1 Tbsp	=2 Tbsp flour (for thickening)
daikon	=a large white turnip
egg, 1 whole	=2 egg whites (in soups and liquid mixtures)
fish sauce	=low-sodium soy sauce (but the taste will be quite different)
five-spice powder	=combination of ground star anise, cinnamon, and fennel, or of anise, pepper, and cloves
garlic, fresh, 1 clove	=¼ tsp powdered, or to taste
ginger, fresh, green root, grated, 1 Tbsp	=preserved ginger with syrup washed off, or ¼–½ tsp powdered ground ginger
herbs, fresh, chopped, 1 Tbsp	=1 tsp dried or ½ tsp powdered
milk, fresh, 1 cup	=½ cup evaporated milk + ½ cup water
nonfat, 1 cup	=1 cup reconstituted nonfat dry milk
sour, 1 cup	=1 Tbsp lemon juice/white vinegar + enough milk to make 1 cup
mirin, 1 teaspoon	=1 teaspoon saké + scant ⅛ teaspoon sugar
rice vinegar	=mild white vinegar
rice wine, Chinese (*lao-jiu*)	=pale dry sherry
Japanese (saké)	=medium-dry white wine
sansho	=black pepper (but the taste is very different)
shichimi togarashi	=crushed dried chilies or cayenne
Sichuan pepper	=half and half dried basil and black pepper, or just black pepper; Japanese *sansho* is a good substitute

Planning and Serving an Asian Meal

Each of the main dishes included in this book allow about 3 ounces of cooked meat (4 ounces uncooked) per serving. However, the number of people that a dish will serve will also depend on whether you are planning to serve it as the main course of a Western meal or as one of a number of dishes in an Asian meal. Side dishes and some soups can become main courses as one wishes, since many are substantial and the distinction is a matter of quantity. Perhaps the best way to begin cooking these foods is to choose a single dish that can be worked in with a more familiar menu. The nutrient analysis given at the end of each recipe should be of help in determining what other foods you can serve with it and still reduce your intake of fats and sodium.

The introduction to each chapter tells what the typical ingredients and seasonings are for that country, and the recipes themselves contain clear and precise explanations as well. The recipes may seem formidable at first glance because there are so many ingredients in them. But every effort has been made to simplify them and to use ingredients that can be found in any supermarket. In practice they are not difficult to manage if you have your collection of spices and seasonings arranged handily by your stove. The actual process of cooking is quick and easy, but, as with so many Asian dishes, preparation is as important as cooking.

Moreover, for the fast pace of contemporary life, Asian cooking styles are marvelously flexible, and the key is the ability to change recipes based on available ingredients. Keep in mind the fact that there are no precise recipes for any of these dishes. Asian cooks rarely measure their ingredients but cook by instinct, taste, and past experience. Seasonings are adjusted to individual taste, so the "correct" amount is the one that tastes best to the cook or those the cook is endeavoring to please.

Recipes and Their Nutrient Values

The computer analysis for calories and for fat, cholesterol, and sodium content that follows each recipe is for one serving. These counts are for the basic recipe and do not include the optional ingredients unless stated. For example, if a recipe calls for green beans and says that carrots may be substituted, the analysis is for green beans. If the recipe says it will yield 4–6 servings, the count is based on the first number, that is, 4, unless otherwise stated.

All of the figures have been rounded *up* to the nearest 5 or 10 milligrams, and to the nearest one-half gram. In reading these figures, you will find a difference between the total fat in a recipe and the sum of the values listed for saturated and polyunsaturated fats. This is because there are other fatty acids in the food that are not included in the nutrient analysis.

All of these nutrient values should be regarded as estimates. There are often minor (but sometimes major) discrepancies from one source to another as well as variations in the foods themselves. For example, the actual amount of fat in the preparation of chicken could vary with the quality of the meat and how much care you take in removing the skin and the fat. As for sodium values in Asian condiments, there is a tremendous disparity from sample to sample and brand to brand. Still another consideration is the fact that most Asian foods are served on large platters that are placed in the center of the table, and that diners freely help themselves from these platters. This makes the notion of an exact analysis for a single serving even more imprecise than it already is, since how big a "single" serving is depends upon the diner's appetite at the time. Under these conditions, the analyses can be but approximations at best.

Please note that the nutrient analysis for meats, chicken, and fish is based on only the leanest portions. For example, if a recipe calls for fillets of fish, the analysis is for a lean fish such as sole, not for a more fatty variety such as salmon, and the figure used is an averaged, rounded-up figure.

Sources for the data given in the nutrient computer analyses can be found in the section titled "Major Sources for the Nutrient Content of the Recipes" found in the back of this volume on page 335.

The
Good-for-Your-Health
All-Asian Cookbook

Japan

The Japanese Kitchen

Japan needs no introduction. With its gross national product accounting for 11% of world production, Japan ranks third after the United States and West Germany as a world trader. It has also become a major partner in many American industries and is giving failing U.S. auto and steel companies a fresh start with infusions of Japanese capital and management. With these economic successes has come a broad series of steps on the part of the Japanese government, education, and business sectors to encourage the development of an international perspective in every aspect of Japanese life. When compared with other nations, Japan has far more knowledge about the rest of the world than most other nations, and Japan has also been more receptive to foreign ideas and foreign technologies. Yet despite these strong influences from the outside, the Japanese, while contributing to the international community, have managed to preserve their cultural heritage and to take pride in being Japanese. Their cuisine is part of this cultural heritage and it has not only been kept intact but is finding devotees all over the world.

Japanese cooking, the most elegantly simple cuisine in the world, stands apart from all other Asian cuisines. Unlike other Asian cooking styles, which tend to combine many ingredients in one dish and to rely on exotic foodstuffs or spice blends, Japanese cuisine emphasizes the unique flavor and character of each food so that all will have equal importance in taste as well as appearance. The insistence on the quality and integrity of the natural food derives from a long history of a reverence for nature and a sense of harmony with the seasons. Only the freshest, most perfect specimen will make this possible, and only the simplest cooking methods are necessary. Seasonings are used with restraint because the aim is to enhance, not mask, the intrinsic properties of each food. Additional excitement is imparted when it is brought to the table by serving small portions of each food separately in aesthetic arrangements designed to appeal to the eye as well as to the palate. Just as much attention is given to choosing the right bowl or plate as to the preparation of the food itself.

Because of the recent concern in the United States for health and fitness, more attention has been focused on the virtues of Japanese cooking, with its sparing use of fats and its reliance on fish and soy products rather than beef as a source of protein. Not only is it gaining popularity in the United States, it is also influencing the direction of international cuisine. In some California and New York restaurants, a happy culinary marriage has taken shape combining the Japanese philosophy of aesthetics and simplicity with the French eye for detail of the school of *la nouvelle cuisine*.

The organization of Japanese cooking is not at all like Western cooking, with its main course preceded by soup or an appetizer and ending with a dessert or an assortment of cheeses. Nor is it like Chinese cooking. At a Chinese meal, foods are brought to the table in large serving dishes from which each diner takes a portion. The Japanese serve each food in individual separate bowls or dishes that are set on a tray or on the table in front of each diner according to prescribed rules for their placement. For instance, rice is usually placed on the left and soup to the right, and dipping sauces or condiments are placed to the right of the dishes they are intended for.

In a traditional Japanese meal, it is customary to serve a soup and three other dishes (*ichiju sansai*) followed by rice and pickles. Since foods are generally classified according to their cooking methods, the items in a particular meal are chosen both for their seasonal availability and for the variety of cooking techniques. A typical dinner menu may include both fish and meat or several kinds of fish and vegetables prepared in different ways. The soup is often eaten near the end of the meal. There are no desserts. The meal usually ends with fresh fruit. With the exception of rice and soup, which should be served hot, most Japanese dishes are served at room temperature.

Therefore, preparing a Japanese-style meal can be done in a leisurely manner without the fear that all the dishes may not be finished at the same time. While the presentation of Japanese dishes is artful and elegant, cooking methods are simple and quick. As in Chinese cooking, everything is cooked only until it is just done; not a moment more. Most of the time is spent preparing, cutting, and slicing.

The recipes that follow are arranged as they would appear in a Japanese cookbook, according to their cooking methods. There are foods simmered in seasoned liquids (*nimono*), broiled foods (*yakimono*), steamed foods (*mushimono*), mixed foods with dressings (*aemono*), vinegared foods (*sunomono*), deep-fried foods (*agemono*), and one-pot table-top cookery (*nabemono*). There are also noodles (*menrui*), rice (*gohan*) and sushi, and soups (*dashi, suimono,* and *shirumono*). Mention is made whenever these dishes can double as appetizers (*zensai*).

Adapting Japanese Food to a Low-Sodium, Low-Cholesterol Diet

For those on low-cholesterol diets, Japanese cooking is perfect. The proof lies in the fact that the incidence of heart disease in Japan is very low in comparison to that in the United States, although the recent popularity in Japanese metropolitan areas of hamburgers, butter, cream, and ice cream has been changing these statistics. Unfortunately, the reverse is true for those who wish to cut down on sodium. Of the three most essential of Japanese staples, all derived from the soybean—soybean curd (*tofu*), soy sauce (*shoyu*), and fermented soybean paste (*miso*)—soy sauce and soybean paste pose grave problems for those who wish to cut down on sodium. They are used generously in soups, sauces, dressings, and marinades, as well as in grilled foods. There are approximately 320 mg of sodium in one teaspoon of Kikkoman's standard soy sauce and 170 mg in the low-sodium product. Frequently as much as a quarter of a cup is used in a single dish (which is equal to twelve teaspoons, or 3,840 mg of sodium if you use the standard soy sauce and 2,040 mg if you use the low-sodium product). In contrast, soybean curd, a subtle tasting, custard-like food, is low in sodium and fat and rich in protein. But it is usually cooked with other foods in sauces that contain either soy sauce or soybean paste. The liberal use of these two staples, as well as salt, has affected the health of many Japanese. The incidence of hypertension is high in Japan, but it is highest in the north, where farmers preserve their food in salt.

Since authenticity is not the goal of this book, the quantity of soy sauce in all these recipes has been substantially reduced and has been limited to Kikkoman's low-sodium soy sauce, which has 40% less sodium in it than the standard product. To compensate for this, more reliance has been placed on other typically Japanese flavors such as horseradish, ginger, and sweet-and-sour sauces. Together with these, generous sprinklings are recommended of ground *sansho*, a fragrant, tangy but not hot spice, and *shichimi togarashi* (seven-spice mixture), a powdered blend of red pepper, *sansho*, dried mandarin orange peel, sesame seeds, poppy seeds, *nori* (seaweed bits), and hemp seeds, as effective flavor additions when cooking without salt. The seven-spice mixture is available in small bottles at very modest cost. In Japan it is not uncommon to buy it from a spice merchant who will mix it in proportions to suit your personal taste. If neither of these is available to you, substitute black pepper for the *sansho*, and crushed dried chilies or cayenne pepper for *shichimi togarashi* though, of course, the flavors are not the same.

Perhaps the best way to begin cooking Japanese food is to choose a single dish that can be worked in with a more familiar menu. Don't overlook one-pot meals, which are cooked at the table, or scattered sushi, a cold rice salad with seafood and vegetables. These one-dish meals are by far the simplest to prepare and the most congenial to serve. Whatever you decide, let three words be your guide: freshness, simplicity, and beauty.

◊  ◊

Stocks and Soups
(*Dashi, Suimono,* and *Shirumono*)

Basic Stock
(*Dashi*)

Dashi is a stock made from dried bonito fish (*katsuobushi*) and dried kelp (*kombu*). Equivalent to our chicken and beef stocks, it is used in the cooking of many meat, poultry, and fish dishes. It is what gives Japanese food its most characteristic flavor.

Ichiban dashi, or first *dashi,* is the foundation of clear soups (*sumashi*), to which is added a morsel of fish or chicken, a slice of vegetable or bean curd, and a decorative garnish to aesthetically complement and add fragrance to the whole.

Niban dashi, or second *dashi,* is a weaker stock made from the leftover ingredients of first *dashi* and is used as a cooking stock in place of water when preparing boiled foods.

Dashi is much easier to make from scratch than chicken broth, but just as busy Western cooks use canned chicken broth instead of making their own, so do Japanese cooks use instant *dashi.* Called *dashi-no-moto,* it comes powdered, in cubes, or in bags like tea bags, with instructions in English. However, it is not recommended for frequent use, because it contains added salt and monosodium glutamate. If none of these ingredients is available, you may substitute chicken stock (p. 10). It must be light, crystal clear, and without a trace of fat. If you use canned broth, use the low-sodium kind. Chill it first and skim off the fat; then dilute it with a little water. Serve the soup in a cup-like bowl, not the wide, shallow bowls in which Western soups are served. The Japanese often use a lacquered bowl with a lid, which not only keeps the soup hot but seals in the delicate aroma.

First *Dashi*
(*Ichiban dashi*)

6 *cups water*	1 *cup flaked* katsuobushi
2-*inch square kombu* (*dried*	(*dried bonito*)
kelp)	

1.   Bring water and *kombu* to a boil over high heat. Immediately remove *kombu* and set aside.
2.   Stir in the *katsuobushi* flakes and turn off the heat. Let the *dashi* rest for 2 or 3 minutes or until the flakes sink to the bottom of the pot.
3.   Strain the stock through a colander lined with 2 or 3 layers of cheesecloth. This is the first *dashi*.

Second *Dashi*
(*Niban dashi*)

1.   Add 6 cups of water to the *kombu* and *katsuobushi* used in the first *dashi*.
2.   Add ¼ cup additional *katsuobushi* flakes. Bring to a boil and simmer 10 minutes.
3.   Strain through a cloth-lined colander. Discard the *katsuobushi* and *kombu*.

To ensure full flavor, *dashi* is best used immediately, though it may be refrigerated for 1 or 2 days.

Note: Salt is probably used in the drying of kelp and bonito, but no figures exist for how much sodium is extracted when *dashi* is prepared. Therefore, whenever *dashi* is called for in the following recipes, the sodium count for chicken stock, its substitute, will be used in doing the nutrient analysis.

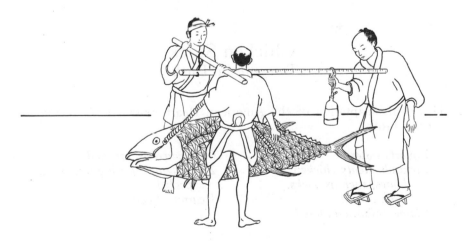

Clear Soup
(*O-sumashi*)

*4 cups first dashi (p. 9), or
    chicken stock (p. 10)
1 teaspoon low-sodium soy
    sauce*

*Powdered sansho (Japanese
    pepper) to taste*

1. Bring the stock to a boil. Reduce heat and add the soy sauce.
2. Add ingredients suggested in the following recipes or create variations of your own. They should provide contrast in shape, color, and texture. One morsel may be a slice of mushroom, bamboo shoot, water chestnut, or lemon peel. Another may be long and thin, such as a strip of carrot, scallion, or green bean. A whole cooked shrimp, an oyster or clam in half-shell, or a cube of tofu or chicken may be used. Finally, a delicate leafy garnish should be added such as trefoil, watercress, parsley, spinach leaf, or green onion top. Three well-chosen morsels per bowl are usually enough.
3. If a thicker soup is desired, 1–2 teaspoons of cornstarch dissolved in a little water may be added.

Yield: 4 servings

Cooking time: 10 minutes

Calories per serving: 40
Saturated fat: 0 g
Cholesterol: 0 mg

Total fat: 0 g
Polyunsaturated fat: 0 g
Sodium: 65 mg

Chicken Stock
(*Tori-gara no Dashi*)

This is an adaptation of the American Heart Association's recipe for chicken broth.

*2 quarts water
2 pounds meaty chicken
    bones, such as backs,
    necks, wings
1 large onion, quartered*

*6 peppercorns, crushed
2-inch length fresh ginger root,
    peeled
1 carrot, sliced*

1.   Combine all the ingredients in a soup kettle, bring to a boil, and simmer partially covered for 1 ½ hours. Skim off froth.

2.   Line a colander with 2 or 3 layers of cheesecloth and strain the stock, discarding the bones. Adjust yield to 4 cups either by adding water or boiling down excess broth.

3.   Strain a second time and chill. Remove the fat that congeals on the surface. Refrigerate and use as required. Result should be a clear, amber-colored stock without a trace of fat.

Yield: About 4 cups

Cooking time: 1 ½ hours

Calories per cup: 40
Saturated Fat: 0 g
Cholesterol: 0 mg

Total fat: 0 g
Polyunsaturated Fat: 0 g
Sodium: 20 mg

Soybean Curd and Scallion Soup
(*Tofu no Suimono*)

½ *inch slice of fresh ginger root*
4 *cups* dashi *(p. 9), or chicken*
    stock (p. 10)
1 *teaspoon low-sodium soy*
    sauce
4 *ounces soybean curd (tofu),*
    cut into 4 equal parts

4 *thin rounds of carrot*
2 *scallions, cut into very thin*
    circles
Powdered sansho *(Japanese*
    pepper), or black pepper, to
    taste

1.   Mince the ginger root and extract the juice (1 teaspoon). Set aside.

2.   Bring *dashi* to a boil. Add the soy sauce and tofu and simmer 3 or 4 minutes.

3.   Add carrots and simmer 1 more minute. Add the ginger juice.

4.   Garnish with scallions and sprinkle pepper to taste.

Yield: 4 servings

Cooking time: 10 minutes

Calories per serving: 75
Saturated Fat: 0.5 g
Cholesterol: 0 mg

Total fat: 2 g
Polyunsaturated fat: 1 g
Sodium: 70 mg

Shrimp and Snow Pea Soup
(*Ebi no Suimono*)

4 medium shrimps
4 cups dashi (*p. 9*), or chicken
    stock (*p. 10*)
1 teaspoon low-sodium soy
    sauce
4 snow peas

4 small sprigs watercress
4 thin strips lemon peel
    Powdered sansho (*Japanese
    pepper*), or black pepper to
    taste

1.   Bring 2 cups water to a boil. Drop in the shrimp and boil 2–3 minutes or until they turn pink. Drain, shell, and devein. Set aside.
2.   Bring the *dashi* to a boil. Add the soy sauce, snow peas, and shrimps and cook 30 seconds.
3.   Arrange a shrimp, snow pea, and watercress sprig at the bottom of each bowl in a pleasing design. Pour hot soup on top being careful not to disturb the arrangement. Float a strip of lemon peel on top and sprinkle a dash of *sansho* over all. Serve hot.

Yield: 4 servings

Calories per serving: 60
Saturated fat: Trace
Cholesterol: 15 mg

Cooking time: 10 minutes

Total fat: 1.4 g
Polyunsaturated fat: 0.5 g
Sodium: 85 mg

Variation: Cooked chicken may be substituted for the shrimp.

Clam Soup
(*Hamaguri Ushiojitate*)

8 small live cherrystone
    clams in shells
4 cups dashi (*p. 9*), chicken
    stock (*p. 10*), or water
4 mushrooms
1/4–1/2 teaspoon low-sodium
    soy sauce

1 tablespoon Japanese saké
4 sprigs trefoil (mitsuba), or
    watercress leaves
4 very thin slices lemon or lime
    Powdered sansho (*Japanese
    pepper*) or black pepper to
    taste

1. Scrub clams thoroughly under cold running water to remove sand.
2. Combine clams and water and bring to a boil over high heat. Continue to boil until clam shells open. Skim off froth.
3. Add mushrooms, soy sauce and saké and simmer 1 minute. Remove from heat.
4. Place 2 clams in their shells in each of 4 bowls Decoratively garnish with a mushroom, trefoil or watercress leaf, and lemon slice. Strain the broth as you fill each bowl, being careful not to disturb the arrangement. Serve hot.

Yield: 4 servings   Cooking time: 10 minutes

Calories per serving: 70   Total fat: 0.5 g
Saturated fat: Trace   Polyunsaturated fat: Trace
Cholesterol: 15 mg   Sodium: 75 mg

Variation: Parboiled snow peas or asparagus tips may be included or substituted for the mushrooms.

Clear Soup with Soybean Paste
(*Misoshiru*)

Breakfast would not be breakfast for most Japanese without *misoshiru*. A simple soup flavored with soybean paste, it is also served at the end of a formal Japanese meal. Like soy sauce, *miso* is used as a flavoring in many Japanese dishes. Unfortunately it is very high in sodium, though exact counts are difficult to ascertain because of tremendous variation in its production.* Two types are usually available, white and red. The white is sweet and less salty than the red. To exclude *miso* completely from Japanese cuisine would be unthinkable, so for the purposes of this book, only two recipes are included, *miso* soup and *dengaku* (pp. 32–33). The quantity of *miso* in both recipes has been considerably reduced. For example, one recipe for *miso* soup calls for 1 cup of *miso* paste to make 6 cups of soup. Simple arithmetic will show the astronomical amount of sodium contained in a single cup. As there are about 284 mg of sodium in one teaspoon of *miso* paste (1 cup = 16 tablespoons or 48 teaspoons), there are 284 × 48 teaspoons = 13,632 mg of sodium in a pot of 6 cups of soup, or 2,272 mg in a single serving of *miso* soup. That is the amount the American Heart Association recommends for a single day, not a single cup of soup! One can see that for strict sodium watchers, *miso* should be eaten only occasionally, if at all. Perhaps the best solution is for the producers of *miso* to put out a low-sodium product with reliable labeling. Although such a product is available in Japan, I have looked in the U.S. but have not been able to find one.

> *4 cups* dashi *(p. 9), or chicken stock (p. 10)*
> *2 tablespoons* shiro *(white) or* aka *(red)* miso
> *1 scallion, thinly sliced*

1. Heat the *dashi*. Add a tablespoon or two to the soybean paste to liquify it and remove lumps before stirring it into the soup.
2. Cook until it comes to a simmer but do not allow it to boil. Garnish with chopped scallions and serve hot.

Yield: 4 servings   Cooking time: 5 minutes

Calories per serving: 130   Total fat: 1 g
Saturated fat: — g   Polyunsaturated fat: — g
Cholesterol: 0 mg   Sodium: 450 mg

*   An approximate sodium count was arrived at by averaging four kinds of *miso* listed in the *Standard Tables of Food Composition in Japan*, Fourth Revised Edition, 1982, Resources Council, Science and Technology Agency, Government of Japan. Per teaspoon: 58 calories; 284 mg sodium; 0.4 mg total fat. No data was given for individual fats. A dash (—) indicates data not available.

Variations:
1. Four ounces of soybean curd (tofu), cut into bite-sized cubes, may be simmered in the soup for 1 to 2 minutes.
2. Shrimps, clams, or scallops may be simmered briefly in the soup.
3. Soak ½ ounce *wakame* (dried seaweed) in water for 15 minutes. Rinse in running cold water for 3 minutes to rid it of salt. Discard the tough center sections and cut into small pieces. Simmer in the soup for 1 minute.

◊  ◊

Steamed Foods
(Mushimono)

Cold Saké-Steamed Chicken
(Tori no Sakamushi)

This is an especially good dish for summer weather that is easy to prepare. It also makes an excellent hors d'oeuvre. Serve it with this simple soy-and-lemon sauce, or, if you have more time, with the sesame dipping sauce given on pages 59–60.

2 whole chicken breasts, boned
    but with skin left on
4 tablespoons saké
1 teaspoon low-sodium soy
    sauce

2 tablespoons lemon juice
Powdered sansho (Japanese
    pepper), or freshly ground
    black pepper

1. Bring water in the bottom of a steamer (pp. xxxii–xxxiii) to a boil and place the chicken, skin side up, on a heat-proof dish. Score the skin and pour the saké over the chicken. Steam for 20 minutes.
2. When cool, remove and discard the skin and cut the meat into thin slices. Sprinkle with Japanese pepper.
3. Mix soy sauce, lemon juice, and 3–4 tablespoons broth from the steaming and pour over the chicken pieces after you slice them.

Yield: 4 servings,
    or about 20 appetizers

Cooking time: 20 minutes

Calories per serving: 215
Saturated fat: 2 g
Cholesterol: 90 mg

Total fat: 6 g
Polyunsaturated fat: 2 g
Sodium: 115 mg

Clams Steamed in Saké
(*Hamaguri no Sakamushi*)

These clams make an elegant appetizer.

*12 shucked littleneck clams
    on open half-shells*
¼ cup saké

*6 thin slices of lemon cut in
    half*

1.   Bring the water in the bottom of a steamer (pp. xxxii–xxxiii) to a boil.
2.   Arrange clams in open half shells on a heat proof dish. Pour ½ teaspoon saké on each clam and steam 2 or 3 minutes.
3.   Remove and garnish each shell with a lemon slice.

Note: If desired, clams may be served with a dipping sauce made with 1 teaspoon low-sodium soy sauce and 2 tablespoons lemon juice. The soy sauce will add 43 mg of sodium to each serving.

Yield: 4 servings,
    or 12 appetizers

Cooking time: 3 minutes

Calories per serving: 65
Saturated fat: Trace
Cholesterol: 20 mg

Total fat: 0.5 g
Polyunsaturated fat: Trace
Sodium: 60 mg

Shrimp and Chicken Custard
(*Chawan Mushi*)

This savory dish may be served either as a soup course or as a side dish. Morsels of chicken, shrimp, and mushrooms lie beneath an intriguingly flavored unsweetened custard. Any small heat-proof cup, preferably of ceramic glaze, will do if you don't have the special Japanese lidded china cups that are made for this purpose. Feel free to use other meats and vegetables that would harmonize both visually and gastronomically with custard, such as tender french-cut beans and thinly sliced carrots. Keep in mind that some may have to be parboiled or blanched first. Serve the custard hot on cold days and chilled in summer weather. Normally 4 whole eggs are used to make 4 servings. However, since a single egg yolk contains about 274 mg of cholesterol, only 2 yolks and 4 whites are used in this recipe. If further reduction is desired, use 1 yolk and 5 whites. However, a very stiff custard will result.

4 small shrimps, shelled and deveined

4 ounces boneds, uncooked chicken breast, all skin and fat removed, cut into 1/4 inch cubes

8–12 thin slices of mushrooms

12 ginkgo nuts (ginnan), shelled and peeled, or 8 snow peas

Marinade:

1 tablespoon saké
1/4 teaspoon low-sodium soy sauce
A dash of seven-spice mixture (shichimi togarashi)

Custard:

2 whole eggs
2 egg whites
2 3/4 cups cold chicken stock (p. 10), or Ichiban Dashi (p. 9), if preferred
1/8 teaspoon low-sodium soy sauce

1 tablespoon mirin
2–4 teaspoons fresh ginger root, grated
Trefoil, watercress, or flat parsley sprigs

1. Combine the saké, soy sauce, and a generous sprinkling of seven-spice mixture, and marinate shrimp and chicken for a few minutes. Drain and discard marinade.

2. Beat the eggs. Stir in the chicken stock, soy sauce, and *mirin*. Strain the mixture to remove air bubbles (optional).

3. Place a shrimp, some chicken cubes, mushroom slices, and ginkgo nuts or snow peas in each of 4 bowls.

4. Pour the egg mixture on top. Put a bit of ginger root on top and cover with aluminum foil.

5. Bring water in the bottom of a steamer (pp. xxxii–xxxiii) to a boil. Place cups of custard on a heat-proof plate and cook over low heat 10–15 minutes. To test for doneness insert a knife or toothpick near the edge (not the center) of the cup. If the blade comes out clean remove from the heat. There is enough stored heat in the cups to complete the cooking process. Overcooking and high heat produce a tough, dry custard. Alternatively, the custard may be baked. Set the covered bowls in a 2-inch deep baking pan. Fill the pan with 1 1/2 inches of hot water. Bake for about 30 minutes in a 325° F oven. Test for doneness.

Yield: 4 servings

Cooking time: 15 minutes

Calories per serving: 155
Saturated fat: 1.5 g
Cholesterol: 175 mg

Total fat: 4.5 g
Polyunsaturated fat: 1 g
Sodium: 140 mg

Turnip Clouds
(Kabura Mushi)

This is a subtly seasoned dish that is quick and easy to prepare. Chicken breast or fish fillets and shrimps are steamed with a topping of beaten egg white and grated turnips, then garnished with a very tangy green horseradish.

12 ounces chicken breast meat, boned, all fat and skin removed, cut into 1-inch pieces, or firm fish fillets
4 shrimps, shelled and deveined

4 small mushrooms, finely chopped
1–2 white turnips, peeled and finely grated
1 egg white

Sauce:

½ cup dashi (p. 9), or chicken stock (p. 10)
½ teaspoon low-sodium soy sauce

1 teaspoon saké
½ teaspoon cornstarch, mixed with 1 tablespoon cold water

Garnish:

1 tablespoon wasabi (green horseradish) powder mixed to a paste with a few drops of cold water

Parsley sprigs

1.   Bring water in bottom of a steamer (pp. xxxii–xxxiii) to a boil.
2.   In the bottom of each of 4 small heat-proof bowls, place chicken pieces or fish, with a shrimp on top.
3.   Place grated turnip in a towel and squeeze out moisture.
4.   Beat egg white to the soft peak (not dry) stage. Fold grated turnip (about ¾ cup) gently into beaten egg white. Divide among the 4 bowls, carefully covering chicken and shrimp. Steam 7–10 minutes.

5. Meanwhile, in a small saucepan, bring the stock to a boil. Reduce heat to low and add soy sauce and saké. Stir in the cornstarch mixture and simmer until sauce thickens slightly and clears. Spoon a little sauce over the chicken and garnish with a round dollop of *wasabi* paste and a parsley spring. Serve hot.

Yield: 4 servings	Cooking time: 10 minutes

Calories per serving: 195 Total fat: 4.5 g
Saturated fat: 1.5 g Polyunsaturated fat: 1 g
Cholesterol: 90 mg Sodium: 125 mg

Steamed Fish with Soybean Curd
(*Sakana no Sakamushi*)

*8 ounces white meat fish, with
    skin left on, cut into 8
    pieces
4 ounces soybean curd (tofu)
    cut into 1-inch cubes
¼ cup saké
4 dried shiitake mushrooms,
    soaked in warm water for
    30 minutes, then thinly slic-
    ed, or fresh mushrooms •
4 thin slices lemon*

Garnish:

*4 trefoil (mitsuba), watercress,   4 lemon wedges
    or parsley sprigs*

1. Bring water in bottom of a steamer (pp. xxxii–xxxiii) to a boil.
2. Cut fish, bean curd, and mushrooms.
3. In each of separate heat-proof bowls arrange 2 pieces of fish, 2 cubes of bean curd, and sliced mushrooms. Douse each with 1 tablespoon of saké. Top with lemon slice.
4. Cover with lid or foil and steam 8–10 minutes. Garnish with trefoil and lemon slice. Serve with *ponzu* (p. 58) or *chirizu* (p. 57) dipping sauces.

Yield: 4 servings   Cooking time: 10 minutes

Nutrient analysis does not include dipping sauce.

Calories per serving: 90   Total fat: 3 g
Saturated fat: 1 g   Polyunsaturated fat: 1 g
Cholesterol: 30 mg   Sodium: 41 mg

◇  ◇

Vinegared Salads
and Mixed Dressed Foods
(Sunomono and Aemono)

Both of these categories accompany main dishes. Vegetables may be used alone or mixed with fish or poultry. Salt is usually added to vegetables to extract as much moisture as possible before dressing them. For the purposes of this book I have eliminated this step. A compromise solution, if you wish to salt them, is to rinse them in cold running water for 3 minutes after salting to remove as much of it as possible. Squeeze and drain on an absorbent towel before mixing with the dressing. Keep in mind that 1 teaspoon of salt contains about 2,000 mg of sodium.

Vinegared Cucumbers
(Kyuri no Sunomono)

2 Japanese cucumbers, or 1
    medium cucumber
¼ cup rice vinegar
¼ teaspoon low-sodium soy
    sauce
1 teaspoon sugar
1 tablespoon white sesame
    seeds

1.   Peel cucumber lengthwise, leaving some green skin in ¼-inch widths for color. Remove seeds and slice thinly. Wrap in a towel or paper towels for a few minutes to drain off the moisture.

2.   Mix vinegar, soy sauce, and sugar. Pour over cucumbers, toss, and divide among 4 small bowls.

3.   In a hot dry skillet, toast sesame seeds briefly and sprinkle over cucumbers.

Yield: 4 servings

Preparation time: 10 minutes

Calories per serving: 30
Saturated fat: 0.5 g
Cholesterol: 0 mg

Total fat: 1.5 g
Polyunsaturated fat: 0.5 g
Sodium: 15 mg

Red-and-White Carrot and Radish Salad
(Kohaku Namasu)

Red and white are the colors of joyous occasions such as weddings and New Year celebrations.

2 cups Japanese white radish
    (daikon), peeled and grated
1 carrot, peeled and grated

½ recipe amazu (sweet-and-sour
    dressing; see p. 58)

1.   Place grated vegetables in separate bowls. Gently turn and squeeze with hands to extract water. Squeeze and drain on an absorbent towel. Please read the introductory paragraph to *sunomono* on page 50 about salting vegetables to extract moisture.

2.   Combine the vegetables in one bowl and pour *amazu* on top. Mix well and marinate at least 30 minutes. Flavor will be stronger (too strong for my taste) if allowed to marinate longer.

3.   Drain and serve in small quantities on individual dishes.

Yield: 6–8 servings

Preparation time: 10 minutes

Nutrient analysis includes *amazu*.

Calories per serving: 35
Saturated fat: 0 g
Cholesterol: 0 mg

Total fat: 0 g
Polyunsaturated fat: 0 g
Sodium: 15 mg

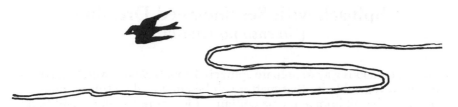

Cucumber Stuffed with Crabmeat
(*Kani Kyuri Ikomi*)

This attractive tidbit makes a tempting appetizer as well as a refreshing side dish. Lobster or shrimp may be used in place of crab.

2-inch piece fresh ginger root
2 ounces cooked flaked
   crabmeat
1 Japanese cucumber (12 inches
   long) or 2 thin cucumbers

½ recipe sanbaizu (p. 59)
½ cup watercress or flat-leafed
   parsley, blanched in boiling
   water for 10 seconds

1. Mince ginger root. Extract 2 teaspoons juice. Discard pulp.
2. Combine ginger-root juice with crab flakes and set aside.
3. Wash and trim ends of cucumber. Peel it lengthwise leaving some green skin in ¼-inch widths for color. Cut cucumbers in half crosswise into 2 short cylinders. With a small spoon or knife remove all pulp and seeds from center to make a hollow for stuffing.
4. Slit one side of cucumber. Hold the slit cucumber open with one hand and using chopsticks or a small spoon, fill the hollowed shell down its length, first with crabmeat, and then stuff greens next to it.
5. Cut filled cucumbers into ½-inch slices. As a side dish, place 4 slices on each of 6 small plates. Spoon *sanbaizu* over each serving.
6. As an hors d'oeuvre, arrange slices on a platter. Sprinkle *sanbaizu* over all and garnish with green leaves artistically placed.

Yield: 6 servings,
   or 24 appetizers

Preparation time: 10 minutes

Nutrient analysis includes *sanbaizu*.

Calories per serving: 30
Saturated fat: Trace
Cholesterol: 10 mg

Total fat: 0.5 g
Polyunsaturated fat: Trace
Sodium: 55 g

Spinach with Sesame-Seed Dressing
(*Horenso no Hitashi*)

This is a delicious way to prepare spinach, though cauliflower, broccoli, or any green vegetable for that matter will be enhanced by this sesame-seed dressing. The traditional recipe contains a lot more soy sauce and hence has a stronger flavor, but this is very good, too. Busy cooks may simplify this recipe by omitting the grinding of the sesame seeds (step 3): in that case, you should combine the sauce ingredients, mix into the spinach, and then sprinkle all the toasted sesame seeds on top of each serving.

1 pound spinach (6 cups), washed and trimmed
¼ cup black or white sesame seeds
¼ cup dashi (p. 9), or unsalted chicken stock (p. 10)

1 teaspoon mirin, or 1 teaspoon saké and less than ⅛ teaspoon sugar
½ teaspoon low-sodium soy sauce
1–2 tablespoons rice vinegar or mild white vinegar

1.   Bring a large pot of water to the boil. Add the spinach and cook until the leaves are barely wilted. Drain and cool immediately under cold water to stop the cooking process. Drain thoroughly and chop into 1-inch lengths.

2.   In a heated skillet, lightly toast the sesame seeds over moderate heat. Shake the pan to avoid scorching. Reserve a few for garnish.

3.   Pound the remaining toasted seeds to a paste in a mortar (*suribachi*) or blender. The grinding of the sesame seeds releases the oil and converts the seeds into a paste. If you use a blender, you may need to add a bit of oil to keep the mass moving.

4.   Combine remaining ingredients in a bowl with the sesame paste. Toss spinach with sauce until leaves are thoroughly coated. Divide among 4 small bowls. Garnish with reserved sesame seeds. Serve at room temperature.

Yield: 4 servings

Cooking time: 10 minutes

Calories per serving: 85
Saturated fat: 1 g
Cholesterol: 0 mg

Total fat: 4.5 g
Polyunsaturated fat: 2 g
Sodium: 60 mg

Variation: Eggplant is very tasty in sesame dressing. If you can find Japanese eggplants, which are small and thin with tender skins, do not peel them. The large American variety is coarser and needs to be peeled. Leave a strip of skin here and there for color if you wish. To prepare the eggplants, cut them into 1–inch cubes and boil them for 1 or 2 minutes or until just tender. Then toss them in the sesame dressing.

◊  ◊

Foods Simmered in Seasoned Liquids
(Nimono)

Saké-Simmered Fish
(Sakana no Nitsuke)

Any fish is suitable for simmering in this saké-based sauce, including shrimp and scallops. Cut a large fish in slices or use very thick fillets.

1 whole fish (about 2 pounds),
   cleaned, scaled, and scored,
   or 1½ pounds thick fillets
   cut into 6 pieces

2 teaspoons low-sodium soy
   sauce
   Seven-spice mixture (shichimi
   togarashi)

Nitsuke sauce:

⅓ cup saké
1 tablespoon sugar, dissolved
   in ¼ cup stock or water

¼ cup chicken stock (p. 10),
   or water
2 tablespoons fresh ginger root,
   finely minced

Garnish:

2 scallions, both white and
   green part, cut into thin
   circles

1 teaspoon fresh ginger root,
   finely grated
   Lemon slices and parsley
   sprigs

   1.   Combine the saké, sugar mixture, chicken stock, and ginger in a pan large enough to hold the fish. Bring to a boil.
   2.   Lay the fish on the boiling sauce and turn heat down to low. Set a

small pot lid inside directly on top of the fish to keep it from falling apart. (In Japan this inner lid, called *otoshibuta,* is made of wood.) Then cover the pot with its own lid.

3. Simmer for 5 minutes, or until fish is just done.

4. Transfer to a plate. Add soy sauce and a generous sprinkling of seven-spice mixture to the sauce in the pan and cook 1–2 minutes. Pour over fish and serve either hot or at room temperature. If desired, cut fish into 6 pieces and place a piece in each of 6 bowls. Arrange garnishes decoratively.

Variations:

1. Two minutes before fish is done, add grated Japanese white radish (*daikon*) over fish and top with thinly sliced green scallions. Steam 1 minute more and serve.

2. After removing fish from saucepan, place six 1–ounce pieces of soybean curd in pan and cook in remaining sauce until heated through. Turn a few times to coat with the sauce. Place a cube of soybean curd in each bowl with the fish.

3. After fish is removed, any vegetable may be simmered briefly in remaining sauce and added to bowls with fish.

Yield: 6 servings

Cooking time: 15 minutes

Calories per serving: 130
Saturated fat: 0.5 g
Cholesterol: 60 mg

Total fat: 1.5 g
Polyunsaturated fat: 0.5 g
Sodium: 135 mg

Simmered Squash
(*Kabocha no Nimono*)

1 pound Japanese squash
(kabocha; *often called
pumpkin*), or acorn or
butternut squash, sweet
potatoes, or yams
½–¾ cup dashi (p. 9), or
unsalted chicken stock
(p. 10). Water may be us-
ed if stock is not handy.

1½ tablespoons sugar (Not so
much sugar is necessary if
using sweet potatoes or
yams.)
1 teaspoon mirin, or saké
(if you prefer less sugar)
½ teaspoon low-sodium
soy sauce
Parsley for garnish

1.   Cut squash into 1½-inch pieces. Leave some skin on for color, or peel completely if skin is tough.

2.   In a medium saucepan, combine *dashi*, sugar, and mirin. Add squash and stir to coat with sauce. Cover and simmer over low heat 8–12 minutes or until tender.

3.   Stir in soy sauce. If needed, add more liquid. However, mixture should be fairly dry, not soupy, when done. Serve in 4 individual bowls and garnish with parsley.

Yield: 4 servings

Cooking time: 12 minutes

Calories per serving: 90
Saturated fat: Trace
Cholesterol: 0 mg

Total fat: 0.5 mg
Polyunsaturated fat: Trace
Sodium: 25 mg

◇  ◇

Broiled and Pan-Fried Foods
(Yakimono)

Broiled Fish with Sesame Seeds
(Sakana no Gomayaki)

Here is a very simple but elegant way to prepare fish. Grilled fillets dipped in egg white and toasted sesame seeds are served with a delicious lemony sauce.

¼ cup white sesame seeds
  (goma)
1 pound firm fish fillets, cut
  into 1-inch slices
1 egg white, lightly beaten

2 teaspoons safflower oil
Watercress, trefoil (mitsuba),
  or parsley for garnish
Ponzu dipping sauce (p. 58)

1. Preheat broiler
2. In a preheated small skillet, toast the sesame seeds, using no oil, very lightly. Do not brown. Lift and shake pan frequently to avoid scorching.
3. In a lightly oiled baking dish, place the cut fillets skin side down and broil 2 minutes. Turn and broil 2 more minutes or until barely done.
4. Remove fish from baking pan and dip flesh side only into beaten egg white, then into toasted sesame seeds.
5. Return to pan and broil until sesame seeds are a golden brown.
6. Place in 4 individual bowls garnished with a sprig of watercress. Serve with small bowls of ponzu set at each diner's place.

Yield: 4 servings   Cooking time: 10 minutes

Nutrient count does not include dipping sauce.

Calories per serving: 185   Total fat: 6 g
Saturated fat: 1 g   Polyunsaturated fat: 4 g
Cholesterol: 60 mg   Sodium: 90 mg

Skewered Chicken and Vegetables
(*Yakitori*)

Yakitori is a popular snack in Japan as well as a favorite appetizer. But it also makes an excellent meal. If I had to choose one dish that I would be happy to dine on most frequently, this would be it. It is perfect for an outdoor cookout on a hot summer day or broiled indoors at any time. Chicken livers are often grilled with the chicken, but I have left them out because of their high cholesterol count. (Three ounces of liver contains 372 mg of cholesterol as compared to about 75 in 3 ounces of chicken without skin and fat.) The liver is said to be one of the animal's chief production sites for cholesterol, but if you are not on a strict low-cholesterol diet, one or two chicken livers can be included, not only for variety but also for their very high nutritional content of vitamins and iron.

36–40 bamboo skewers at least 8 inches long
11½ pounds boneless, skinless chicken, all fat removed, cut into 1-inch cubes
12 scallions cut into 2-inch lengths; use white part with some of the green
6 small Japanese eggplants, about 4–5 inches long

18 cherry tomatoes
18 whole mushrooms
2 tablespoons safflower oil for basting
Powdered sansho (Japanese pepper), or black pepper
Seven-spice mixture (shichimi togarashi)
Lemon wedges
4 green peppers, cut into 1-inch squares

Basting sauce:

½ cup saké
½ cup mirin
1 tablespoon sugar
4 teaspoons low-sodium soy sauce

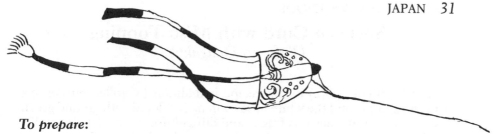

To *prepare*:

1. Soak bamboo skewers in water for at least an hour. Preheat broiler or start charcoal fire.
2. On each of 18 skewers, string 4 or 5 pieces of chicken alternated with 1-inch lengths of scallion.
3. To cook the eggplants, prick them in 3 or 4 places with a fork or a toothpick. Skewer them whole. Hold 2 skewers in a V position and insert them sideways into each eggplant. This will allow you to hold the eggplant securely in one hand.
4. String on skewers, in any order you wish, green pepper squares, tomatoes, and whole mushrooms.

To *cook*:

1. Start cooking eggplant first. Brush with oil and broil about 4–5 inches from fire until skin shrivels and eggplants get soft. This will take 15–20 minutes.
2. Using a small pastry brush, baste chicken with sauce and cook about 3 inches from heat for 5–8 minutes, basting and turning several times until the chicken is tender and brown. Do not overcook.
3. Brush the skewers of vegetables with oil and broil very briefly or just enough to lightly brown them and heat them through. If desired, you may brush them with the marinade.
4. Sprinkle *sansho* or seven-spice mixture to taste. Serve yakitori with boiled rice (p. 48) and vinegared cucumbers (p. 21).

Yield: 6 servings,
   or 36 appetizers

Cooking time: About 20
   minutes

Calories per serving: 420
Saturated fat: 2.2 g
Cholesterol: 100 mg

Total fat: 12 g
Polyunsaturated fat: 5.3 g
Sodium: 220 mg

Variation: Chunks of beef or fish, or whole shrimps may also be cooked in this way.

Soybean Curd with *Miso* Topping
(*Tofu no Dengaku*)

The soybean curd (*tofu*) in this recipe is traditionally grilled on skewers over an open fire and the white *miso* topping is colored with ground green *sansho* leaves. But since it is fragile and difficult for the novice to handle, pan broiling or frying is suggested in this highly adapted recipe.

Remember that *miso* is high in sodium—approximately 284 mg in 1 teaspoon. Normally, this recipe would be prepared with as much as ½ cup of *miso*, which would add up to 6,816 mg of sodium (24 teaspoons × 284 mg), or 1,704 mg per serving. That's nearly as much sodium as a person should have in a single day. For more on *miso*, see the recipe for Clear Soup with Soybean Paste on pages 13–14.

1 pound fresh firm soybean curd (tofu)
1 tablespoon safflower oil

White (*shiro*) *miso* topping:	**Red (*aka*) *miso* topping:**
2 teaspoons white miso *paste*	*2 teaspoons red* miso *paste*
1 teaspoon mirin	*1 teaspoon saké*
½ teaspoon sugar	*½ teaspoon sugar*
Dashi, *or water*	Dashi, *or water*

Garnish:

Powdered sansho (*Japanese pepper*), *or black pepper* *Sesame seeds*	*Seven-spice mixture* (shichimi-togarashi) *Watercress or parsley sprigs*

1.   Wrap bean curd in a cloth and weight with a board or plate for 30 to 40 minutes to press out moisture. This step is optional.

2.   In two separate sauce pans, mix ingredients for each of the *miso* toppings and cook over low heat until well blended. Add a little *dashi* or water to thin to spreading consistency.

3.   Cut the tofu into 8 pieces. Heat oil in a nonstick frying pan and brown lightly on both sides for 1 to 2 minutes. Alternatively, place in one layer in a baking dish. Add cold water to come halfway up the sides of the tofu and sear for a few seconds under the broiler. Turn and sear the other side.

4.   Spread the tops of 4 pieces of tofu with the white dressing and 4 with the red. If you are broiling the bean curd, place dressed sides under the broiler to heat. If pan frying, cover pan briefly to heat.

5.   Sprinkle *sansho*, sesame seeds, or seven-spice mixture as desired. Serve on 4 small plates with a green garnish.

Yield: 4 servings

Cooking time: 10 minutes

Calories per serving: 150
Saturated fat: 1 g
Cholesterol: 0 mg

Total fat: 6 g
Polyunsaturated fat: 3 g
Sodium: 292 mg

Variation: Eggpant is delicious cooked with *miso* dressing. If available, use small Japanese eggplants. Do not peel. Cut into ½-inch slices. Brown both sides lightly in a tablespoon of safflower oil, turning once. Add a tablespoon or two of water or saké, cover, and cook 2 or 3 minutes or until tender. Then spread *miso* dressing, heat and garnish as above. Alternatively, eggplant may be left unpeeled, cut in half lengthwise and grilled on a skewer over an open fire, then coated with *miso* dressing.

Thin Omelets
(*Usuyaki Tamago*)

1 whole egg and 2 egg whites, or
 2 whole eggs
¼ teaspoon sugar

¼ teaspoon mirin
1 teaspoon safflower oil

1. Beat eggs thoroughly with sugar and *mirin*.
2. Heat a nonstick frying pan until a drop of water sprinkled into it instantly evaporates. Using a paper towel, lightly grease the bottom and sides of the skillet with safflower oil. Pour just enough egg to coat the bottom of the pan.
3. Tilt the pan from side to side to cook. Turn over when firm and cook a few more seconds. Do not brown. Remove to a plate. Repeat the procedure, stacking the omelets on top of one another.
4. If using the thin omelets in Scattered Sushi (p. 52) or in Hand-Wrapped Sushi (p. 54), slice into very thin strips with a very sharp knife.

Yield: About 6 omelets
 (to serve 6)

Cooking time: 10 minutes

Calories per omelet: 30
Saturated fat: 0.5 g
Cholesterol: 45 mg

Total fat: 2 g
Polyunsaturated fat: 1 g
Sodium: 30 mg

◇  ◇

Deep-Fried Foods
(Agemono)

Deep-Fried Shrimp, Fish, and Vegetables in Batter
(Tempura)

Deep-fried foods have been left out of this book because they require the use of large quantities of oil. But tempura, one of my favorite dishes, is an exception. An enchanting tale of how deep-frying was introduced into Japan is told by the eminent linguist Mario Pei. Actually, it is the derivation of the word *tempura*, the name by which the Japanese call this dish, that tells the story. In his *Talking Your Way Around the World*, Pei says that this method of cooking was brought to Japan by the Portuguese in the sixteenth century. The Portuguese, who were good Catholics, did not eat meat on Fridays, during Lent, or on the Ember Days, which, since they constitute any Wednesday, Friday, or Saturday in four designated weeks of the year, are called in Latin the Quatuor Tempora, the "four times" of the year. They ate seafood instead, usually shrimp. Thus, the name tempura, coming from the Latin word for "times," became attached to the shrimp deep-fried in batter. But the tempura that the modern Japanese make bears no resemblance to Western deep-fried foods (or even to most of the so-called tempura available in the West).

Tempura is *not* fish and chips, but something miraculously transformed both gastronomically and visually. Nowhere outside of Japan do restaurants produce the light, delicate, and lacy coating that is served in Japan. Whatever the secret—a combination of the freshest ingredients, the lightest cooking oil, and perfect timing—tempura is food for the gods.

Close attention to the condition of the oil and batter is necessary to produce the delicacy that Japanese fried foods are noted for. For the lightest batter, sift the flour and use ice-cold water. Cooling the bowl and egg in the refrigerator helps to keep the batter cold longer. It should be mixed just before it is used. If it must be kept, it should not be allowed to stand more than eight to ten minutes or it will become gluey. Keep it away from the stove or put it in the refrigerator while food is cooking. Do not hesitate to discard it and mix a second batch midway during the frying process. Only vegetable oil should be used and it must be fresh and kept at the right temperature. Skim off the surface frequently to remove droppings from the frying process. Drain on several thicknesses of paper towels, arranging the food in a single layer to prevent a soggy result. Serve immediately after frying.

12 large shrimp (about
    ½ pound)
½ pound firm fish fillets
1 medium eggplant (about
    ½ pound)
1 medium sweet potato (about
    ½ pound)

16 snow peas
16 asparagus stalks
4 scallions
    Flour for dredging
    Safflower or other vegetable
    oil for deep frying

Preparation:

1.   Shell and devein shrimp, leaving tails attached. To prevent curling during cooking, make 2 or 3 short cuts along inner curve of shrimp. Wash and dry thoroughly.
2.   Cut fish fillets into ¼-inch slices.
3.   Cut eggplant into quarters and slice into ½-inch slices, leaving skin on for color. Peel potato, and slice into ¼-inch slices.
4.   Remove strings from snow peas. Cut off tough ends of asparagus stalks and discard. Use 3-inch length of bulb portion of scallions. Wash and dry ingredients thoroughly.
5.   Arrange shrimp and fish on one platter and vegetables on another.

*   *   *

Dipping Sauce:

1 cup first dashi (p. 9)
2–4 tablespoons low-sodium soy
    sauce

2–4 tablespoons mirin

Garnishes:

½ cup Japanese white radish
    (daikon), finely grated
    (white turnip may be
    substituted)

2–3 tablespoons fresh ginger
    root, finely grated
    Lemon wedges

1.   Bring *dashi*, soy sauce, and *mirin* to the boiling point. Remove from heat and cool.

2.   Place small mound of grated *daikon* in each of four small bowls. Top with grated ginger. Pour ¼ cup of dipping sauce on top of each mound and place bowls at the table, which has been set with chopsticks.

*   *   *

Batter:

1 *egg yolk*	1 *cup all-purpose flour, sifted*
1 *cup ice-cold water*	

1.   In a large bowl, beat egg slightly with chopsticks or a fork. Add ice-cold water and give the mixture a *few* strokes.

2.   Add sifted flour all at once. Stroke a few times with chopsticks or fork. Do not overmix. Ingredients should just be combined, but batter will appear very lumpy. *Do not overmix*, as a smooth batter will be sticky and will make tempura that is too heavy and oily.

3.   For a thin, lacy coating, batter should be thin and run off the spoon easily. Add more water if necessary.

Note:

1.   Mix the batter with the least amount of movement possible.

2.   Do not make the batter until just before you are ready to begin deep-frying.

3.   Use batter, once mixed, immediately.

*   *   *

To deep-fry:

1.   To keep tempura warm as you are deep-frying, heat oven to 250°F.

2.   In a wok, a deep-fat fryer, or a large deep pan, heat enough oil for deep frying over high heat to about 375°. (Oil should be about 3 inches deep.) If you do not have a thermometer, test oil by dropping a small piece of bread or a teaspoon of batter into it. Oil should be sizzling hot.

3.   Prepare batter while oil is heating.

4.   Cook vegetables first in the following order: eggplant, sweet potato, scallions, snow peas, and asparagus. Fry fish and shrimps last. Dredge each piece to be fried lightly with flour and shake off excess. Dip into batter, shake off excess, and slip into hot oil. Do not fry too many pieces at a time (since that would cause the oil temperature to fall too drastically and result in poor tempura). There should be ample space between the pieces

as they fry. Turn the pieces after one minute and fry the other side another minute, or until crisp and lightly golden.

5.   Drain on several layers of paper towels placed atop a wire cake rack and keep warm in preheated oven. Skim the oil occasionally to remove droppings. Be sure to mix a new batch of ice-cold batter midway in the deep-frying process. Serve tempura immediately for a light and crispy taste treat. How much fat will be absorbed by the tempura is difficult to predict, since it depends upon a number of variables, such as the temperature of the oil, how long the food remains in it while frying, how well you succeeded in making a light batter, and how well the pieces are drained.

I measured the amount of oil left over after I prepared tempura according to this recipe and found that only 4 tablespoons were missing from the original quantity (which is equivalent to only one tablespoon per serving). That was quite a surprise to me. Still, I do not recommend deep-fried foods except as an occasional treat.

Yield: 4 servings

Nutrient analysis does not include dipping sauce.

Calories per serving: 445   Total fat: 25 g
Saturated fat: 5 g   Polyunsaturated fat: 15 g
Cholesterol: 155 mg   Sodium: 180 mg

Dipping Sauce:

Calories per serving: 40   Total fat: 0 g
Saturated fat: 0 g   Polyunsaturated fat: 0 g
Cholesterol: 0 mg   Sodium: 265 mg

Variation: Other vegetables may be used. For example, carrots (thinly sliced), string beans, mushrooms, cauliflower, and broccoli. Also, a variety of fish may be used to make tempura, including squid or small fish such as smelts.

◊  ◊

Table-Top Cooking
(Nabemono)

Nabemono consists of one-pot do-it-yourself cooking. Fresh, artfully cut and arranged ingredients are simmered at the table and eaten with tasty dipping sauces. Sukiyaki, one example of a popular *nabemono*, is known throughout the world, but there are many other such dishes that are beginning to enter foreign cuisines. One-pot cookery makes giving a party a friendly, comparatively effortless occasion. If you don't have the traditional Japanese cooking pot (*do-nabe*) or a Mongolian hot-pot, any heavy flame-proof casserole set on an alcohol burner will do. An electric frying pan is an excellent substitute, so long as it is not too shallow.

Beef and Vegetables Cooked in Stock
(Shabu Shabu)

Because of Japan's Buddhist tradition, red meat was excluded from the Japanese diet until about a century ago. But aside from the religious prohibition, perhaps Japan's limited grazing lands and geographical location reveal a more logical explanation. Why should a nation of islands surrounded by waters that teem with such an astonishing variety of seafood need beef? Of course it doesn't, and fish remains the "meat" of preference.

Yet the most perfect beef in the world comes from Japan. In a unique method of raising cattle, the animal enjoys an unbelievably relaxed and pampered existence. When it isn't eating a diet of rice and beans, it is babied and massaged to produce the larding that is so prized in good

Japanese beef. Toward the end of its life, it will surrender further to its sybaritic existence by imbibing daily rations of beer. Even the proverbial life of Riley is no match for the life of Kobe's steer. Though larding makes delicious beef, it is 100% saturated animal fat. The name of this dish comes from the swishing sound that is made as the food is cooked.

1 pound lean fillet of beef or sirloin steak, frozen for 1 hour before being cut into paper-thin slices
6 ounces harusame (cellophane noodles; optional)
8 ounces soy bean curd (tofu), cut into 1-inch cubes
12 large leaves Chinese cabbage, cut into 2 or 3 pieces

16 medium spinach leaves, tough stems trimmed
8–12 small fresh mushrooms, washed and trimmed
12 asparagus tips in season, or substitute other vegetable
3 cups first dashi (p. 9), or chicken stock (p. 10), or vegetable stock (p. 41)

Dipping sauces:

Ponzu (*p. 58*)
2/3 cup white radish (daikon), finely grated

Sesame sauce (goma-dare), (*p. 59*)
2 scallions, finely chopped

1. Prepare the dipping sauces in advance. Pour 2 or 3 tablespoons of each of the dipping sauces into separate bowls for each person. Place chopped scallions and grated daikon in separate bowls. Refrigerate until ready for use. Guests will add scallions to sesame sauce and *daikon* to *ponzu* as they wish.
2. If using cellophane noodles, soak in hot water for 15–20 minutes. Rinse, drain, and cut noodles into 4- or 5-inch lengths. For best results be sure to also consult cooking instructions on noodle package.
3. Slice the meat across the grain in paper-thin slices. Partially frozen meet is eesier to cut. The slices should be large enough to be held securely with a chopstick while cooking, approximately 3 × 5 inches.
4. Arrange all the ingredients on a large platter and place it on the table within each diner's reach.
5. In a flame-proof pot, place 3 cups *dashi* or stock and bring it to a boil. Adjust the heat so the liquid simmers throughout the meal.
6. To eat *shabu-shabu*, select a piece of food from the platter with chopsticks and swish it about in the stock for 2 or 3 seconds without letting go of it. When it is barely done, dip it in one of the dipping sauces and eat it. Skim the broth from time to time if froth forms on the surface. Add more stock to the pot if needed. When all the food has been eaten, ladle

the broth into bowls and drink as soup. Since *shabu shabu* is a complete meal in itself, no other dishes need be served with it except perhaps an appetizer, a bowl of rice, and fresh fruit for dessert.

Yield: 4 servings

Nutrient analysis does not include dipping sauces.

Calories per serving: 395
Saturated fat: 6 g
Cholesterol: 105 mg

Total fat: 14 g
Polyunsaturated fat: 4 g
Sodium: 130 mg

Vegetable Stock:

Use approximately twice as much water as vegetables. Wash, peel, and slice a combination of onions (skins may be left on to give color to the stock), carrots, celery ribs, leeks, and a bay leaf or two. Cover, bring to a boil, and simmer for 1 ½ hours. Strain.

Seafood and Vegetables Cooked in Stock
(*Yosenabe*)

Yosenabe means "a pot full of everything." A variety of seafood and vegetables in season is cooked at the table and eaten with piquant dipping sauces. Allow ½ pound of seafood per person and select ingredients that will add texture and color contrasts to the dish. Lobsters, or large prawns, are often cooked in this dish.

½ pound firm white-meat fish fillets, cut into 1-inch pieces
18 medium shrimps, shelled and deveined
½ pound scallops
12 cherrystone clams, shucked and scrubbed
2 carrots
12 small fresh mushrooms, washed and trimmed

4 ounces harusame (*cellophane noodles*)
6 scallions, cut into 2-inch lengths
6 Chinese cabbage leaves, cut into 2 or 3 pieces
3 cups first dashi (*p. 9*),
or vegetable stock (p. 41),
or chicken stock (p. 10)

Dipping sauces:

Chirizu (*p. 57*)   1 *cup white radish* (daikon),
Ponzu (*p. 58*)   *grated*

1.   Prepare the dipping sauces in advance. Pour 2 or 3 tablespoons of each of the sauces into separate small dishes for each person. Place grated *daikon* in separate bowls. Refrigerate until ready for use. Guests will mix *daikon* with the sauces as they wish.

2.   Peel and cut carrots obliquely. Make a diagonal slice first, then roll the carrot a quarter of a turn and slice again. Repeat. Blanch in boiling water for 2 minutes. Drain.

3.   Soak cellophane noodles in hot water for 15–20 minutes. Rinse, drain, and cut noodles into 4- or 5-inch lengths.

4.   Arrange all ingredients attractively on a large platter and place at the dining table.

5.   In a heat-proof dish, bring stock to a boil. Adjust the heat so that the liquid simmers throughout the meal. To eat *yosenabe*, select a piece of food from the platter, cook it 1 or 2 minutes, and dip it in a dipping sauce. Skim the broth if froth forms on the surface. Add more stock, if needed. When all the food has been eaten, ladle the broth into bowls and drink it as soup. Rice may be served as a final course with a side dish of vinegared cucumbers (p. 21) if desired.

Yield: 6 servings

Nutrient count does not include dipping sauces.

Calories per serving: 205   Total fat: 2 g
Saturated fat: 0.5 g   Polyunsaturated fat: 0.5 g
Cholesterol: 85 mg   Sodium: 250 mg

Noodles
(Menrui)

Noodles, the fast food of Japan, are the most popular snack and lunch food in the country. As ubiquitous as the hamburger places in the United States, noodle shops can be found *everywhere* in Japan. There are several kinds of noodles, and they are eaten in a variety of ways with a variety of soups and sauces. Contrary to popular belief, most noodles are not high in calories, nor do they contain fat or sodium. It's what you add to them that puts them off-limits for dieters. In case you did not know, noodles are eaten with chopsticks in Japan. If you cannot master how to use them elegantly, do not be embarrassed. Slurping is not considered bad manners, so just enjoy yourself!

Moon-Viewing Noodles
(Tsukimi Udon)

This tasty noodle dish contains all the nutrients necessary for a complete meal. The name of the dish is poetically descriptive: the full moon is represented by a poached egg surrounded by clouds of noodles. Served steaming hot, *tsukimi udon* is comforting on a cold winter day. This recipe usually contains as much as ¼ cup of soy sauce. Even if you used the low-sodium variety, this would add up to 2,040 mg per serving. In the following recipe, seven-spice mixture (*shichimi togarashi*) and green horseradish (*wasabi*) compensate very nicely for the missing soy sauce.

12 ounces dried udon (white
 wheat-flour noodles; thick
 spaghetti may be
 substituted)
4 cups first dashi (p. 9),
 or chicken stock (p. 10)
1 ½ teaspoons low-sodium soy
 sauce
1 teaspoon sugar
2 tablespoons mirin
4 ounces spinach, washed
 and trimmed

4 ounces soybean curd (tofu),
 cut into bite-sized pieces
4 whole mushrooms
4 whole eggs
2 scallions, finely chopped
 Nori (dried laver), crumbled
 A dash of seven-spice mixture
 (shichimi togarashi)
2 tablespoons green horseradish
 (wasabi) powder

1. To cook noodles in the Japanese way, put them in a large pot of at least 5–6 quarts boiling water and bring back to a boil. Stir to keep from sticking. Add 1 cup of cold water and bring back to a boil again. Repeat this process 2 or 3 times, adding no more than 3 cups of cold water in all. Test for doneness. The noodles should be firm to the bite. Drain and rinse under cold running water. To reheat just before serving, immerse colander of noodles into boiling water.

Of course, the noodles can also be cooked in the Western way. Put them into a large quantity of rapidly boiling water and cook until they are done but still firm to the bite—just a little bit softer than the state that any Italian recognizes as al dente. Drain and rinse as above. (For best results, be sure to also consult cooking instructions on noodle package.) When ready to serve, divide noodles among 4 flameproof bowls.

2. Bring stock to a boil. Add soy sauce, mirin, spinach, and tofu. Cook 1 to 2 minutes. Divide among 4 bowls of noodles and return bowls to the stove and simmer on low heat.

3. Break an egg in the center of each bowl. Cover and cook egg to desired doneness. The Japanese like their egg barely set. If you would like to try it this way, turn the heat off after you break the eggs into the bowls and allow the heat of the bowls to cook the eggs. Then stir the loose eggs into the broth, which will further cook them.

If you are using an electric stove, remove the bowls from the burner after you break the eggs. If you do not have individual flameproof bowls, you may poach the eggs separately and slide them gently on top of each bowl of soup and noodles.

4. Sprinkle chopped scallions, nori, and seven-spice mixture (shichimi togarashi) on top of each serving.

5. Just before serving, mix the wasabi powder with a little water to make a stiff paste. Serve in 4 small individual dishes as a condiment.

Yield: 4 servings   Cooking time: 15 minutes

Calories per serving: 375 Total fat: 7 g
Saturated fat: 2.5 g Polyunsaturated fat: 2.5 g
Cholesterol: 275 mg Sodium: 175 mg

Note: Just that one egg yolk added 275 mg of cholesterol to each serving.

Variation: Add leftover meats or other vegetables. Some may need to be parboiled or blanched first if they are raw.

Iced Summer Noodles
(Hiyashi Somen)

This perfect hot-weather dish is usually eaten garnished simply with chopped scallions. It is traditionally served in glass bowls with matching smaller bowls for the dipping sauce.

16 ounces somen *(fine
    white wheat-flour noodles;
    a very fine vermicelli may
    be substituted)*

*16–20 ice cubes
    12 shrimps, or enough to
        make 6 ounces (op-
        tional)*

Garnishes:

*2 tablespoons scallions, finely
        chopped
8 thin slices of cucumber*

*4 sprigs trefoil (mitsuba),
        watercress, or parsley*

Noodle dipping sauce:

1½ cups first dashi *(p. 9),
        or chicken stock (p. 9)
3 tablespoons* mirin

*½–1 teaspoon low-sodium soy
        sauce
Seven-spice mixture
        (shichimi togarashi), to
        taste*

Condiments:

*4 tablespoons fresh ginger root,
        peeled and grated*

*½ cup scallions, finely chopped
1 tablespoon* wasabi *powder*

1.   Mix noodle dipping-sauce ingredients in a small saucepan, bring to a boil and simmer 1 minute. Remove from heat and chill.
2.   Grate ginger and chop scallions. Refrigerate until ready to serve.
3.   Mix *wasabi* powder with a little water to make a stiff paste. Keep covered until serving time.
4.   Drop shrimp into boiling water and cook until pink (2–3 minutes). Shell, devein, and chill.
5.   Cook noodles according to directions on package. Rinse and drain. Divide them equally among four serving bowls. Place 4 or 5 ice cubes around the edge of the bowl to keep the noodles cold.
6.   Arrange shrimp and garnishes decoratively on top.
7.   Serve the noodles with individual bowls of dipping sauce as well as with small individual dishes containing ginger root, scallions, and *wasabi* to be added to the dipping sauce as each diner wishes.

Yield: 4 servings   Cooking time: 15 minutes

Calories per serving: 250   Total fat: 1 g
Saturated fat: 0.5 g   Polyunsaturated fat: 0.5 g
Cholesterol: 50 mg   Sodium: 145 mg

◇  ◇

Rice Dishes and Sushi
(*Gohanmono* and *Sushi*)

Rice Dishes
(*Gohanmono*)

The Japanese prefer a short-grain rice that is slightly glutinous, and they like it to be cooked so that it remains moist but firm. This recipe should be used only as a guide. Because of the differences in the many varieties of Japanese rice on the market, it would be wise to follow the cooking instructions on the rice package.

The debate continues over whether or not to wash rice before cooking. Some say that it must be done to rid the rice of its starchy powder coating, which produces a gummy texture and affects the absorption of seasonings that may be added to the cooked rice. Others do not wash rice because they believe that many of the nutrients are lost with the water. Aside from true glutinous rice, which must actually be soaked before it can be cooked, I tend to side with the nonwashers (which would probably cause most Japanese to shudder with horror). My view, however, is reinforced by the producers of Kokuho Rose Rice, the Japanese rice that I use. The package plainly says in very large letters, WASHING NOT NECESSARY. Putting the debate aside, however, the best way to make perfect rice is to use a Japanese automatic rice cooker and to follow the directions that come with it to the letter. The rice is not washed in the following recipe.

Boiled Rice
(*Gohan*)

To make 3 cups cooked rice:

1 cup short-grain Japanese rice   1 ¼ cups cold water

1. In a heavy pot with a tight-fitting lid, measure rice and add water. Bring to a full, hard boil over high heat.
2. Reduce heat to low, cover, and simmer for 25 minutes. Do not remove lid at any time during cooking. Because electric stoves respond so slowly, to avoid scorching, move the pot to a second burner that has been preheated to its lowest setting.
3. Fluff lightly with a wooden paddle or spoon before serving. For softer, clingier rice, increase amount of water slightly. Reduce water for a firmer rice. Use at least one cup of raw rice at a time. Less rice and water will not produce the steam required for proper cooking.

If you have an automatic Japanese rice cooker, place the water and rice in the cooker and prepare according to the manufacturer's instructions.

Yield: 3–4 servings   Cooking time: 25 minutes

Calories per serving: 225   Total fat: 0.5 g
Saturated fat: Trace   Polyunsaturated fat: Trace
Cholesterol: 0 mg   Sodium: 5 mg

Note: Contrary to popular belief, rice is not high in calories. It contains virtually no fat and only a trace of sodium. The same is true of the potato. It is what you add to the rice and potatoes that makes the difference.

Rice Cooked with Vegetables
(*Maze Gohan*)

White rice speckled with colorful vegetables makes a delicious and wonderfully light one-dish meal. Feel free to improvise. You may substitute other vegetables or add chunks of fish or chicken. Serve *maze gohan* as a main course with perhaps a clear soup and/or a salad.

2–3 shiitake *mushrooms, or* ½
   cup fresh mushrooms,
   thinly sliced
1 *carrot, peeled and finely*
   shredded
½ *cup green beans, thinly*
   sliced on the diagonal
1 *red or green bell pepper,*
   cut into thin strips, or zuc-
   chini, cut into small
   cubes
16 *ginkgo nuts* (ginnan), *or*
   slivered almonds or
   chestnuts
1¾ *cups first* dashi (*p. 9*),
   or chicken stock (*p. 10*)

2 *tablespoons* mirin
1–1½ *teaspoons low-sodium*
   soy sauce
1½ *cups Japanese short-grain*
   rice (*Read preceding*
   recipe for boiled rice
   first. It is best to use the
   amount of liquid called
   for in the instructions
   on the rice package.)
½ *cup fresh green peas*
   (*Frozen green peas do*
   well in this recipe if
   fresh ones are not
   available.)
Seven-spice mixture
   (shichimi togarashi)

1.   If using dried Japanese mushrooms, soften by soaking in warm water for 30 minutes. Discard the hard stems and slice mushrooms finely.

2.   If you decide to wash the rice, drain and place in a heavy pot with a tight-fitting lid, or in an automatic rice cooker. Add all the solid ingredients except the green peas.

3.   Combine stock, *mirin*, and soy sauce, and a generous sprinkling of seven-spice mixture and add to the rice pot. (Adjust the amount of liquid to match that called for on the rice package if you wish.) Stir gently, bring to a boil over high heat. Reduce heat to low, cover, and simmer for 10 minutes, or until all liquid is absorbed.

4.   Turn heat down to lowest point and cook 5 more minutes. Because electric stoves respond so slowly, to avoid scorching, move the pot to a second burner that has been preheated to its lowest setting.

5.   Turn off heat and let pot stand covered for 10 to 15 minutes before fluffing. Do *not* remove lid at any time during cooking.

6.   One or 2 minutes before serving, stir in the green peas. The heat of the pot will cook them. Sprinkle with additional seven-spice mixture (*shichimi togarashi*) to taste and serve hot.

Yield: 4 servings

Cooking time: 30 minutes

Calories per serving: 335
Saturated fat: 0.5 g
Cholesterol: 0 mg

Total fat: 1 g
Polyunsaturated fat: 0.5 g
Sodium: 75 mg

Sushi
(Sushi)

Sushi, the glory of Japanese cuisine, is perhaps the best-known food of Japan. The word originally meant simply vinegared rice; but there is more to it these days than rice. There are various wrappings, toppings, and fillings—some vegetable, others fish (uncooked), shrimp, caviar, and more. Some years ago, only a few devotees cared for sushi because of a Western aversion to raw fish. That's all changed now. Judging from the number of sushi bars (not all first-rate) in the metropolitan areas of the United States, especially in California, Americans have not only overcome their bias against eating raw fish, but have actually become addicted to it. And what a heathful addiction it is.

Recent medical studies suggest that certain fatty acids in fish have a protective effect on the heart and blood vessels and that shellfish, once considered to be high in cholesterol, also contain a fair amount of these protective substances. On the basis of these studies, health practitioners believe that eating fish at least twice a week instead of meat, eggs, and butterfats, may diminish the risk of cardiovascular and coronary heart diseases. (More details on these studies can be found in the ingredients section of this book on page xxiv.) For sushi lovers, this comes as good news, and, if one takes care to use the soy-sauce-and-*wasabi* dip sparingly, then sushi is a perfect food.

Sushi has a long history. It originated as a way to preserve fish by salting it and allowing it to ferment in layers of rice. However, the rice was discarded when the fermentation process was completed. A successor to this process is a kind of sushi known as *oshi-zushi*,* or pressed sushi, in which vinegared fish and rice are pressed into a shallow mold and cut into bite-sized pieces to eat. Many different combinations and methods of serving sushi have evolved since. The most commonly eaten type of sushi today is called *nigiri-zushi*, or hand-shaped sushi, which originated in Edo (Tokyo) in the early nineteenth century. Together with this perennial favorite, which consists of a small "finger" of vinegared rice that is topped with some delicious morsel, there are also other types that are equally popular, the most famous being *maki-zushi*, or rolled sushi, with its many variations. Strips of seafood, vegetables, or pickles are placed on a bed of rice that is then rolled into a cylinder, covered on the outside by a sheet of dried toasted seaweed (*nori*) and cut into ½-inch thick slices.

Learning how to make sushi is a formidable and time-consuming task. A sushi master must complete a long and exacting period of training before he can properly learn how to select, fillet, and slice the fish, as well as to arrange these artful combinations of food with a manual dexterity akin to a magician's. Some of the kinds of seafood usually used to make sushi include tuna, yellowtail, flounder, halibut, sea bream, salmon roe, and shrimp. I recommend that the fish be purchased already filleted from a trustworthy fishmonger. One cannot overstress the necessity for absolute freshness. Frozen fish cannot be used. It must be obtained from a handler who has the strictest standards. If a fish smells, it is not only too old to be eaten raw—it is too old to be eaten cooked.

Another word of caution is that only saltwater fish be used; one reason for this is that freshwater fish often contain parasites that cannot exist in saltwater. Another is that lakes and rivers are often, unfortunately, polluted.

For the purposes of this book, recipes are given for only two types of sushi: a do-it-yourself sushi called *temaki-zushi* and a lovely dish called *chirashi-zushi*, or scattered sushi, which is served in a bowl like a salad. Both are within the capabilities of every cook. The ingredients are the same, but no expert dexterity is required. For an aesthetically rewarding experience, eat the delectable fingers of *nigiri-zushi* in a sushi bar, where the taste is reminiscent of heaven and the performance of the sushi master makes the meal a more than memorable event.

Note: The Japanese word *sushi* becomes *-zushi* in compounds.

Vinegared Rice
(*Su-meshi*)

2 cups short-grain rice	3 cups water

Vinegar dressing:

⅓ cup rice vinegar, or mild white vinegar	¼ cup sugar

1.   In a small saucepan, dissolve the sugar in the vinegar over low heat. Cool.

2.   Cook rice according to recipe for boiled rice on p. 48. While still hot, sprinkle vinegar dressing on it. Simultaneously fluff rice gently with a wooden paddle or spoon, being sure to use a cutting motion rather than a stirring motion. Fan the rice to cool it down quickly. You may not need all of the dressing. Be careful not to add too much liquid or the rice will become soggy. Grains should be separate; the rice should never become mushy.

Note: It is usual to vary amount of vinegar or sugar to suit individual taste. The salt that the Japanese use (about 3 tsps for this amount) has been left out of this recipe, but it is not missed when the rice is eaten with other things that are dipped in flavorful sauces.

Yield: 6 cups cooked rice   Cooking time: 45 minutes

Calories per cup: 260   Total fat: 0.5 g
Saturated fat: Trace   Polyunsaturated fat: Trace
Cholesterol: 0 mg   Sodium: 5 mg

Scattered Sushi
(*Chirashi-zushi*)

Scattered sushi is the simplest kind of sushi to prepare and is well within the skills of every cook. Boiled crab and shrimp and a colorful assortment of vegetables and egg are mixed in and scattered on top of vinegared rice. A complete one-dish meal, much of which can be cooked in advance, scattered sushi makes a delicious and beautiful hot weather dish. Feel free to alter the selection of ingredients to suit taste and availability. You may leave out the seafood altogether and just mix the vinegared rice with as few or as many vegetables—with or without the egg—as you wish. The combinations are limitless.

*1 recipe vinegared rice
(su-meshi; p. 51)
12 ounces cooked crabmeat
6 cooked medium shrimps
4–5 shiitake mushrooms, or
1 cup fresh mushrooms*

*2 carrots, peeled and cut
into very thin strips
4 ounces lotus root (renkon),
peeled and cut into ⅛-inch
slices. Soak in water with 1
tablespoon vinegar to prevent discoloring.*

1 zucchini squash, cut into
matchstick strips
1 green or red bell pepper,
deribbed and cut into thin
strips
4 ounces snow peas. If not
available, use string beans or
green peas. Some green color
is desirable as an accent in
this dish.
1 recipe thin omelet (p. 33;
optional)
1 lemon, cut into 6 wedges

Garnishes:

1 sheet nori (dried laver)
Packaged pickled ginger
(beni shoga), cut into thin
bits

2 tablespoons white sesame
seeds

1. Boil rice according to the recipe on p. 48. Prepare vinegar dressing
called for and mix into rice. Cool and set aside.
2. Shred the crabmeat, leaving a few choice pieces to scatter on top.
Squeeze a little lemon juice on the crabmeat.
3. Drop shrimp into boiling water and cook uncovered 2 or 3 minutes.
Rinse in cold water and shell and devein. Dry and set aside.
4. If using dried *shiitake*, soak in warm water for 30 minutes to soften.
Discard hard stems and slice mushrooms into fine strips.
5. Parboil vegetables in the following manner: bring to a boil 1 cup
first *dashi* (p. 9), or chicken stock (p. 10), combined with 1 teaspoon sugar,
2 teaspoons saké, and 1/4 teaspoon low-sodium soy sauce; add thinly sliced
lotus root, carrots, zucchini, bell pepper, and mushrooms, and simmer 1
minute, or until tender but crisp; drain and set aside.
6. Make thin omelets, cut into thin strips, and set aside.
7. Trim snow peas and blanch in boiling water for 1 minute. Drain
and rinse in cold water. Dry and cut into matchstick strips.

To assemble:

1. Gently fold the shredded crabmeat and parboiled vegetables into
the vinegared rice. Place the mixture in a large shallow serving bowl or into 6 individual bowls.
2. Scatter decoratively on top the reserved crab pieces, cooked
shrimps, omelet strips, and snow peas.

To garnish:

1.   Sprinkle the chopped pickled ginger on top.
2.   Hold sheets of *nori*, one at a time, with tongs and toast over very low heat over a burner on top of the stove, waving it slowly back and forth, until it looks translucent and green when held up to the light. You can also toast it in a toaster oven, but you will have to be careful, since it burns easily.
3.   Toast the sesame seeds for a few seconds in a dry skillet over medium heat. Shake the pan to keep the seeds from scorching. Sprinkle all over the top.

Serving suggestion:

Serve scattered sushi at room temperature; a clear soup makes a nice accompanying dish.

Yield: 6 servings   Preparation time: 45 minutes
                                                                to 1 hour

Nutrient count does not include omelets or pickled ginger.

Calories per serving: 410   Total fat: 25 g
Saturated fat: 0.5 g   Polyunsaturated fat: 0.5 g
Cholesterol: 65 mg   Sodium: 100 mg

Variation: For everyday fare, select 2 or 3 vegetables you may have on hand. For example, carrots, mushrooms, and green peas. Blanch them for 1 or 2 minutes and cut them into thin strips. Prepare vinegared rice, add the cooked, drained vegetables, and mix well. If you include diced leftover meat in the mixture, you will have a complete meal.

Hand-Wrapped Sushi
(*Temaki-zushi*)

No manual dexterity whatsoever is need to make this delightful and delicious variety of sushi. Each diner wraps his own cone-shaped package, making this a pleasant, informal occasion for friends to share a meal. The ingredients are cut and arranged on a platter along with a bowl of vinegared rice and side dishes of dipping sauces and condiments. The wrapper is a sheet of *nori* (dried laver). For those who do not like the taste of *nori*, lettuce or spinach leaves make a good substitute. *Temaki-zushi* may be served as a first course, a lunch, as an hors d'oeuvre course, or as party food.

1 recipe vinegared rice (p. 51)
12 medium shrimps
8 ounces very fresh raw fish
    fillets, cut into pieces 1/4-
    inch thick and about 2 in-
    ches long (Red snapper, sea
    bream, tuna, and
    yellowtail are suitable.)
2 cucumbers, cut into very
    thin 2-inch matchstick
    lengths

1 recipe thin omelet
    (p. 33; optional)
Watercress, or flat-leaved
    parsley or young spinach
    leaves
8–12 sheets dried laver (nori)
    Lettuce leaves, raw, and
    large spinach leaves
    blanched for 30 seconds
    (to be used as wrappers)

Condiments and dipping sauce:

Packaged pickled ginger
2 tablespoons green horseradish
    (wasabi) powder, mixed with
    a little water to form a stiff
    paste

1–2 recipes chirizu dipping
    sauce (p. 57)

1.   Prepare vinegared rice and set aside.

2.   Before cooking the shrimp, insert a toothpick lengthwise along the inner curve to prevent curling and cook in boiling water for 2 to 3 minutes. Drain, shell, and devein.

3.   If possible, have a fishmonger fillet and slice the fish. Handle as little as possible and keep in refrigerator until ready to eat.

4.   Slice cucumber. Make omelets and cut into thin strips.

5.   Hold sheets of *nori*, one at a time, with tongs and toast over very low heat over a burner on top of the stove, waving it slowly back and forth, until it looks translucent and green when held up to the light. You can also toast it in a toaster oven, but you will have to be careful, since it burns easily. Cut into quarters.

6.   Arrange all ingredients attractively on the table. The procedure is to take a sheet of *nori* and to place a tablespoon or two of rice on it. Then select a piece of fish, a sprig of watercress, cucumber, ginger, or whatever appeals to you. Add a bit of horseradish and roll into a cone-shaped bundle. Eat as is, or dip into the dipping sauce; or you can eat this as the Japanese usually do, by leaving the horseradish out of the cone and dipping it into a little dish of low-sodium soy sauce to which a bit of horseradish has been added (but watch out, since it is much hotter than you think).

Yield: 6 servings   Preparation time: About 1 hour

Nutrient analysis does not include pickled ginger, thin omelet, or dipping sauce.

Calories per serving: 345   Total fat: 1.5 g
Saturated fat: Trace   Polyunsaturated fat: 0.5 g
Cholesterol: 65 mg   Sodium: 95 mg

Dipping Sauces
(Tare)

All the following dipping sauces contain less soy sauce than would normally be used in Japan. For extra bite, ¼ to ½ teaspoon of Japanese mustard (Wa-garashi) or any hot dry mustard may be added. You may also want to experiment with adding green horseradish (wasabi) or seven-spice mixture (shichimi togarashi) to give your sauce a little more kick. Be careful to add only a little of these at a time, however, since they are hotter than you might think. You probably do not want to use more than one of these in any dish, either, as their flavors do not mix well, as least not to the Japanese palate.

White Radish-and-Soy Dipping Sauce
(Chirizu)

4 tablespoons saké
⅓ cup Japanese white radish
    (daikon), finely grated
2 scallions, white and some
    tender green portions,
    thinly sliced

2 tablespoons low-sodium soy
    sauce
¼ cup freshly squeezed lemon
    (or lime) juice
¼ teaspoon seven-spice mixture
    (shichimi togarashi)

Heat the saké. When it cools, mix it with the other ingredients and serve it in small individual dishes at each diner's place.

Yield: ¾ cup   Preparation time: 1 minute

Calories per tablespoon: 10   Total fat: 0 g
Saturated fat: 0 g   Polyunsaturated fat: 0 g
Cholesterol: 0 mg   Sodium: 90 mg

Lemon-and-Soy Dipping Sauce
(*Ponzu*)

3 tablespoons freshly squeezed   6 tablespoons first dashi
    lemon (or lime) juice   (p. 9), chicken stock (p. 10),
3 tablespoons low-sodium soy   or water
    sauce

Mix all ingredients and serve in small individual dishes at each diner's place.

Yield: ¾ cup   Preparation time: 1 minute

Calories per tablespoon: 5   Total fat: 0 g
Saturated fat: 0 g   Polyunsaturated fat: 0 g
Cholesterol: 0 mg   Sodium: 130 mg

Sweet-and-Sour Sauce
(*Amazu*)

½ cup Japanese rice vinegar   ¼ cup sugar
    (mild white vinegar may   2 tablespoons freshly squeezed
    be substituted)   lemon (or lime) juice

Combine all ingredients in a saucepan and bring to a boil. Cook until sugar dissolves. Cool.

Yield: ⅔ cup   Preparation time: 1 minute

Calories per tablespoon: 20

Total fat: 0 g

Saturated fat: 0 g

Polyunsaturated fat: 0 g

Cholesterol: 0 mg

Sodium: 0 mg

Vinegar-and-Soy Dipping Sauce
(*Sanbaizu*)

¼ cup Japanese rice (or mild
   white) vinegar
¼ cup first dashi (*p. 9*), or
   chicken stock (*p. 10*), or
   water

1–2 tablespoons sugar
2 tablespoons low-sodium soy
   sauce

Combine all ingredients in a saucepan. While stirring, bring to a boil and immediately remove from heat. Cool and set aside. Serve in small individual serving dishes as a dipping sauce.

Yield: ⅔ cup

Preparation time: 1–2 minutes

Calories per tablespoon: 10

Total fat: 0 g

Saturated fat: 0 g

Polyunsaturated fat: 0 g

Cholesterol: 0 mg

Sodium: 105 mg

Sesame Sauce
(*Goma-dare*)

½ cup white sesame seeds
3 tablespoons saké
1 teaspoon sugar
1 tablespoon low-sodium soy
   sauce

2 tablespoons first dashi (*p. 9*),
   chicken stock (*p. 10*), or
   water

1.   In a heated dry skillet, lightly toast the sesame seeds over moderate heat. Shake the pan to avoid scorching. Remove quickly and pound the

seeds in a mortar and pestle (or in a Japanese *suribachi*), or process in an electric blender until oil is released.

2. Add the remaining ingredients one at a time and mix thoroughly.

Yield: ½ cup   Preparation time: 1–2 minutes

Calories per tablespoon: 65   Total fat: 4.5 g
Saturated fat: 1 g   Polyunsaturated fat: 2 g
Cholesterol: 0 mg   Sodium: 65 mg

Korea

◊  ◊

The Korean Kitchen

Korea first became familiar to Americans during the Korean War. A peninsula just 600 miles long, Korea borders on Manchuria and the Soviet Union in the north, faces China to the west, and looks toward Japan to the east. It is a land of rugged mountains and a heavily indented coastline, along which lie some thousands of tiny islands, most of them rocky and uninhabited. Its strategic position and its natural resources have made it several times a battleground for its more powerful neighbors.

Though Chinese and Japanese influences have been strong in Korean history, the Korean people belong to a racial and cultural group that is distinct from both the Japanese and Chinese. The Korean language is also unique. Though it is akin to Japanese in its grammatical structure, it is thought by some linguists to be related to the Altaic family of languages and by others to be of uncertain origin. Once written in Chinese characters, modern Korean has its own phonetic alphabet (*hangul*), which was devised in the fifteenth century by a Korean king and his scholars. It is so scientifically matched to the sound system of the language that the Korean alphabet is considered by scholars to be a remarkable linguistic achievement. Also developed in the fifteenth century was printing with movable type. A little known fact is that a half-century before it was used in Europe, movable type made from metal molds was already in use in Korea.

Through the centuries, Korea came under the influence of China's civilization and religions. Chinese influence remained strong until the Japanese occupation, which continued until the end of World War II. During its history, repeated invasions by surrounding countries compelled the Korean government to shut its doors to the outside world, and for a time Korea's complete isolation earned it the name "Hermit Kingdom." It was after Japan's defeat in World War II that Soviet and U.S. forces arbitrarily

divided the country into two zones, thereby establishing two rival govern-
ments.

Most Koreans are Confucianists or Buddhists, although the people tend
to be eclectic in their religious practices. For example, Korean Confu-
cianism has developed into more of an ethical system than a religion and
its influence is wide and pervasive. The Christian religion had a particular
appeal during the years of the Japanese occupation, again after World War
II, and even more so after the Korean War. In South Korea, Christianity is
said to be growing at a rapid rate, and, next to the Philippines, Korea has
more Christians than any other Asian country.

What has astonished the world in recent years is South Korea's deter-
mination to become an industrialized nation. Its achievements have been
impressive. It has produced and exported automobiles, personal com-
puters, and other consumer goods of very high quality, thus
demonstrating to the already industrialized countries how close it is to
becoming a world-class economic power.

While Korean food bears some resemblance to Chinese and Japanese
cuisine, it retains a definite character of its own that distinguishes it from
both. It is a hearty cuisine characterized by a fondness for beef, for rich
warming soups, and for its lavish use of garlic, sesame oil, and sesame
seeds. The seeds are toasted and then crushed, thus imparting a rich nutty
aroma entirely missed when the toasting process is omitted. Another
seasoning frequently used is chili pepper, but, unlike the fiery hot dishes
of Thailand and India, Korean dishes are more discreetly spiced. Soy
sauce, scallions, and fresh ginger root are also frequently used. Some
Korean dishes are obviously related to Chinese and Japanese cooking. For
example *manduguk*, a soup made with meat, soybean curd, and vegetable-
filled dumplings, is similar though decidedly different from Chinese *wonton* soup. Koreans use beef stock for the broth and season the filling with
sesame oil and sesame seeds.

A typically Korean dish is *kimchi*, a highly seasoned and fermented
pickle of cabbage and turnips. Probably developed as a way of preserving
vegetables without refrigeration, *kimchi* accompanies every meal, including breakfast. Another food that appears frequently on the Korean
table is *kim*, the Korean name for the seaweed called *nori* in Japanese.
These thin sheets of seaweed are lightly toasted then either crumpled and
used as a condiment over food or kept intact and used as a wrapper for a
roll known as *kim bap*. To prepare this roll, a thin layer of rice is spread on
a sheet of seaweed, over which is placed cooked ground beef seasoned
with sesame and vegetables. The whole is wrapped like a jelly roll and cut
into thin slices. This is reminiscent of Japanese *temaki-zushi*, but Koreans
prefer to use beef. Who influenced whom is debatable, though sushi in all
its elaborate forms remains a Japanese invention.

Of course, the cornerstone of Korean cooking is, as elsewhere in Asia, a
dish of perfectly cooked rice—not the fluffy long-grain rice of China but

the short-grain rice that the Japanese favor. To make good rice by Korean standards, cook it as directed on page 48 in the Japanese section. Rice is also often cooked with other things such as beans, millet, and even *kim-chi*. Soybean products common to all three countries are also staple foods in Korea. But there are two varieties of Korean bean paste. One type, *twenjang*, resembles the *miso* pastes of Japan. The second variety, *kochu-jang*, contains ground hot red chili pepper.

Unlike China and Japan, Korea is not a tea drinking nation, at least not the usual type of tea. Rather, the beverage that often accompanies a Korean meal is barley tea, drunk cold in summer and hot in winter. Perhaps the most famous beverage unique to Korea is a tea brewed from ginseng, a root shaped like the human body. Its healthful effects have been prized for centuries, not only in the Far East but also in Europe, and at one time ginseng was worth its weight in gold because it was believed to cure certain illnesses and to have aphrodisiac and rejuvenating benefits. Now it is produced commercially in three forms—a powdered herb tea, a powdered capsule to take as one would take a vitamin, and a liqueur. Like coffee, it is an acquired taste.

A typical Korean meal consists of rice, a bowl of soup, and as many side dishes as the purse allows. Three would be an average number and would include a meat or fish dish, *kimchi*, and one or two vegetable dishes. Preparing a Korean meal is very much like preparing a Chinese meal, with the main job being chopping and slicing. But Koreans slice and shred meats and vegetables more finely than Chinese cookery requires. However, most of the cooking is quite simple and requires only a frying pan and a saucepan or two. Serving a family-style Korean meal is like serving a Chinese meal. All the dishes are set in the middle of the table at once. Rice and soup are served in individual bowls that are placed before each diner. Chopsticks are used as well as spoons.

Adapting Korean Food to a Low-Sodium, Low-Cholesterol Diet

In keeping with the purposes of this book, the selection of Korean recipes has been limited to those that could be appetizingly adapted to a low-salt, low-fat diet. Chicken has sometimes been substituted for beef, and the use of soy sauce and bean pastes has been kept to a minimum. However, a few beef dishes have been included because they are so typical of Korean cooking. It is suggested that care be taken to trim away all fat and to drain any that may be rendered in the cooking process.

To further compensate for the absence of salt and for the reduced quantity of soy sauce in these recipes, it is suggested that extra freshly ground black pepper, cayenne pepper, or chili pepper flakes be added. Also mustard sauce (*keja*; p. 68), used in small quantities, does wonders to liven up certain dishes.

◊  ◊

Appetizers
(Pan)

Nine Delicacies Hors d'Oeuvres
(Ku Jeol Pan)

This inspired creation usually served on festive occasions makes a wonderful hors d'oeuvre as well as a main dish. A variety of finely shredded vegetables and meats is stir-fried separately and arranged in mounds around a pile of pancakes. The fillings are rolled in the pancakes and eaten with a hot mustard sauce. Koreans use an octagonal-shaped serving platter with eight compartments for the savory dishes and a center one for the pancakes. Since *ku jeol pan* is served at room temperature, it is an ideal dish for advance preparation. Almost any fresh vegetable will substitute for the ones suggested here. If the recipe seems too elaborate, substitute lettuce leaves for the pancakes.

Pancakes:

Korean cooks use whole eggs in the batter. This is a low cholesterol adaptation. For a more tender pancake, use 3 egg whites and 3 yolks.

2 cups flour	1 cup water
6 egg whites	1 tablespoon safflower oil, or
1 cup nonfat milk	melted unsalted margarine

1. Sift flour into a bowl.
2. Beat together remaining ingredients.
3. Make a well in the center of the flour and add liquid. Beat until smooth. Use an electric blender if desired.
4. Cover and refrigerate at least 2 hours or overnight if possible. Do

not omit this important step. The batter should be thin. Add a little water
if the batter does not seem thin enough.

5.   Heat a small nonstick pan over moderate heat. Grease lightly with
oil or margarine. Pour enough batter to make a thin pancake 3–4 inches in
diameter. When firm, turn and cook on other side. Pancakes should not
brown. If uniform size is desired, cook large pancakes and cut them into
smaller circles with a water glass or cookie cutter.

Note: The pancakes can be made ahead of time and frozen between
layers of wax paper.

Yield: About 36 pancakes	Cooking time: About 1 hour
Calories per pancake: 30	Total fat: 0.5 g
Saturated fat: 0 g	Polyunsaturated fat: 0.5 g
Cholesterol: 0 mg	Sodium: 15 mg

Fillings:

6 ounces lean sirloin, or flank steak	2 green or red bell peppers, or 2 zucchini squashes
6 ounces chicken breast meat, or cooked crabmeat, or shrimps	6 scallions
3 cups Chinese (Napa) cabbage	3 tablespoons sesame oil
1 ½ thin cucumbers	1 teaspoon low-sodium soy sauce
2 carrots	3 tablespoons toasted sesame seeds (kkaesokum; p. 86)
½ pound green beans	Freshly ground black pepper

1.   Cut the beef and chicken meat into thin slices, then cut slices into
thin matchstick strips. Partially frozen meat is easier to cut. Heat a teaspoon of oil and stir-fry beef and chicken separately, adding one-half teaspoon soy sauce, 1 tablespoon sesame seeds, and a generous grinding of
pepper to each. Meats should be well done and dry. Set aside in separate
bowls.

2.   Cut vegetables into thin matchstick strips. There should be about 1
cup of each. Keep separated. Do not peel zucchini or cucumber unless it
has been waxed. Heat oil and stir-fry each vegetable separately adding
generous grindings of black pepper to each. Do not overcook. Do not add
soy sauce because it is important that vegetables retain their bright color.
Garnish with remaining sesame seeds.

3.   Place vegetables and meats in separate mounds on a large serving
platter with pancakes in the center. Take a pancake, brush a bit of
mustard sauce (keja; p. 68) on it, then add some filling, roll, and eat.

Yield: 8–12 servings   Cooking time: 15–20 minutes

Nutrient analysis is for fillings only. Obviously, this is the sort of dish that is difficult to measure with any degree of accuracy.

Calories per serving: 170   Total fat: 10 g
Saturated fat: 2.5 g   Polyunsaturated fat: 5 g
Cholesterol: 35 mg   Sodium: 65 mg

Mustard Sauce (*Keja*):
(About ¼ cup)

¼ cup dried mustard   1 teaspoon low-sodium soy
  1 teaspoon sugar   sauce

Combine all ingredients with 3 or 4 tablespoons of water and let sauce mellow before serving. Sauce should have a paste-like consistency.

Yield: 16 teaspoons   Preparation time: 1 minute

Calories per teaspoon: 10   Total fat: 0 g
Saturated fat: 0 g   Polyunsaturated fat: 0 g
Cholesterol: 0 mg   Sodium: 15 mg

Soups
(*Tang, Kuk,* and *Tchigae*)

Beef Stock
(*Sokogi Tang*)

This is an adaptation of the American Heart Association recipe for beef broth.

2 pounds boneless lean beef, all
    fat removed
1 tablespoon safflower oil
1 large onion, quartered

4 large slices fresh ginger root
3 or 4 bay leaves
2 quarts water
10 peppercorns

1. In a large sauce pan, heat oil and lightly brown meat. Pour off fat.
2. Add remaining ingredients and bring to a boil. Skim off the froth. Turn heat down to low, cover, and simmer 2–3 hours. Remove meat and use for another recipe.
3. Strain stock and measure. Adjust yield to 6 cups by adding water or boiling down excess stock. Refrigerate. When ready to use, discard layer of fat that congeals on the surface.

Yield: About 6 cups

Calories per cup: 10
Saturated fat: 0 g
Cholesterol: 0 mg

Cooking time: 2–3 hours

Total fat: 0 g
Polyunsaturated fat: 0 g
Sodium: 35 mg

White Radish Soup
(Mu Tang)

The giant white radish (*mu*), also called Chinese turnip or *daikon* (in Japanese), has a crisp texture and a flavor similar to a turnip. Most supermarkets carry this white-fleshed root in their produce section.

1 teaspoon sesame oil
4 large cloves garlic, minced
1/4 pound very lean beef, cut across the grain into thin strips
4 cups beef stock (p. 69)
2 cups white radish, peeled and thinly sliced

1 teaspoon low-sodium soy sauce
1/2–1 teaspoon freshly grated black pepper
2 scallions, finely chopped

1.   Heat oil over high heat and saute garlic and beef until meat changes color.
2.   Add beef stock and bring to a boil. Add radish, reduce heat, and simmer until tender, about 10 minutes.
3.   Add soy sauce, black pepper, and scallions and simmer 1 more minute.

Yield: 4 servings

Cooking time: 15 minutes

Calories per serving: 110
Saturated fat: 1.5 g
Cholesterol: 30 mg

Total fat: 4.2 g
Polyunsaturated fat: 2 g
Sodium: 125 mg

Variation: Four ounces soybean curd cut into 1/2 inch cubes may be added before step 3. Cook 2 or 3 minutes longer.

Soybean Sprout Soup
(Kong Namul Kuk)

This excellent soup is best made with soybean sprouts, which have a large body and a distinctive nutty flavor. If they are not available in your area, the small common mung bean sprout may be substituted, but it is not nearly as good.

1 teaspoon sesame oil
3 large cloves garlic minced
¼ pound lean tender beef, cut
    across the grain into very
    thin strips
4 cups beef stock (p. 69)

3 cups soybean sprouts,
    trimmed and washed
2 scallions, finely chopped
1 teaspoon low-sodium soy
    sauce
½–1 teaspoon freshly ground
    black pepper

1.   Heat oil over high heat and saute garlic and beef about 2 or 3 minutes or until meat changes color.

2.   Add stock and bring to a boil. Add sprouts and simmer 5–7 minutes, or until tender.

3.   Add scallions, soy sauce, and pepper and serve hot.

Yield: 4 servings

Cooking time: 15 minutes

Calories per serving: 120
Saturated fat: 1.5 g
Cholesterol: 30 mg

Total fat: 4.5 g
Polyunsaturated fat: 2 g
Sodium: 100 mg

Beef-and-Fish Soup with Hot Bean Paste
(Sokogi wa Saengsun Tchigae)

A *tchigae* is a hot and spicy soup seasoned with red soybean paste (*kochujang*), a soy product similar to Japanese soybean paste (*miso*). The big difference between the two is that the Korean bean paste is generously laced with hot chilies. Various combinations of ingredients may be put into a *tchigae*, including beef, fish, vegetables, and soybean curd. How much sodium Korean bean paste contains is unknown, but I am assuming that it is close to the amount in Japanese bean paste, which averages approximately 284 mg per teaspoon. In any case, the quantity that this recipe calls for makes a very mild soup. Though higher in sodium than is recommended for strict dieters, as occasional fare a *tchigae* is a zesty treat. In this recipe, meat and fish are combined, a rare practice in Western cooking but common in Korea. Served with rice and a vegetable, this soup is substantial enough to be the main course.

5 Chinese mushrooms, or 1 cup sliced fresh mushrooms	4 cups beef stock (p. 69)
1 ½–2 teaspoons red bean paste (kochujang), (Japanese-style red miso paste with cayenne pepper added to taste may be substituted.)	¼ pound very lean beef, cut across the grain into thin strips
4 large cloves garlic, minced	½ pound firm fish fillets, cut into 1-inch chunks
	4 ounces soybean curd, cut into ½-inch cubes
	2 scallions, finely chopped

Garnish:

2 sheets kim (*dried seaweed; like the Japanese* nori)

1.   Soak dried mushrooms in hot water to cover for 30 minutes. Cut off and discard stems and thinly slice caps.
2.   Combine bean paste, garlic, and stock and bring to a boil. Cover and simmer 10 minutes.
3.   Add mushrooms and beef and cook 5 minutes.
4.   Add fish fillets and cook 30 seconds or until barely done.
5.   Add bean curd and scallions and cook 1 to 2 minutes more. Serve immediately.
6.   Hold each sheet of seaweed with tongs over very low heat from a burner on top of the stove until it turns a greenish color, or toast very briefly in a toaster oven. Be careful or it will burn in a matter of seconds. Crumble over the soup.

Yield: 4–6 servings

Cooking time: 18 to 20 minutes

Calories per serving: 180

Total fat: 5 g

Saturated fat: 1.5 g

Polyunsaturated fat: 2 g

Cholesterol: 55 mg

Sodium: 205 mg

Variation: Shrimps may be substituted for the beef. Add them in step 4 with the fish.

◊  ◊

Fish
(Saengsun)

Grilled Fish with Sesame Sauce
(Saengsun Kui)

Quick and easy to prepare, the sesame sauce used in this recipe is excellent on fish.

1 pound firm fish fillets or a whole fish

Sesame Sauce:

*1 teaspoon low-sodium soy
    sauce
½ teaspoon sugar
2 tablespoons sesame oil
2 large cloves garlic, minced
2 scallions, finely chopped*

*2 tablespoons toasted sesame
    seeds (kkaesokum; p. 86)
Dried crushed chili peppers,
    or cayenne pepper to taste,
    or ½ teaspoon hot red bean
    paste (kochujang)*

1.   Combine all sauce ingredients and coat fish on both sides.
2.   Grill under the oven broiler 3 or 4 minutes on each side, or bake in a lightly greased baking dish until just done. Do not overcook.

Yield: 4 servings

Cooking time: 6–8 minutes

Calories per serving: 205
Saturated fat: 1.5 g
Cholesterol: 60 mg

Total fat: 11 g
Polyunsaturated fat: 7 g
Sodium: 120 mg

Fish Fillets and Vegetables Wrapped in Egg Batter
(Saengsun Sanjuk Chunya)

Skewers of fish and vegetables seasoned in a garlic-sesame marinade are wrapped in egg batter and cooked on top of the stove in a frying pan. Nothing could be more tasty, but with the amount of cholesterol in egg yolks, the recipe was obviously not appropriate for a book of this sort. I decided to try it using the American Heart Association's recipe for egg substitute, which is made from egg whites, and immediately changed my mind. I also tried the recipe with commerical egg substitute and was surprised at how good it turned out. Also made from egg whites, egg substitutes are sold in the dairy section of most markets. Read the labels carefully, however, and do not buy any that contain coconut or palm oil or other saturated fat. (Please read about eggs on page xxvi) This dish also makes an excellent hors d'oeuvre.

1 pound thin fillet of sole, or
   other firm white-flesh fish
1 green bell pepper
6 large mushrooms
12 scallions

2 cups egg substitute (p. 76),
   or commercial egg
   substitute
1 tablespoon sesame oil
Flour for dredging
12 wooden skewers

Marinade:

4 large cloves garlic
1 teaspoon low-sodium soy
   sauce
1 teaspoon sesame oil
1 teaspoon black pepper

3-4 tablespoons rice wine (sool),
   or pale dry sherry
2 teaspoons toasted sesame
   seeds (kkaesokum; p. 86)

1.   Cut fish into 24 thin strips approximately ½ × 2 inches long.
2.   Combine marinade ingredients in a bowl, coat fish fillets with mixture, and set aside.
3.   Cut 2-inch lengths from the white ends of the scallions.
4.   Cut green pepper into 12 pieces approximately ½ × 2 inches long. Cut mushrooms in half.
5.   Pour egg batter in a shallow bowl.
6.   Alternate vegetables with 2 pieces of fish on each skewer. Dredge threaded skewers with flour and dip in egg.
7.   Heat a nonstick pan over low heat and lightly grease it with oil. Place a skewer in the pan, pouring 2 or 3 tablespoons more egg batter on the skewer, letting it run away from the skewer in a thin sheet. Use a spatula to gently fold excess cooked egg over skewer to wrap it into a neat package. Turn skewer over and brown other side. Sprinkle with freshly

ground pepper. Keep warm while you repeat process with remaining skewers. Two frying pans may be used to speed things up. Egg should be golden brown and fish just tender.

Yield: 4–6 servings, or about 12 hors d'oeuvres

Cooking time: 30 to 45 minutes

Calories per serving: 320
Saturated fat: 2 g
Cholesterol: 60 mg

Total fat: 15 g
Polyunsaturated fat: 11 g
Sodium: 275 mg

Note: The seasoning on the fish is so tasty that the recipe is worth repeating even without the egg batter: simply saute the marinated fish in a tablespoon of oil. It's quick, easy, and much lower in calories and sodium.

Egg Substitute
(¼ cup = 1 whole egg)

6 *egg whites*
4 *tablespoons powdered nonfat milk*

1 *tablespoon oil*
1 *or 2 drops yellow food coloring (optional)*

Combine all ingredients and blend until smooth. May be stored in a covered jar in the refrigerator for a few days.

Yield: 1 cup

Preparation time: 2 minutes

Calories per ¼ cup: 70
Saturated fat: 0.5 g
Cholesterol: 0 mg

Total fat: 3.5 g
Polyunsaturated fat: 3 g
Sodium: 100 mg

Variation: Lean slices of beef may be substituted for fish.

Chicken
(T'akkogi)

Mixed Vegetables, Noodles, and Chicken
(Chapchae)

Tender marinated chicken slices combine with a variety of colorful vegetables in this attractive stir-fry. Served over transparent noodles, this healthful one-pot dish is a meal in itself.

1 pound chicken breast meat,
    all fat and skin removed, cut
    into thin slices (Partially
    frozen meat is easier to
    slice.)
2 ounces cellophane noodles
4 Chinese mushrooms, or ¾
    cup fresh mushrooms

2 small carrots
1 green or red bell pepper
1 medium onion
1 cup green beans, or 1 zucchini
1 tablespoon sesame oil
    Dried chili pepper flakes, or
    cayenne pepper, to taste

Marinade:

2 teaspoons low-sodium soy
    sauce
3 tablespoons rice wine (sool),
    or pale dry sherry
2 large cloves garlic, minced

2 tablespoons toasted sesame
    seeds (kkaesokum; p. 86)
½ teaspoon sugar
1 scallion, finely chopped

1.   Combine marinade ingredients, using only ½ the sesame seeds, and marinate the chicken for 1 hour.
2.   Soak the noodles in a bowl of warm water to cover for 30 minutes. Rinse and drain.

3.   Soak dried mushrooms in hot water for 30 minutes to soften. Cut off and discard stems and thinly slice caps.

4.   Cut vegetables into thin matchstick strips.

5.   Heat a teaspoon of oil in a wok or nonstick skillet over high heat until very hot and stir-fry meat 1 to 2 minutes or until it is just done. Remove from pan.

6.   Heat ½ teaspoon of oil and stir-fry vegetables one at a time over high heat until tender but still crisp. Remove from pan. It is important to stir-fry the vegetables separately to be sure they retain their color and will not be overcooked.

7.   Stir-fry noodles tossing and turning to heat evenly. Place in warmed shallow serving bowl.

8.   Return meat and vegetables to pan. Add hot pepper to taste. Mix together and cook a minute or so to heat through and blend flavors. Mound atop noodles and sprinkle with sesame seeds. Toss at the table if desired.

Yield: 4 servings   Cooking time: 12–15 minutes

Calories per serving: 260   Total fat: 10 g
Saturated fat: 2.5 g   Polyunsaturated fat: 4 g
Cholesterol: 75 mg   Sodium: 175 mg

Variation: Lean beef (sirloin or top round) cut against the grain and sliced into thin strips may be substituted for the chicken.

Beef
(Sokogi)

Barbecued Beef Strips
(Bul Kogi)

This delicious way to marinate and grill beef appeals to everyone. In Japan, where Korean restaurants abound, it is cooked at the table and is the most popular dish on the menu. The meat is sliced very thin and soaked in a spicy marinade, then grilled very quickly to seal in the juices. Grilling may be done under an oven broiler, on a Japanese hibachi, or on an outdoor barbecue. Beef is not recommended as everyday fare, since a low cholesterol diet should make sparing use of red meat in favor of fish and chicken. But occasionally, if one restricts oneself to a few lean pieces, it will do no harm. *Bul kogi* is also very good served as an hors d'oeuvre.

1 pound lean sirloin or top round, cut across the grain into ⅛-inch thick strips (Partially frozen meat is easier to cut.)

Marinade:

1 teaspoon fresh ginger root, minced
3 large cloves garlic, minced
2 scallions, finely chopped
1 tablespoon sesame oil
2 teaspoons low-sodium soy sauce

4 tablespoons Korean rice wine (sool), or pale dry sherry
1 teaspoon sugar
1 tablespoon toasted sesame seeds (kkaesokum; p. 86)
1 teaspoon black pepper
Dried crushed chili peppers, or cayenne pepper, to taste

1.   In a large bowl stir together marinade ingredients.

2.   Add meat strips and mix well to coat all sides. Cover and marinate in the refrigerator for 1 to 2 hours. Some cooks grill the meat immediately but best results are obtained when it is marinated.

3.   Grill quickly about 4 inches above glowing coals. Turn once. Serve immediately with rice.

Yield: 4 servings

Cooking time: About 5 minutes

Calories per serving: 325
Saturated fat: 6 g
Cholesterol: 105 mg

Total fat: 16 g
Polyunsaturated fat: 6 g
Sodium: 165 mg

Variation: Substitute chicken breast meat cut into 2 × 3 inch slices for another tasty treat even lower in cholesterol and saturated fats.

Stir-Fried Beef Strips
(Kogi Bokkum)

Instead of cooking the meat over a grill, the marinated beef in the recipe for Barbecued Beef Strips (p. 79) may be stir-fried, a few at a time, in a tablespoon of very hot oil. Cook only a few seconds. Serve with rice.

Soybean Curd with Ground Beef Topping
(Tubu Tchim)

It is best to use firm bean curd for this recipe.

4–6 ounces very lean beef,
    ground
1 ½ teaspoons low-sodium soy
    sauce
1 scallion, finely chopped
2 large cloves garlic, minced

1 teaspoon black pepper
1 ½ tablespoons sesame oil
12 ounces firm bean curd, cut
    into ½-inch slices
1 teaspoon sugar
3 tablespoons water

2 tablespoons rice wine (sool),
or pale dry sherry
1 tablespoon toasted sesame
seeds (kkaesokum; *p. 000*)
1–3 dried chili peppers, seeded
and chopped, or cayenne
pepper to taste
1 scallion, finely chopped for
garnish

1.   Combine ground meat with ½ teaspoon soy sauce, scallion, garlic, and pepper.
2.   In a nonstick pan heat ½ tablespoon oil over high heat and stir-fry ground meat until it changes color. Remove and set aside. Wipe pan clean with paper towel.
3.   Heat remainder of oil over moderate heat and brown bean curd on both sides. Try to keep it intact, but don't worry if it tends to fall apart. It is sometimes unavoidable.
4.   Spread meat on top of each slice of bean curd.
5.   Mix remaining soy sauce, sugar, water, and wine and pour over top. Sprinkle generously with pepper, chopped scallion, and sesame seeds. Cover and simmer gently until done, about 15 minutes.

Yield: 4 servings

Cooking time: 30 minutes

Calories per serving: 205
Saturated fat: 3 g
Cholesterol: 30 mg

Total fat: 13 g
Polyunsaturated fat: 7 g
Sodium: 90 mg

Vegetables
(Ch'aeso)

Various seasonings are used in the preparation of vegetables from the most assertively hot pickling flavors of *kimchi* to the more subtle sauces that go into the making of *namuls.* All are simple to make and are further-more excellent fare for a low-fat diet. Koreans also flavor vegetables with a meat sauce of ground beef, soy sauce, garlic, and sesame oil. Thus, a small quantity of meat is used as a condiment rather than ingested in large quantities by itself. Of course, this is the rule for most of the people in Asian countries where meat, especially beef, is beyond the means of an average family. For low-fat diets, this is an excellent way to cut down on meat consumption. If you decide to cook vegetables with a beef sauce, then eliminate the meat course. Two or three vegetables prepared this way served with rice would provide ample protein for any one meal. It is important to use the leanest possible meat and to remove any fat that results from the cooking process.

Sauteed Soybean Sprouts
(Kong Namul)

Either soybean sprouts or mung bean sprouts (*sookju namul*) may be used in this recipe.

*4 cups soybean sprouts, washed
and trimmed*

*1 teaspoon sesame oil
2 large cloves garlic, minced*

½ *teaspoon low-sodium soy*
  sauce
1 *tablespoon toasted sesame*
  seeds (kkaesokum; *p. 86*)

½ *teaspoon sugar*
1 *scallion, finely chopped*
½–1 *teaspoon black pepper*

1. Blanch bean sprouts for 30 seconds. Drain.
2. Heat oil and saute garlic.
3. Add soy sauce, sesame seeds, sugar, scallions, and pepper and blend thoroughly.
4. Add bean sprouts and cook 1 or 2 minutes tossing and turning to blend flavors. Serve hot or at room temperature.

Yield: 4 servings

Cooking time: 5 minutes

Calories per serving: 70
Saturated fat: 0.5 g
Cholesterol: 0

Total fat: 4 g
Polyunsaturated fat: 1.5 g
Sodium: 30 mg

Variation: Add ⅛ pound very lean ground beef after step 2 and saute until well done. Drain fat that results from the cooking process. Proceed as above.

Sauteed Spinach
(*Sikumchi Namul*)

1 pound spinach, washed and
   shredded (about 6 cups)
1 teaspoon sesame oil
2 large cloves garlic, minced
½ teaspoon low-sodium soy
   sauce

1 tablespoon toasted sesame
   seeds (kkaesokum; p. 86)
½ teaspoon sugar
1 scallion, finely chopped
½–1 teaspoon black pepper

Blanch spinach in boiling water (unsalted) for 30 seconds and proceed as
for Sauteed Soybean Sprouts (p. 82). Cabbage may also be prepared this
way.

Yield: 4 servings

Cooking time: 4–5 minutes

Calories per serving: 55
Saturated fat: 0.5 g
Cholesterol: 0 mg

Total fat: 2.5 g
Polyunsaturated fat: 1.5 g
Sodium: 60 mg

Sauteed Eggplant
(*Kaji Namul*)

1 medium eggplant, peeled and
   cut into thin strips (About 4
   cups)
1 teaspoon sesame oil
2 large cloves garlic, minced
½ teaspoon low-sodium soy
   sauce

1 tablespoon toasted sesame
   seeds (kkaesokum; p. 86)
½ teaspoon sugar
1 scallion, finely chopped
½–1 teaspoon black pepper

Blanch eggplant in boiling water to soften. Drain. Heat oil and proceed as
for Sauteed Soybean Sprouts (p. 82).

Yield: 4 servings

Cooking time: 7–10 minutes

Calories per serving: 70
Saturated fat: 0.5 g
Cholesterol: 0 mg

Total fat: 3 g
Polyunsaturated fat: 1.5 g
Sodium: 25 mg

Spicy Pickled Cabbage
(*Kimchi*)

Few people who have tasted *kimchi* are neutral on the subject. They either love it or hate it. This hot and pungent pickle is basic to Korean cooking and is served at every meal—including breakfast. There are countless varieties, some strong, some mild, some more pungent, and there are just as many cooks who have their own versions. In Korea, autumn is the time when families drop everything to make large quantities of *kimchi* to last them through the long winter months when fresh vegetables are scarce. The most common type of *kimchi* is made with cabbage. The usual procedure is to soak slices of cabbage in salted water overnight and season them the following day with onions, garlic, scallions, and red pepper. Then the cabbage and the spices are packed in huge earthenware crocks and stored underground for several weeks to ferment. The longer they ferment the more pungent they become. The basic recipe is varied by adding radishes, cucumbers, dried shrimp, and even bits of meat. Commercially prepared *kimchi* is available in oriental grocery stores as well as in some supermarkets. Hotness, pungency, and salt content vary in ready-made varieties of *kimchi*, though all contain far too much salt for a low-sodium diet. Generally, for a yield of 2 cups of *kimchi*, 1 tablespoon of salt is used to prepare 4 cups of fresh cabbage. That's 6,000 mg of sodium! Even if two-thirds of it is eliminated by a 3–minute rinse,* that would still leave 2,000 mg to be ingested. The recipe offered here—though not the real thing in content—is remarkably successful, and it is prepared without a grain of salt.

---

* Reference: Rita T. Vermeulen, R.D., Frank A. Sedor, Ph.D., and Sue Y. S. Kimm, M.D., "Effect of Water Rinsing on Sodium Content of Selected Foods," *Journal of the American Dietetic Association*, 82(4):394–96.

1 small head Chinese (Napa) cabbage	2 tablespoons vinegar
	½ teaspoon sugar
3 large cloves garlic, minced	1 teaspoon low-sodium soy
3 tablespoons scallions, both white and green parts, finely chopped	sauce
	⅛–1½ teaspoons cayenne pepper

1. Wash and cut cabbage into 1 × 2 inch pieces. There should be about 4 packed cups.

2. Cover with boiling water and blanch for 1 minute or until cabbage wilts to one half its original volume. Drain thoroughly and remove remaining moisture by wrapping briefly in a towel.

3. Combine remaining ingredients and mix into the cabbage. Set aside until ready to serve.

Yield: 4 servings
(approx. 2 cups)

Cooking time: 1 minute

Calories per serving: 35
Saturated fat: 0 g
Cholesterol: 0 mg

Total fat: 0.5 g
Polyunsaturated fat: 0.5 g
Sodium: 65 mg

Toasted Sesame Seeds
(Kkaesokum)

Place sesame seeds in a dry skillet and cook over medium heat 5–10 minutes or until golden brown. Crush slightly using a mortar and pestle or whirl in a coffee or pepper grinder or an electric blender. May be kept in the refrigerator in an airtight jar, but for only a few days. In Korea, sesame seeds are usually prepared with salt to keep them from spoiling.

China

The Chinese Kitchen

Chinese cuisine, with a history that spans over 3,000 years, is the most complex and sophisticated in the world. It is vaster in scope and more demanding in its use of cooking techniques and ingredients than any in the West. It is generally considered, along with French *haute cuisine*, as one of the two greatest cuisines in the world. No society on earth has been so inventive in terms of preparing food. Every possible taste sensation is relished, and all edible foodstuffs—both those common and those not usually even considered edible in the West—are incorporated in this remarkable cuisine, from the humble cabbage to the improbable bird's nest. This is not because the Chinese have been in search of exotic ingredients, though this may have been so in the palace kitchens, but because they have had to be resourceful and use everything edible in order to survive.

With only a small proportion of its total land area (about 7%) suitable for farming, producing an adequate food supply for its huge population has always been a serious problem for China. Early cooking styles developed from two important aspects of Chinese life. The first was religion. Taoism, which taught mankind to seek union with natural forces, encouraged a simple, vegetarian existence. Vegetables are still an integral part of the Chinese diet. The second determinant of Chinese cuisine was the country's chronic fuel shortage: stir-frying small chunks of food for a short period of time is more energy efficient than baking.

Chinese cuisine is usually divided roughly into four regional styles, each determined primarily by the size and population of the country and its sharp contrasts in climate. Of China's four main regions, the North, with Beijing (Peking) as its center, was long dominated by the court and by the offices of government. It attracted visitors from distant lands, among whom was the Venetian traveler Marco Polo, who reached Peking in 1275. He became a favorite of Kublai Khan, who employed him to conduct business in central and northern China and in Southeast Asia and India. Marco Polo was so wonderstruck by Oriental splendors, including the astonishing variety of foods in Chinese produce markets, that he described them in great detail in his celebrated account of life in China. The cooking from this region, often referred to as classic or mandarin cuisine, has an eclectic, cosmopolitan character with a high gastronomic reputation that was enjoyed mainly by the upper classes. The area has a short, dry growing season with a limited variety of ingredients. For the common people rice was a luxury and the staple food was wheat. Hence, the variety of noodles and steamed breads for which the Peking cuisine is so famous. Some say all the good dishes in China were first concocted in the North, while others claim that the North simply adopted all the best of Chinese cuisine as its own. Onions and garlic are commonly used and seasonings are restrained. The most famous dish is Peking duck, served with mandarin pancakes.

The Southeast, with Guangdong (Canton) as its center, has the most varied cuisine because its semitropical climate allows an abundant production of crops. Seasoning is light and is restricted to highlighting the taste of the main ingredients, though some Cantonese restaurants in the United States do not follow this rule and tend to be heavy handed in their use of condiments and cornstarch. Sweet-and-sour dishes make use of tropical fruits grown in the area such as pineapple and lichee. It is Cantonese cooking that excels in the various kinds of steamed dumplings that are known as *dim sum,* as well as in the art of stir-frying. The Cantonese style of cooking is the best known of China's cuisines because in the nineteenth century large numbers of Chinese emigrated from Canton to many countries in Southeast Asia and Japan, as well as to the United States and western Europe, and introduced their cooking to these regions. Canton's location made it the gateway to China, and it has been the center of trade since the fourth century, when Arab merchants served as trade intermediaries beween the Chinese and Europeans and established a steady commerce between China, India, Africa, and Europe. It was via this route that the noodle found its way from China through the Middle East to Europe. When the Portuguese began to arrive in the sixteenth century, they brought with them plants from the New World. Among them was the chili pepper, which was to make such a dramatic change in Chinese as well as Indian and Southeast Asian cooking.

The southwestern inland region of Sichuan (Szechuan), with the Chengdu (Ch'eng-tu) area as its center, is noted for its use of incredibly fiery, highly seasoned dishes, an incomprehensible practice to many Chinese not from this region The fire comes mainly from the chili that the Portuguese introduced and that the Sichuanese embraced with such ardor. How food was seasoned before its arrival remains a matter of conjecture. The climate of this inland region is an excellent environment for agriculture, with abundant rain, hot, humid summers, and moderate winters. This is also the land of Sichuan peppercorns, an unusual spice with a mildly hot flavor and a pleasant scent. The best of Sichuanese cooking is characterized by the contrasting of different flavors in a single dish. Cooked meats and vegetables are rarely surrounded by abundant sauces but are cooked until they are dry. South of Sichuan and abutting Thailand and Laos lies Yunnan Province, where the Chinese are a minority. The majority of the population here is made up of the non-Han minority peoples of the Tai, Shan, Lolo, Miao, Yao, Yi, Nasi, Liao, and Lisu groups, as well as a substantial number of Tibetans and Moslems. These same peoples populate the northern hills of Burma and Thailand. The cooking of Yunnan, though not highly developed, reflects these various influences: hot dishes from Sichuan to the north and curried dishes from Burma, Thailand, and India to the south and west.

The fourth region is the coastal area to the east, dominated by Shanghai. As a seacoast city in touch with the outside world, it developed a cosmopolitan cuisine of its own. The fish and seafood dishes of the area are remarkable for their variety. The region is known for slowly simmered, robust sauces using large quantities of soy sauce and brown sugar, for its longer-cooked stir-fry dishes, and for its salted greens. Lion's Head, a dish from this area in which meatballs and cabbage are simmered in a soy-and-ginger sauce, is included in this book, though highly adapted. Fujian (Fukien), the coastal area to the south of Shanghai, is renowned for producing the best soy sauce, which is used unsparingly in a form of stewing known as "red cooking." As in Shanghai, fish and seafood abound.

The northeastern areas of Mongolia and Shandong (Shantung) have given a fifth cooking style to China, one that owes little debt to traditional Chinese gastronomy. Moslem influences predominate, with lamb dishes and a fiery shishkebab being the most renowned specialties.

Lesser known is a highly developed vegetarian cuisine among Chinese Buddhists and Taoists who do not eat meat for religious reasons. Some of these vegetable dishes are prepared in such a way that they even resemble meats in taste as well as in texture.

Though all these cooking styles cannot be found everywhere outside of China, the remarkable fact is that Chinese food has become the most international cuisine in the world and that some form of it can be found even in the most remote corners of the earth. There is hardly a country, town, or city that cannot claim to have a Chinese restaurant. In some areas of the world, such as Southeast Asia, where the Chinese have emigrated in large numbers, the impact of Chinese cooking goes further than a few local restaurants. For example, in Thailand Chinese food is not only firmly entrenched but has influenced and blended with Thai cuisine. Some Indonesian dishes are a mixture of Chinese and Indian cooking styles, and in Vietnam and Singapore the food is primarily Chinese.

Preparing and Serving a Chinese Meal

There are two main styles for serving Chinese food: one for family and one for special occasions. At family meals, all the dishes are placed in the center of the table at the same time. In banquet style, the dishes are served in succession with soup served in the middle or the end; rice is also served at the end. At some banquets, a sweet dish may be offered at the midway point and a beautifully garnished fish of immense proportions is saved for last. A typical meal would include one poultry dish, one fish dish, and one meat dish, and these would be complemented by appropriate vegetables chosen for their color appeal as well as for their taste and texture. The dishes selected would contrast spicy with bland dishes, delicate with robust flavors, and soft-textured with somewhat crisp textures. For the novice cook, it would be wise to cook only a single dish at first. To go with this dish, rice and perhaps a soup can be made ahead and kept hot. Have the table set ahead of time. Besides chopsticks you'll need a plate, a bowl for rice, and a bowl for soup. And for it to be a truly Chinese-style meal, include a pot of hot tea. Everyone helps himself from the serving platters in the center of the table. Use soy sauce and other condiments sparingly or not at all. Never use monosodium glutamate. Fresh wholesome foods do not need carcinogenic chemical flavor enhancers.

Adapting Chinese Food to a Low-Sodium, Low-Cholesterol Diet

For the person who would like to limit his consumption of fats, cholesterol, and calories, Chinese food is ideal. Very tasty dishes can result from fresh vegetables cooked in such a way as to make small amounts of meat go as far as possible. But as in other Asian cuisines the reverse is true when it comes to salt. Chinese seasonings and condiments are notoriously high in sodium. For example, monosodium glutamate, a flavor enhancer used liberally by Chinese cooks, has 492 mg of sodium in one teaspoon alone. It has also been found to be the cause of a condition called the Chinese Restaurant Syndrome. Symptoms develop within half an hour of starting a meal. A burning sensation is felt in the back of the neck and forearms, and there is also a tight feeling in the chest, as well as a headache. Many have experienced this condition. A team of doctors traced the syndrome to the MSG that is added to foods in large quantities in many Chinese restaurants. The symptoms disappear quickly and have no lasting effect.

Recently, Chinese condiments have been the subject of study in the United States and their sodium values have been analyzed by Teresa Chew in an article on planning effective low-sodium diets for Chinese patients (published in the *Journal of the American Dietetic Association*). Her philosophy is "limitation" over "elimination" as "a more realistic approach." She asks for "small, gradual changes in long-held dietary habits."

In selecting the recipes for this section of the book, I was more severe than her article recommends. Only those recipes that were adaptable to a diet low in fat and sodium have been included and only those condiments that contained the least sodium were used. The quantities of these condiments, including soy sauce, have been drastically reduced, while those of other seasonings have been adjusted. The result is light and very tempting nevertheless.

Insofar as fat is concerned, Chinese cooks use quite a bit of oil for stirfrying and deep-frying, as well as lard, which is made from rendered pork fat. However, in the recipes selected for this book, if a nonstick skillet, or a well-seasoned wok, is used, only a tablespoon or less of oil is required to make a light and very lean stir-fry.

Tips for Cooking Chinese Food

Everyday Chinese cooking is easy and can be cooked with available Western utensils. Though a steamer would be handy, especially for cooking a whole fish, it is not essential, since one can be easily improvised. In a large tightly-covered pot or roasting pan, place two small heat-proof bowls or small empty tuna cans. On top of these bowls set the heat-proof food-laden plate. The plate ought to stand at least two inches above the level of the water. Before attempting to prepare any of the recipes in this part of the book, be sure to go back and read the cooking tips on stir-frying given in the introductory material on pages xxxiii–xxxiv.

The Transliteration and Pronunciation of Chinese

The transliteration of Chinese sounds into English may be confusing because we learned Chinese words through the Wade-Giles or Yale system. Since 1958, *pinyin* (meaning phonetic transcription) has been the officially endorsed phonetic system of romanizing Chinese sounds, and the Western media are increasingly adopting the odd-looking spelling. Peking seems strange as Beijing; Mao Tse-tung as Mao Zedong; and Tsingtao as Qingdao. Sooner or later this new system will supplant all others and we will have to learn it. To help in this transition, this book offers the more familiar form in parenthesis after the *pinyin* spelling, and the following chart is offered as a very rough approximation of some of the sounds and their phonetic equivalents.

Pinyin Transliteration	Pronounced	
x	=sh	as in squa<u>sh</u>
sh	=sh	as in squa<u>sh</u>
ch	=ch	as in chur<u>ch</u>
q	=ch	as in chur<u>ch</u>
j	=dg	as in ju<u>dg</u>e
zh	=dg	as in ju<u>dg</u>e
z	=dz	as in groun<u>ds</u>
c	=ts	as in studen<u>ts</u>

◊  ◊

Snacks and Appetizers
(Xiao Chi)

Chilled Soybean Curd Appetizer
(Mala Doufu)

8 ounces very fresh soybean curd

Sauce:

1 teaspoon low-sodium soy
   sauce
1 tablespoon rice vinegar
1 teaspoon fresh ginger root,
   minced
½ teaspoon sugar, dissolved in 1
   tablespoon water

1 teaspoon chili oil (p. 96), or
   to taste
Dried red chili flakes, or
   cayenne pepper, to taste
2 tablespoons coriander leaves,
   finely chopped, or parsley or
   scallions, for garnish

1. Blanch bean curd in boiling water for 30 seconds. Chill until ready to serve.
2. Cut into ½-inch cubes and place in a serving bowl.
3. Combine sauce ingredients and pour over bean curd. Garnish with coriander leaves.

Yield: 8–10 servings

Calories per serving: 30
Saturated fat: 0.5 g
Cholesterol: 0 mg

Total fat: 2 g
Polyunsaturated fat: 1 g
Sodium: 25 mg

Red Chili Pepper Oil
(*Lajiaoyou*)

Used as both an ingredient in cooking as well as a condiment, red chili pepper oil, or hot oil, as it is also called, is available in bottles in Chinese shops and in some supermarkets. But it is easy to make and keeps well.

½ cup safflower or sesame oil
2 tablespoons dried crushed red chili peppers

Heat a skillet over very high heat. Add oil. Just before it begins to smoke, remove it from the heat and add the peppers. The oil ought to turn red. If it doesn't, heat it again. Strain the oil and discard the flakes.

Yield: About ½ cup

Calories per teaspoon: 40
Saturated fat: 0.5 g
Cholesterol: 0 mg

Cooking time: 5 minutes

Total fat: 5 g
Polyunsaturated fat: 4 g
Sodium: Trace

Pot Stickers
(*Guotie*)

Dim sum, the Cantonese pronunciation of the word *dian xin*, meaning literally "a touch of heart," consists of a plethora of small taste treats that are a joy to eat. Traditionally, they are eaten as a snack in teahouses all during the day and evening. Today they are served in special restaurants in the middle of the day as brunch or lunch. Anyone who has been to a *dim sum* restaurant has experienced the exquisite anticipation one feels as the serving carts approach each diner, offering what seems like a limitless variety of delights. I doubt whether many Chinese make the many kinds of *dim sum* at home, because they are tricky and time-consuming to prepare, though the dough for pot stickers is much easier to handle than wonton dough. The commercial varieties of wonton wrappers available, either fresh or frozen, in Chinese groceries and supermarkets, are so good that a busy cook might wish to buy them ready made. Some factory-made wrappers are not always thin enough, however. Naturally, the thinner the wrapper, the more delicate the dumpling. Buy either round or square 3½-inch wrappers. For best results, be sure they are fresh and supple. The pork in the traditional filling is usually quite fatty, which makes for a more succulent dumpling. To cut down on saturated fat, this recipe substitutes chicken for pork, and sesame oil is added to replace the pork fat. Serve Pot Stickers with Hot-and-Sour Soup (p. 102) or Velvet Corn Soup (p. 104).

> 1 recipe Jiaozipi dough (p. 99), or 3 dozen commercially made 3½-inch round wrappers

Filling:

1 pound very lean ground
    chicken, or a combination of
    ½ pound ground chicken
    and ½ pound shrimp,
    shelled, deveined, and finely
    minced
1 cup finely minced Chinese
    (Napa) cabbage, blanched in
    boiling water for 1–2
    minutes and thoroughly
    drained
2 Chinese black mushrooms
1 tablespoon fresh ginger root,
    minced

1 large clove garlic, minced
2 scallions, white part only,
    minced
1 tablespoon Chinese rice
    wine, or pale dry sherry
1 teaspoon low-sodium soy
    sauce
2 teaspoons sesame oil
½ teaspoon sugar
2 tablespoons coriander
    leaves, or parsley, minced
½–1 tablespoon pepper
1 tablespoon cornstarch

1.   Soak mushrooms in warm water for 30 minutes. Discard tough stem and finely mince.

2.   Combine the filling ingredients and mix thoroughly. The filling should be soft and sticky, not crumbly. Add another teaspoon of oil if it is not. Let stand 15–20 minutes or longer to blend flavors.

To fill wrappers:

1.   Place 2 rounded teaspoons of filling off-center in the wrapper, spreading it to shape it into a half moon.

2.   Fold the wrapper in half to make a half-moon shape and pinch the two edges together at the center of the wrapper. A drop of water will help seal edges if dough is dry.

3.   Seal the curved edges, making 3 pleats at each end of the side facing you, and pinch along the top of the dumpling to seal the two edges together. The crescent-shaped dumpling should sit solidly on its middle with the edges up. Keep the finished dumplings covered with plastic wrap or a damp towel while you fill the rest. (May be frozen on a flat baking sheet, then transferred to a plastic bag and cooked without thawing at another time.)

Cooking the Pot Stickers:

1.   Heat a nonstick skillet or other heavy skillet over moderately high heat. Cook 12 at a time or use 3 skillets so they will all be done at the same time. Add 1–2 tablespoons oil. When hot, place the dumplings on their bottoms crowded side by side just touching each other with pleated edges up. Cook until bottoms brown, 5 to 10 minutes.

2.   Add ½ cup unsalted chicken stock or water to each skillet. Cover pan tightly and cook over low heat for about 10 minutes (15 minutes or longer if frozen). Be careful not to burn them. If liquid evaporates too soon, add more.

3.   Remove lid and let dumplings cook until liquid is absorbed. The bottoms should be crisp. Add more oil if necessary to keep from sticking.

4.   Gently remove dumplings to heated platter, browned bottoms up. Do not separate them from each other. The traditional serving is of 5–6 dumplings attached to one another. Serve them plain or with Vinegar Dipping Sauce (p. 98) and Mustard Sauce (p. 99).

Note: To steam the dumplings, put them in one layer on an oiled heatproof plate and steam over boiling water for 10–15 minutes.

Yield: 36 dumplings   Cooking time: 25-30 minutes

Nutrient analysis includes wrapper but not dipping sauces.

Calories per dumpling: 50	Total fat: 1 g
Saturated fat: 0.5 g	Polyunsaturated fat: 0.5 g
Cholesterol: 15 mg	Sodium: 15 mg

Vinegar Dipping Sauce for *Guotie*:

¼ cup Chinese rice vinegar, or
    other vinegar
1 teaspoon low-sodium soy
    sauce
1 teaspoon fresh ginger root,
    minced

½ teaspoon sugar
1 large clove garlic, minced
1 tablespoon hot chili oil
    (p. 96)
Dried chili pepper flakes, or
    cayenne pepper, to taste

Combine all ingredients and let stand 20 minutes to blend flavors.

Yield: About ⅓ cup

Calories per teaspoon: 10	Total fat: 1 g
Saturated fat: 0 g	Polyunsaturated fat: 1 g
Cholesterol: 0 mg	Sodium: 15 mg

Mustard Sauce for *Guotie*:

Combine ¼ cup (4 tablespoons) dry hot mustard with enough hot water to make a paste. Let stand at least 20 minutes before serving, which will make the mustard hotter.

Yield: ¼ cup

Calories per teaspoon: 9	Total fat: 0 g
Saturated fat: 0 g	Polyunsaturated fat: 0 g
Cholesterol: 0 mg	Sodium: Trace

Wrapper Dough (*Jiaozipi*) for *Guotie*:

2 cups all-purpose white flour   ¾ cup boiling water

1.   Blend the boiling water into the flour a little at a time, stirring constantly. The dough should just hold together when pressed into a ball.
2.   Knead on a lightly floured board 5 to 10 minutes or until a stiff dough is formed. Put the ball of dough in a bowl and cover it with a sheet of plastic or a damp towel. Let it rest 30 minutes or longer.
3.   Knead the dough again for 5 minutes or until it becomes smooth and elastic. Keep the board and your hands floured so the dough won't stick.
4.   Divide the dough in half and roll it into 2 sausage-shaped cylinders about ½ inch in diameter. Place one end under a sheet of plastic or a damp towel while you work with the other.
5.   Cut the cylinder into 18 slices. Shape the slices into balls about 1 inch in diameter. Repeat the process with the other cylinder. You should have about 36 balls.
6.   Flatten each ball and roll it into a thin 3 to 3½-inch round. Place the rounds side by side on a lightly floured surface. Cover them with a sheet of plastic or a damp towel to keep them from drying out. Stuff with filling as directed above.

Yield: 36 wrappers

Calories per wrapper: 22	Total fat: 0 g
Saturated fat: 0 g	Polyunsaturated fat: 0 g
Cholesterol: 0 mg	Sodium: Trace

Steamed Dumplings
(*Shaomai*)

The filling for these dumplings is the same as that used in Pot Stickers (p. 96); it can also be used in the dumplings for *wonton* soup (p. 000).

> 30 *homemade (p. 101) or commercial wonton wrappers cut into 3-inch*
> *rounds*
> *Chopped fresh coriander leaves for garnish*

Filling:

> 1 *recipe filling for pot stickers (p. 96)*
> 1 *egg white, very slightly beaten*

Combine the filling ingredients and mix thoroughly. Let stand 20 minutes or longer to blend flavors.

To fill dumplings:

1. Cut *wonton* wrappers into circles using a round cookie cutter or water glass about 3 inches in diameter.
2. Place 1 tablespoon filling in the center of a *wonton* wrapper. Gather the sides of the wrapper around the filling, pleating the wrapper and squeezing it in the middle to give it the form of a waist. The finished dumpling should be cup-shaped and filled up to the edge of the pastry, and the filling should be exposed at the top.
3. Flatten by tapping on a flat surface so the dumpling will stand upright in the steamer. Garnish the tops with the chopped coriander leaves.

Cooking:

1. Place the dumplings on an oiled heatproof plate and steam over boiling water 25–30 minutes.
2. Serve plain or with Vinegar Dipping Sauce (p. 98), Red Chili Pepper Oil (p. 96), and Mustard Sauce (p. 99).

Yield: 30 dumplings   Cooking time: 25–30 minutes

Nutrient analysis includes wrapper but not dipping sauces.

Calories per dumpling: 65   Total fat: 2 g
Saturated fat: 0.5 g   Polyunsaturated fat: 1 g
Cholesterol: 25 mg   Sodium: 25 mg

Wonton Wrappers:

Rolling this dough thin enough takes time and patience. Be sure the rolling pin, the board, and your hands are floured or the dough will stick.

2 cups all-purpose white flour   *1 teaspoon safflower oil*
1 egg, slightly beaten   *½ cup cold water*

1.   Sift flour into a bowl and make a well in the center.
2.   Combine remaining ingredients and pour into the flour. Knead with your hands until smooth, about 10 minutes. Divide into 4 balls. Cover with plastic wrap or a damp towel and let stand for 30 minutes or longer.
3.   On a lightly floured board roll dough out paper thin. Cut into 3½–4-inch squares for *wonton* soup (p. 105) and 3-inch rounds for Steamed Dumplings (*Shaomai*) (p. 100). Dust with flour and stack. Cover with plastic wrap to keep from drying out. May be refrigerated wrapped in plastic wrap for 2 or 3 days, or may be frozen until ready to use.

Yield: Approx. 30 wrappers   Preparation time: 15–20 minutes

Calories per wrapper: 30   Total fat: 1 g
Saturated fat: 0.1 g   Polyunsaturated fat: 0.2 g
Cholesterol: 10 mg   Sodium: 5 mg

◇  ◇

Soups
(Tang)

Hot-and-Sour Soup
(Suanlatang)

It is said that this Pekinese soup originated as a way of using leftovers. Marvelously comforting, this thick, tart, and peppery soup contains all the ingredients necessary for a complete meal. Pork is usually used to make the stock, but chicken has been substituted in this recipe to cut back on fat. For Chinese who don't eat pork, the soup is made with beef, which makes it the Moslem version. If one or two ingredients are not on hand, leave them out or substitute something else. The soup will be just as good as long as the bean curd, mushrooms, and the hot and sour seasonings are included. Pot Stickers (p. 96) go very well with this dish.

4–5 cups unsalted chicken stock
    (p. 10)
4–6 ounces boneless chicken, all
    fat removed
¼ cup dried cloud ears.
    (optional)
8 dried Chinese black mush-
    rooms, or 1½ cups fresh
    mushrooms
1 teaspoon low-sodium soy
    sauce
1 tablespoon Chinese rice
    wine, or pale dry sherry
1 teaspoon cornstarch
8 ounces firm soybean curd

½ cup bamboo shoots, or
    1 cup shredded Chinese
    (Napa) cabbage
½ cup water chestnuts
2 tablespoons cornstarch,
    dissolved in ¼ cup water
1 teaspoon sesame oil
½–1 tablespoon freshly ground
    black pepper
Cayenne pepper to taste
1 tablespoon fresh ginger
    root, minced
3 tablespoons rice wine vinegar,
    or other mild vinegar
1 teaspoon sugar

2 *egg whites, or 1 whole egg,*
    slightly beaten
2 *scallions, both green and*
    white parts, chopped into
    very thin circles
3 *tablespoons fresh coriander*
    leaves, chopped

Preparation:

1.   Cut chicken into ¼ inch shreds. Combine soy sauce, wine, and cornstarch, and marinate 20–30 minutes.
2.   Soak cloud ears and dried mushrooms in warm water 30 minutes to soften. Discard hard stems and cut into thin shreds. Reserve soaking liquid and add to stock.
3.   Cut bean curd into thin matchstick lengths, about ¼ inch thick.
4.   If using canned bamboo shoots and water chestnuts, rinse them for 3 minutes in cold water to remove salt and cut into thin shreds. Have all ingredients within easy reach of the stove.

Cooking:

1.   Put chicken stock and mushroom soaking liquid in a large soup kettle and bring to a boil.
2.   Add chicken with marinade and boil 1 minute.
3.   Add the cloud ears, mushrooms, and bean curd and let soup come to a boil again. Add bamboo shoots and water chestnuts and cook 30 seconds.
4.   Add cornstarch mixture, sesame oil, pepper, ginger root, vinegar, and sugar, and cook until soup thickens.
5.   Slowly stir in the beaten egg in a thin stream. Taste and adjust the seasonings. Soup should be very hot and very sour. Add more pepper or vinegar if necessary. More soy sauce may be added if desired, keeping in mind that there are 170 mg of sodium in 1 teaspoon of the low-sodium product. Garnish with scallions and coriander leaves and serve from a heated soup tureen.

Yield: 6–8 servings   Cooking time: 20-25 minutes

Calories per serving: 150   Total fat: 3.5 g
Saturated fat: 0.5 g   Polyunsaturated fat: 0.5 g
Cholesterol: 20 mg   Sodium: 95 mg

Velvet Corn Soup
(*Xumitang*)

This soup from South China and Indochina is not only quick and simple to prepare but has several variations, all easy and elegant. Shredded ham is very good in it, but is generally too salty.

1 teaspoon safflower oil
½ tablespoon fresh ginger root, minced
2 cups unsalted chicken stock (p. 10)
One 17-ounce can low-sodium cream-style corn

1 tablespoon Chinese rice wine, or pale dry sherry
½–1 teaspoon white pepper
2 egg whites, beaten until frothy but not stiff
3 tablespoons fresh watercress or coriander leaves, chopped

1. Heat oil in a soup kettle. Stir-fry ginger for 10 seconds. Add chicken broth and bring to a boil.
2. Add corn, wine, and pepper, and cook until heated.
3. Slowly stir in the beaten egg whites. Serve immediately, garnished with watercress.

Yield: 4–6 servings

Cooking time: 15 minutes

Calories per serving: 140
Saturated fat: 0.5 g
Cholesterol: 0 mg

Total fat: 3 g
Polyunsaturated fat: 2 g
Sodium: 35 mg

Variation: Four ounces shredded cooked chicken, ham, crab, or lobster may be added after step 2.

Wonton Soup
(*Huntuntang*)

This is a delicate but satisfying full-meal soup that is not so time consuming to prepare if you use ready-made wrappers.

30 *homemade (p. 101) or commercial wonton wrappers*
1 *recipe filling for Pot Stickers (p. 96)*

6 *cups unsalted chicken stock (p. 10)*
3–4 *scallions, thinly sliced for garnish*

1.   Place a strip of filling straight across the *wonton* wrapper just below the center. Roll one side of the wrapper over the filling. Continue rolling into a tube, leaving ½ inch unrolled. Pull the two ends of the cylinder around until they meet and overlap. Pinch ends firmly together to seal. Cover with plastic wrap or damp towel until all wrappers are filled.
2.   Bring chicken stock to a boil and keep hot.
3.   In the meantime, bring 4 quarts of water to a boil. Drop half the *wontons* in and wait until they float to the surface. Add a cup of cold water and bring to a boil again. With a slotted spoon transfer the *wontons* to the chicken stock. Drop the remaining *wontons* into the remaining water and repeat the procedure. Transfer to the stock. Be sure to bring soup to a boil again to ensure that fillings are thoroughly cooked. Serve garnished with chopped scallions.

Yield: 6 servings

Cooking time: 20–30 minutes

Nutrient analysis includes wrapper.

Calories per serving: 300
Saturated fat: 1 g
Cholesterol: 115 mg

Total fat: 4.5 g
Polyunsaturated fat: 2 g
Sodium: 125 mg

Tomato and Egg Soup
(Fanqiedantang)

4 medium tomatoes
1 teaspoon safflower oil
2 large cloves garlic, minced
1 tablespoon fresh ginger root,
   minced
2 scallions, finely chopped
4 cups unsalted chicken stock
   (p. 10)

½–1 tablespoon Sichuan
   peppercorns, or black
   pepper
1–2 teaspoons cornstarch,
   dissolved in 3 tables-
   poons water
2 egg whites, beaten until
   frothy but not stiff

Preparation:

1.   Soak the tomatoes in boiling water for 5 minutes. Peel and coarsely chop them.
2.   Prepare remaining ingredients and place within reach of the stove.

Cooking:

1.   Heat oil in a soup kettle. Stir-fry garlic, ginger, and scallions 10 seconds.
2.   Add tomatoes and stir-fry 2–3 minutes.
3.   Add chicken stock and pepper, bring to a boil and cook 5 minutes.
4.   Stir in cornstarch mixture and cook 2 more minutes.
5.   Fold in beaten egg whites and serve immediately.

Yield: 4–6 servings

Cooking time: 15–20 minutes

Calories per serving: 110
Saturated fat: 0.5 g
Cholesterol: 0 mg

Total fat: 2 g
Polyunsaturated fat: 1 g
Sodium: 55 mg

◊  ◊

Seafoods
(Haiwei)

Stir-Fried Fish Fillets with Vegetables
(Chaoyupian)

Fresh fish fillets are wonderful when they are stir-fried. This recipe is one that is popular all over China. Oyster sauce, which can be purchased in most supermarkets, is actually made from oysters, but does not taste at all fishy. Oddly enough, it goes well with chicken and beef too, and either may be substituted for the fish in this recipe. But it should be used sparingly, since 1 teaspoon contains about 260 mg of sodium.

1 pound firm white fish fillets, cut into 1-inch slices	4 dried Chinese mushrooms, or ¾ cup fresh mushrooms
1 tablespoon cornstarch	1 cup Chinese or American broccoli, cut into bite-sized pieces (snow peas, asparagus, or green peas may be substituted)
½ teaspoon low-sodium soy sauce	
1½ tablespoons Chinese rice wine, or pale dry sherry	
1½ tablespoons safflower oil	½–1 teaspoon oyster sauce
3 large cloves garlic, minced	½–1 teaspoon black pepper
2 tablespoons fresh ginger root, minced	

Preparation:

1.   Combine cornstarch, soy sauce, and wine. Coat fish slices evenly and marinate 10–20 minutes.

2. Soak mushrooms in warm water 30 minutes to soften. Discard tough stems and cut into thin slices.

3. Prepare remaining ingredients and place within easy reach of the stove.

Cooking:

1. Heat a wok or nonstick skillet over very high heat. Add half the oil. Just before it begins to smoke, stir-fry garlic and ginger root 10 seconds.

2. Add fish pieces and stir-fry 30–60 seconds, or until white and firm. Remove from pan.

3. Heat remaining oil and stir-fry mushrooms and broccoli for 1 to 2 minutes.

4. Mix in oyster sauce, pepper, and 2 or 3 tablespoons water (if mixture seems dry). Broccoli should be crisp but not raw. If needed, cover pan for a minute or so to steam broccoli to desired tenderness.

5. Return fish and stir and toss for 30 seconds, or until heated through. Serve on heated plate.

Yield: 4–6 servings   Cooking time: 6 minutes

Calories per serving: 190   Total fat: 6.5 g
Saturated fat: 1 g   Polyunsaturated fat: 5 g
Cholesterol: 60 mg   Sodium: 140 mg

Stir-Fried Fish Fillets with
Hoisin Sauce, Sichuan Style
(Haixianjiang Chaouyupian)

Hoisin sauce is substituted for brown bean sauce in this recipe because there is much less sodium in it. It tastes rather different from the original Sichuanese dish, but it is very tasty.

1 pound firm white fish fillets, cut into 1-inch slices
1 tablespoon cornstarch
½ teaspoon low-sodium soy sauce
2 tablespoons rice wine, or pale dry sherry
1 tablespoon safflower oil

3 large cloves garlic, minced
2 tablespoons fresh ginger root, minced
1–4 fresh or dried chili peppers, seeded and chopped, or cayenne pepper, to taste
4 scallions, thinly sliced

Sauce:

1 teaspoon hoisin sauce
1 tablespoon rice vinegar, or mild white vinegar

½ teaspoon sugar
2 teaspoons Chinese rice wine, or pale dry sherry

Preparation:

1. Combine cornstarch, soy sauce, and wine. Coat fish slices evenly and marinate 10–20 minutes.
2. Mix sauce ingredients in a small bowl and set aside.
3. Prepare remaining ingredients and place within easy reach of the stove.

Cooking:

1. Heat a wok or nonstick skillet over high heat. Just before it begins to smoke, stir-fry garlic, ginger, and peppers 10 seconds.
2. Add fish slices and stir-fry 30–60 seconds, or until white and firm.
3. Add scallions and stir-fry 30 seconds longer.
4. Mix in sauce ingredients and stir and toss about 1 minute or until heated through.

Yield: 4–6 servings

Cooking time: 3 minutes

Calories per serving: 170
Saturated fat: 0.5 g
Cholesterol: 60 mg

Total fat: 5 g
Polyunsaturated fat: 3.5 g
Sodium: 120 mg

Steamed Whole Fish with Black Beans
(Doushi Zheng Xianyu)

This dish served with rice and a salad makes a distinctive, healthful meal that can be prepared in less than half an hour. Traditionally, a whole fish is served at the end of a Chinese banquet.

1 whole snapper, sea bass, rockfish, rock cod, or other firm-fleshed fish weighing 1½ to 2 pounds (yield: 1 pound boneless meat)
2 teaspoons fermented black beans
2 tablespoons fresh ginger root, minced
4 large cloves garlic, minced

3 scallions, cut into 2-inch lengths
1 teaspoon low-sodium soy sauce
2 tablespoons Chinese rice wine, or pale dry sherry
½ teaspoon sugar
1 tablespoon safflower oil
Fresh coriander or parsley leaves for garnish

Preparation:

1. Clean, wash, and dry the fish. Make 3 or 4 diagonal cuts on each side.
2. Wash the black beans in running water for 3 minutes to rid them of salt. Drain. Chop the beans coarsely. Mince ginger root and garlic and cut scallions.
3. Combine remaining ingredients with beans, ginger, garlic, and scallions and pour over fish.

Cooking:

1. Boil water in the bottom of a steamer (p. 000). Place fish on a rack, cover tightly, and steam 10 to 15 minutes. Test for doneness. Do not overcook.
2. Garnish with coriander leaves and serve immediately.

Yield: 4–6 servings

Cooking time: 15 minutes

Calories per serving: 165
Saturated fat: 0.5 g
Cholesterol: 60 mg

Total fat: 5 g
Polyunsaturated fat: 3.5 g
Sodium: 180 mg

Shrimps and Green Pepper
with Sweet-and-Sour Sauce
(*Suantian Xiaren*)

The shrimps are usually coated with an egg batter and deep fried, adding unwanted calories and fat. This adaptation is just as tasty and has the added advantage of being quick and simple to prepare.

1 pound shrimps
1 tablespoon safflower oil
3 large cloves garlic, minced
2 tablespoons fresh ginger root, minced

1–4 fresh or dried red chili peppers, minced, or to taste
3 green bell peppers, deribbed and cut lengthwise into ¼ inch strips

Sauce:

½ cup chicken stock (p. 10)
3 tablespoons rice vinegar, or
*   other mild vinegar*

2 tablespoons sugar
2 teaspoons cornstarch, blended
*   with 2 tablespoons water*

Preparation:

1.   Shell, devein, and rinse shrimp without removing tails. Dry and set aside.
2.   Mince garlic and ginger.
3.   Derib and cut green peppers lengthwise into ¼-inch strips.
4.   Combine stock, vinegar, sugar, and cornstarch mixture.

Cooking:

1.   Heat a wok or nonstick skillet over medium heat. Add two teaspoons oil and cook shrimp on both sides about 30 seconds, or until barely done. Do not overcook. Remove from pan.
2.   Heat a teaspoon of oil over high heat and stir-fry green pepper 1 minute.
3.   Add sauce ingredients and bring to a boil.
4.   Return shrimp and stir and toss until heated through. Serve immediately on a heated platter.

Yield: 4–6 servings

Cooking time: 5 minutes

Calories per serving: 190
Saturated fat: 0.5. g
Cholesterol: 115 mg

Total fat: 4.5 g
Polyunsaturated fat: 3 g
Sodium: 90 mg

Stir-Fried Squid with Ginger and Garlic
(*Jiang Suan Bao Youyu*)

Please read about squid in the ingredients section on page xxv before attempting this recipe.

1 pound squid (yield is about ⅔
*   pound edible meat)*
1 tablespoon safflower oil

4 large cloves garlic, minced
2 tablespoons fresh ginger root,
*   minced*

Sauce:

1 tablespoon Chinese rice
   wine, or pale dry sherry
1 teaspoon low-sodium soy
   sauce
1/4 teaspoon sugar

1 teaspoon cornstarch,
   blended with 1 tables-
   poon water
1/2–1 teaspoon black pepper
   Chopped coriander leaves
   for garnish

Preparation:

1. Clean the squid, removing transparent center bone, purple spotted skin and inner matter. Wash and cut along entire length to flatten body, then slice into 1/2-inch strips.
2. Combine sauce ingredients in a bowl and set aside.

Cooking:

1. Heat a wok or nonstick skillet over high heat. Add oil. Just before it begins to smoke, stir-fry garlic and ginger root 10 seconds.
2. Add squid and stir-fry quickly for 1 minute or until squid curls and turns white.
3. Add wine mixture and stir-fry 1/2 to 1 minute.

Note: Be careful to cook the squid no more than 3 minutes or it will toughen.

Yield: 4–6 servings

Cooking time: 3 minutes

Calories per serving: 150
Saturated fat: 0.5 g
Cholesterol: 200 mg

Total fat: 5 g
Polyunsaturated fat: 3 g
Sodium: 125 mg

Stir-Fried Crabmeat with Oyster Sauce
(*Haoyou Xierou*)

This is a delightfully light, agreeable dish from Shanghai that is easy to prepare.

16 ounces fresh cooked crabmeat
1 tablespoon fresh ginger root, minced
2 large cloves garlic, minced
3 scallions, thinly sliced

2 teaspoons safflower oil
½–1 teaspoon oyster sauce
1 tablespoon Chinese rice wine, or pale dry sherry
½–1 teaspoon black pepper
1–2 egg whites, slightly beaten

Preparation:

1. Flake crabmeat.
2. Combine oyster sauce, wine, and pepper.

Cooking:

1. Heat a wok or nonstick skillet over medium heat. Add oil and stir-fry ginger, garlic, and scallions 30 seconds.
2. Add crabmeat and stir-fry 30–60 seconds.
3. Add oyster sauce mixture and cook until well blended.
4. Mix in beaten egg whites and cook for a few seconds longer stirring gently. Serve immediately on a heated platter.

Yield: 4–6 servings

Cooking time: 3 minutes

Calories per serving: 150
Saturated fat: 0.5 g
Cholesterol: 85 mg

Total fat: 4 g
Polyunsaturated fat: 2 g
Sodium: 130 mg

◇  ◇

Chicken
(*Jirou*)

Chicken with Nuts and Hoisin Sauce
(*Jiangbao Jiding*)

Hoisin sauce is an important ingredient in Chinese cooking. It has a spicy-sweet, tangy taste and fortunately has a lower sodium content than most Chinese condiments. The combination of flavors and textures in this northern dish from Shandong is outstanding.

1 pound boneless chicken breast meat, all fat and skin removed, cut into ½-inch cubes	2 zucchini squashes, cut into thin 1-inch strips
1 tablespoon cornstarch	1 tablespoon safflower oil
2 tablespoons Chinese rice wine, or pale dry sherry	2 large cloves garlic, minced
½ teaspoon low-sodium soy sauce	1 tablespoon fresh ginger root, minced
4 dried Chinese mushrooms, or ¾ cup sliced fresh mushrooms	½–1 teaspoon black pepper
	1 teaspoon hoisin sauce, mixed with 2 or 3 tablespoons water
	¼ cup unsalted almonds or walnuts

Preparation:

1. Place chicken cubes in a bowl and dredge with cornstarch. Mix wine and soy sauce. Add to chicken and marinate 20 minutes.
2. Soak mushrooms in warm water for 30 minutes to soften. Trim and discard hard stems. Cut into thin slices.

3. Toast nuts in a small dry skillet or toaster oven until golden. Set aside.

4. Prepare remaining ingredients and place within easy reach of the stove.

Cooking:

1. Heat a wok or nonstick skillet until very hot. Add half the oil. Just before it begins to smoke, stir-fry garlic and ginger root for 10 seconds.

2. Add chicken pieces and stir-fry for 1 or 2 minutes or until chicken turns white and firm. Remove from pan.

3. Add remaining oil and stir-fry zucchini and mushrooms for 1 more minute. Return chicken to pan and stir-fry until chicken is heated through.

4. Stir in pepper, hoisin sauce, and water, and cook until well blended.

5. Mix in nuts and serve immediately.

Yield: 4–6 servings	Cooking time: 6 minutes
Calories per serving: 325	Total fat: 11 g
Saturated fat: 2.5 g	Polyunsaturated fat: 5 g
Cholesterol: 90 mg	Sodium: 140 mg

Variation: Shrimp may be substituted for chicken.

Chicken with Peanuts and Chili Peppers
(Gongbao Jiding)

A Peking Grand Duke supposedly gave his name to this Sichuanese dish, but his identity as well as his connection with distant Sichuan either as emissary or exile remains shrouded with mystery. Fortunately for posterity, Gongbao chicken as well as Gongbao shrimp have become famous the world over as one of Sichuan's outstanding dishes. The combination of textures and seasonings—sour, sweet, hot, and crunchy with velvety chicken—is exceptionally delicious. The dish is meant to be fiery hot, but adjust the heat to suit your own taste.

1 pound boneless chicken breast meat, all fat and skin removed, cut into ½-inch cubes	½ egg white, slightly beaten 1 tablespoon cornstarch ½ teaspoon low-sodium soy sauce

1½ *tablespoons safflower oil*
¼ *cup skinless unsalted*
  roasted peanuts
2 *large cloves garlic, minced*
2 *scallions, thinly chopped*
1 *tablespoon fresh ginger*
  root, minced
1–4 *fresh or dried red chili*
  peppers, seeded and
  chopped, or cayenne pep-
  per, to taste
1 *sweet red bell pepper, cut*
  into thin strips (optional)

Sauce:

1 *teaspoon sugar*
½ *teaspoon low-sodium soy*
  sauce
1 *teaspoon hoisin sauce*
1 *tablespoon Chinese rice*
  wine, or pale dry sherry

1 *tablespoon rice vinegar,*
  or mild white vinegar
1 *teaspoon cornstarch, mixed*
  with 1 tablespoon water

Preparation:

1. Combine egg white, cornstarch, and soy sauce. Coat chicken cubes and set aside.
2. Prepare remaining ingredients and place within easy reach of the stove.
3. Combine sauce ingredients and set aside.

Cooking:

1. In a wok or nonstick skillet, heat 1 teaspoon oil over high heat and stir-fry peanuts until lightly browned. Remove with slotted spoon and spread on paper towels to drain off excess oil.
2. Heat remaining oil and stir-fry garlic, scallions, ginger root, chilies, and bell pepper for 1 minute.
3. Add coated chicken cubes and stir-fry over high heat 1–2 minutes or until chicken turns white and firm.
4. Stir in combined sauce ingredients and cook until slightly thickened.
5. Toss in peanuts, stir-fry briskly until heated through, and serve immediately. Result should yield little or no sauce.

Yield: 4–6 servings

Cooking time: 6 minutes

Calories per serving: 335
Saturated fat: 3.5 g
Cholesterol: 90 mg

Total fat: 16 g
Polyunsaturated fat: 6.5 g
Sodium: 145 mg

Chicken with Sweet Brown Bean Sauce and Vegetables
(Doubanjang Jiding)

This dish from Peking-Shanghai makes a delicious, eye-pleasing one-pot meal. Other vegetables in season may be substituted. Sweet brown bean sauce has approximately 160 mg sodium per teaspoon as compared with brown bean sauce, which has about 425. Amount differs from brand to brand.

1 pound boneless chicken breast meat, all skin and fat removed, cut into ½-inch cubes
1 tablespoon cornstarch
½ teaspoon low-sodium soy sauce
1 tablespoon Chinese rice wine, or pale dry sherry
1 tablespoon safflower oil
2 large cloves garlic, minced

2 tablespoons fresh ginger root, minced
2 bell peppers, 1 green and 1 red, deribbed and cut into ¼-inch strips
1 cup diced water chestnuts, fresh or canned
2 teaspoons sweet brown bean sauce, mixed with 2 or 3 tablespoons water
½ teaspoon sugar
½–1 teaspoon black pepper

Preparation:

1. Dredge chicken with cornstarch. Combine soy sauce and wine and coat chicken pieces evenly with mixture.
2. If using canned water chestnuts rinse them under cold water for 3 minutes to remove salt. Cut into thin slices.
3. Place remaining ingredients within easy reach of stove.

Cooking:

1. Heat a wok or nonstick skillet over high heat until very hot. Add oil. Just before it begins to smoke, stir-fry garlic and ginger root 10 seconds.

2. Add chicken and stir-fry 1–2 minutes, or until white and firm. Remove from pan.

3. Reheat oil and stir-fry green and red peppers 1–2 minutes.

4. Return chicken to pan and stir-fry until heated through.

5. Add water chestnuts, bean sauce, sugar, pepper, and 2 or 3 tablespoons water. Stir until well blended and serve with rice.

Yield: 4–6 servings

Cooking time: 5–6 minutes

Calories per serving: 280
Saturated fat: 2.5 g
Cholesterol: 90 mg

Total fat: 10 g
Polyunsaturated fat: 4.5 g
Sodium: 150 mg

Hot-and-Sour Chicken
(*Mala Ziji*)

Hunan Province, birthplace of Mao Zedong (Mao Tse-tung), is famous for its hot and strongly seasoned dishes, among which this one is well loved.

1 pound boneless chicken breast meat, skin and fat removed, cut into ½-inch cubes
½ egg white, slightly beaten
1 tablespoon cornstarch
2 tablespoons Chinese rice wine, or pale dry sherry
½ teaspoon low-sodium soy sauce
1 tablespoon safflower oil

1–4 fresh or dried red chili peppers, seeded and chopped, or cayenne pepper, to taste
2 tablespoons fresh ginger root, minced
3 large cloves garlic, minced
4 scallions, cut into 2-inch lengths

Sauce:

¼ cup chicken stock
1 teaspoon low-sodium soy sauce
1 tablespoon sugar
2–3 tablespoons rice vinegar, or mild white vinegar

1 teaspoon sesame oil
1–2 teaspoons five-spice powder, or substitute a combination of ground star anise, cinnamon, fennel or aniseed, pepper, and cloves

Preparation:

1.   Combine egg white, wine, and soy sauce and coat chicken pieces evenly with mixture. Marinate 20–30 minutes.
2.   Combine sauce ingredients in a bowl and set aside.
3.   Prepare remaining ingredients and place within easy reach of the stove.

Cooking:

1.   Heat a wok or nonstick skillet over high heat until very hot. Add oil. Just before it begins to smoke stir-fry chicken cubes 1–2 minutes. Add chilies and stir-fry 30 seconds. If you use enough chilies, chicken will turn slightly pink.
2.   Add ginger root, garlic, and scallions and stir-fry another 30 seconds.
3.   Mix in combined sauce ingredients and cook and stir until well blended. Serve on a heated dish.

Yield: 4–6 servings

Cooking time: 4–5 minutes

Calories per serving: 295
Saturated fat: 2.1 g
Cholesterol: 90 mg

Total fat: 11 g
Polyunsaturated fat: 5 g
Sodium: 150 mg

Lemon Chicken
(Ningmeng-zhi Ji)

This delicious dish seems too good to be good for you, and is very popular in the southern regions of China, especially Sichuan and Canton.

1½ pounds boned chicken
    breast meat, all fat and
    skin removed, cut into
    large serving pieces
1 teaspoon low-sodium soy
    sauce

2 tablespoons lemon juice
1 tablespoon safflower oil
    Lemon slices and chopped co-
    riander leaves for garnish
1 tablespoon rice wine, or pale
    dry sherry

Lemon sauce:

1 teaspoon safflower oil
1 teaspoon fresh ginger root,
    finely minced
1 large clove garlic, minced
4 Chinese dried black
    mushrooms, or 4 fresh
    mushrooms
1 teaspoon grated lemon rind
2 tablespoons sugar

¼ teaspoon black pepper
1 cup unsalted chicken stock
    (p. 10)
½ cup fresh lemon juice
    Dash of cinnamon
    Dash of cayenne pepper
1 teaspoon cornstarch, mixed
    with 1 tablespoon water

Preparation:

1. Soak mushrooms in warm water for 30 minutes, discard tough stems and cut into thin slices. Or wash and slice fresh mushrooms.
2. Combine soy sauce, wine, and lemon juice and marinate chicken 20–30 minutes.

Cooking:

1. Heat a nonstick skillet until very hot. Add oil. Just before it begins to smoke, brown chicken pieces on both sides. Cook 1–2 minutes, or until chicken is white and firm. Remove from heat and keep warm.
2. To make sauce, heat oil and saute mushrooms, ginger root, and garlic for 2 or 3 minutes.
3. Stir in lemon rind, sugar, black pepper, and chicken stock. Bring to a boil and simmer 3–5 minutes.
4. Add lemon juice, cinnamon, and cayenne pepper and cook for 1 minute.
5. Thicken with cornstarch mixture. Return chicken pieces to sauce and cook until heated through and chicken is tender. Do not overcook. Serve on a heated platter and garnish with lemon slices and coriander leaves.

Yield: 6 servings

Cooking time: 15-20 minutes

Calories per serving: 265
Saturated fat: 2 g
Cholesterol: 90 mg

Total fat: 7 g
Polyunsaturated fat: 4 g
Sodium: 105 mg

Sweet-and-Sour Chicken with Pineapple
(Bolo Ji)

In the South where pineapples and lychees grow in a lush tropical climate, Cantonese and Hong Kong cooks make use of fruit and fruit juices in their sweet-and-sour dishes. For those looking for variety in a low-sodium diet, these dishes offer a welcome change.

1 pound boneless chicken
  breast meat, all fat and skin
  removed, cut into ½-inch
  cubes
1 tablespoon cornstarch
½ egg white, slightly beaten
2 tablespoons rice wine, or pale
  dry sherry
1 tablespoon safflower oil

1 tablespoon fresh ginger root,
  minced
2 large cloves garlic, minced
1 cup snow peas, strings
  removed
1 cup drained, canned
  pineapple chunks
4 water chestnuts, fresh or
  canned

Sauce:

⅓ cup pineapple juice
1 teaspoon low-sodium soy
  sauce
1 teaspoon sugar

2 tablespoons rice vinegar
1 teaspoon cornstarch, blended
  with 1 tablespoon water

Preparation:

1. Mix cornstarch, egg white, and wine, and coat chicken pieces evenly. Marinate 10–20 minutes.
2. If using canned water chestnuts, wash under cold water for 3 minutes to remove salt. Cut into small pieces.
3. Combine sauce ingredients and set aside.

Cooking:

1. Heat wok or nonstick skillet over high heat until very hot. Add half the oil. Just before it begins to smoke, add garlic and ginger root and stir-fry 10 seconds.
2. Add chicken pieces and stir-fry 1–2 minutes, or until chicken turns white and firm. Remove from pan.
3. Reheat oil and stir-fry snow peas 10 seconds.
4. Return chicken to pan and stir-fry to heat through. Add pineapple chunks and water chestnuts and stir-fry 1 more minute.
5. Add combined sauce ingredients and stir until slightly thickened.

Yield: 4–6 servings

Cooking time: 6 minutes

Calories per serving: 320
Saturated fat: 2.5 g
Cholesterol: 90 mg

Total fat: 10 g
Polyunsaturated fat: 4.5 g
Sodium: 105 mg

Variation: Pork may be substituted for the chicken.

Mixed Vegetables, Eggs, and Chicken (or Pork) with Mandarin Pancakes
(*Muxu Rou*)

This Pekinese dish has gained enormous popularity in recent years for good reason. A wonderful combination of flavors and textures wrapped in a delicate, steaming pancake, *Muxu Rou* has become everybody's favorite. There are fewer eggs and more vegetables in this recipe, but it remains just as tasty. I have eaten this dish in many different restaurants and each has its own version. Freezing the meat slightly will make it easier to cut. To cut down on fat, I have substituted chicken for pork. If you do use pork, be sure it is very lean. The nutrient analysis is included for both, but it is based on the leanest possible pork. The saturated fat count climbs dramatically when fatty cuts are used. To cut back on cholesterol, only one egg yolk is used.

4 dried Chinese mushrooms, or ¾ cup fresh mush-rooms
¼ cup dried cloud ears
2 large cloves garlic, minced
8 ounces very lean pork or boneless chicken, all fat and skin removed
1 tablespoon Chinese rice wine, or pale dry sherry
1½ teaspoons cornstarch
1 teaspoon low-sodium soy sauce
½ teaspoon sugar
2 tablespoons safflower oil
1 slice fresh ginger root

1 whole egg and 1 egg white, lightly beaten
1 cup Chinese (Napa) cabbage, shredded
½ cup bamboo shoots, cut into thin strips
2 scallions, green and white part, cut into thin strips for garnish
2 teaspoons pepper, or to taste
16 mandarin pancakes (p. 125; optional)
Sauce for Peking Duck and Muxu Rou (p. 127; optional)

Preparation:

1. Freeze the meat slightly. Cut it into thin slices, then into ⅛-inch shreds.
2. Soak mushrooms and cloud ears to soften. Discard hard stems. Wash under cold water and cut into small pieces.
3. Combine wine, cornstarch, soy sauce, and sugar and mix with meat.
4. Beat the eggs and prepare the vegetables. Canned bamboo shoots should be washed for 3 minutes under cold water to rid them of salt. Have all the ingredients within easy reach of the stove.

Cooking:

1. Heat a wok or skillet over high heat. Add 1 teaspoon of oil and the slice of ginger root. Reduce the heat, discard the ginger root, and add the beaten eggs. Scramble them quickly until they are barely set and dry. Transfer them to a bowl. Cut them into small pieces. Wipe the pan with paper towels to remove any trace of egg.

2. Heat the skillet again over high heat. Add remaining oil. Just before it begins to smoke, add garlic and stir-fry 30 seconds. Add the meat and stir-fry for 1 to 2 minutes.

3. Add the mushrooms and cloud ears and stir-fry 1 minute.

4. Add the cabbage and bamboo shoots and stir-fry 1 or 2 minutes or until vegetables wilt. If using pork, be sure it is well done before going on to step 5.

5. Return the eggs and cook another minute, stirring and mixing constantly until heated through.

6. Serve with mandarin pancakes. Each diner spreads a pancake flat on his plate and places 2 or 3 tablespoons of filling in the center and, if desired, a dab of sauce. The pancake is rolled up and eaten with the hands.

Yield: 4–6 servings   Cooking time: 8 minutes

Nutrient analysis does not include pancakes or sauce.

Recipe with chicken:

Calories per serving: 220   Total fat: 11 g
Saturated fat: 2 g   Polyunsaturated fat: 7 g
Cholesterol: 115 mg   Sodium: 125 mg

Recipe with pork:

Calories per serving: 240   Total fat: 16 g
Saturated fat: 5 g   Polyunsaturated fat: 7 g
Cholesterol: 120 mg   Sodium: 120 mg

Mandarin Pancakes
(*Baobing*)

Also known as Peking doilies, these delicate pancakes are traditionally served to enclose Peking duck as well as a variety of fillings made with egg, pork, or chicken. The filling is placed in the center of the pancake, dabbed with a dark, rich sauce, and sprinkled with chopped scallions. Then the pancake is rolled up and eaten with the hands. Not only are mandarin pancakes delicious, but they contain no salt and no cholesterol-rich eggs. They are cooked on a griddle in pairs on one side only, with the inside of the "sandwich" held together with a light coat of oil. When they come out of the pan they are separated. One side should be lightly colored, the other soft and chewy. The recipe may seem formidable at first, but with a bit of practice it is no more difficult than making any other pancake. Mandarin pancakes may be made ahead of time, stacked in foil, then steamed for a few minutes to heat them while the filling is cooking. Or they may be frozen and steamed without thawing 15–20 minutes before serving.

2 cups all-purpose white flour	1–2 tablespoons safflower
¾ cup boiling water	or sesame oil

Preparation:

1.   Stir the boiling water into the flour a little at a time, blending well. The dough should just hold together when pressed into a ball.

2.   Knead on a lightly floured board until it is smooth, about 10 minutes. Put the ball of dough in a bowl and cover it with a sheet of plastic or a damp towel. Let it rest 30 minutes or longer.

3.   Knead the dough again for 5 minutes, adding a little flour if dough seems sticky. With your hands, roll it into a long, uniform cylinder about 1½ inches thick. Cut the cylinder into 8 pieces of equal size. Then divide each piece into 2 equal slices.

4.   Roll each slice between your palms into a ball. Flatten the balls into patties. (Alternatively, dough may be rolled out ⅜-inch thick on a lightly floured surface and cut into 16 rounds with a 3-inch cookie cutter.)

5.   Brush the tops of these patties with a thin coat of oil, being careful to oil the pancake all the way out to the edge of the circle. Oil one side only.

6.   Place one oiled pancake on top of a second, oiled sides together. Repeat the process, carefully matching the pairs in size. You will have 8 pairs of pancakes, oiled sides inside.

7.   Roll each pair of bonded pancakes out as thinly and evenly as possible, to about 7 inches in diameter. To be sure that both cakes stay the same size, turn them over and roll on the other side from time to time. As you finish rolling the pancakes, cover them with a sheet of plastic or a damp cloth.

Cooking:

1.   Heat a heavy ungreased skillet or griddle over moderate heat. Put the flattened pairs in the pan and cook until light brown specks begin to appear on the side touching the pan. This will take about 1 minute. Flip

the pair over and cook another minute. Do not brown. They are done when the pairs begin to show signs of separating from each other.

2.   While still warm, carefully separate the pancakes. Stack them on a heated platter and keep them warm as you cook the remaining pancakes.

Yield: 16 pancakes

Cooking time: 20 minutes

Calories per pancake: 60
Saturated fat: Trace
Cholesterol: 0 mg

Total fat: 1 g
Polyunsaturated fat: 0.7 mg
Sodium: Trace

Sauce for Peking Duck and *Muxu Rou*
(*Xinmeijang*)

There are approximately 160 mg of sodium in 1 teaspoon of hoisin sauce, depending on brand and batch.

¼ cup hoisin sauce
1 teaspoon sesame oil

2 teaspoons sugar
2 tablespoons water

Combine ingredients in a small pan and stir until sugar dissolves. Simmer for 2 to 3 minutes. Pour into dipping sauce dishes and serve at room temperature.

Yield: Approx. 6 tablespoons

Cooking time: 3 minutes

Calories per teaspoon: 11
Saturated fat: 0 g
Cholesterol: 0 mg

Total fat: 0.5 g
Polyunsaturated fat: 0.5 g
Sodium: 110 mg

◇  ◇

Beef
(Niurou)

Stir-Fried Beef with Vegetables
(Niurou Chao Qingcai)

This is the standard meat-and-vegetable dish that is eaten all over China and that can be adapted to suit everybody's taste. Allow 2 to 3 ounces of meat per person and at least twice as much vegetable. The meat is marinated for at least 10 minutes, then stir-fried in ginger-and-garlic-flavored oil. It is removed from the pan to allow the vegetables to be stir-fried separately. Then the two are combined with the sauce. Hoisin sauce is used here because it has the lowest sodium content, but brown-bean sauce or oyster sauce may be substituted. This recipe calls for asparagus, but any fresh vegetable will do. Be sure to freeze the meat slightly to ensure a thinner, more precise slice.

12 ounces very lean beef	2 tablespoons fresh ginger
2 teaspoons cornstarch	root, minced
2 tablespoons Chinese rice	4 large cloves garlic
wine, or pale dry sherry	1 1/2 pounds asparagus
1/4 teaspoon sugar	1 teaspoon hoisin sauce,
1/2 teaspoon low-sodium soy	mixed with 4–5 table-
sauce	spoons water
1 1/2 tablespoons safflower oil	Black pepper to taste

Preparation:

1.   Slice the meat against the grain into thin 2-inch strips.
2.   Combine cornstarch, wine, sugar, and soy sauce, and coat the meat

evenly with the mixture. Marinate at least 10 minutes or longer if you wish.

3.   Snap off and discard tough ends of asparagus. Cut the tender parts diagonally into 1½-inch lengths. Prepare remaining ingredients and place within easy reach of the stove.

Cooking:

1.   Heat a wok or nonstick skillet over high heat. Add half the oil and swirl to coat the pan evenly. Just before it begins to smoke, add the ginger root and garlic and stir-fry 10 seconds. Add the meat and stir-fry 2 to 3 minutes. Remove from the pan. Be sure pan remains hot throughout the entire cooking process.

2.   Heat remaining oil and stir-fry asparagus 15 seconds.

3. Add hoisin sauce, water, and pepper and bring to a boil. Cook until asparagus is almost tender.

4. Return meat and stir-fry and toss until ingredients are combined and heated through. Be sure the vegetable remains crisp and green.

Yield: 4–6 servings

Cooking time: 5 minutes

Calories per serving: 265
Saturated fat: 4.5 g
Cholesterol: 80 mg

Total fat: 14 g
Polyunsaturated fat: 6.5 g
Sodium: 120 mg

Variations:

1. Brown-bean sauce or oyster sauce may be substituted for hoisin sauce.

2. Soybean curd may be added to make a more substantial dish without the addition of more cholesterol. Cut 4 to 6 ounces of soybean curd into ½-inch cubes. Add in step 3, with the hoisin sauce.

3. A Sichuanese variation on these recipes would be to add 2–3 teaspoons of vinegar, crushed chilies to taste, and a teaspoon more sugar, in step 3.

Gingered Meatballs, or Lion's Heads
(Shizitou)

This is a highly adapted recipe for Lion's Heads, or Chinese meatballs, named after the lion-dog statues that stand as guardians of Chinese and other Oriental temples and palaces. Usually made with pork or a mixture of pork and dried shrimp, this dish is so named because the large loosely shaped meatballs look like the lion-dog's head and the cabbage looks like his ruffled mane. It is a tasty and inexpensive one-pot meal that has the advantage of not seeming overcooked if you don't serve it immediately.

12 ounces ground lean beef
2 egg whites, slightly beaten
2 tablespoons water
½–1 teaspoon black pepper
2 teaspoons Chinese rice wine, or pale dry sherry

4 water chestnuts finely chopped, or 1 small carrot, grated
¼ cup scallions, finely chopped
3 tablespoons fresh ginger root, minced

1½ teaspoons low-sodium soy
    sauce
1–2 tablespoons cornstarch
  1 tablespoon safflower oil
  1 pound Chinese cabbage, or
    spinach, cut into 2-inch
    pieces
½ teaspoon sugar
¼ cup stock, or water
½ teaspoon cornstarch,
    blended in 1 tablespoon
    water

Preparation:

1. Combine beef, eggs, water, pepper, water chestnuts, scallions, ginger root, and half the soy sauce. Mix thoroughly and form 4 large meat balls.
2. Roll meatballs in cornstarch and set aside.
3. Line a heavy pot with the cabbage or spinach leaves and set aside.
4. In a small bowl combine remaining soy sauce with sugar, stock, and cornstarch mixture.

Cooking:

1. Heat a skillet over medium heat. Add oil and brown meatballs on all sides. Drain on paper towels and place them on top of the cabbage or spinach.
2. Pour sauce ingredients over meatballs and bring to a boil. Cover, turn heat down to lowest setting and simmer 25–30 minutes.

Yield: 4–6 servings

Cooking time: 30–40 minutes

Calories per serving: 265
Saturated fat: 4 g
Cholesterol: 80 mg

Total fat: 12 g
Polyunsaturated fat: 5 g
Sodium: 170 mg

Stewed Five-Flavor Beef
(*Wuxiang Niurou*)

We are so accustomed to Chinese food being stir-fried that we forget that stews also exist. This one has an unusual combination of flavors. Like most stews it is better the next day.

1 pound very lean stewing beef
1 tablespoon safflower oil
½ teaspoon ground aniseed
½ teaspoon crushed or ground
    Sichuan peppercorns (black
    peppercorns may be
    substituted)
1 teaspoon cinnamon

1 teaspoon five-spice powder
½ teaspoon low-sodium soy
    sauce
4 scallions
1 tablespoon fresh ginger root,
    minced
1 teaspoon sugar
1 to 2 cups water or stock

Preparation:

1.   Remove all fat and cut beef into ½-inch cubes.
2.   Cut scallions into 2-inch lengths. Mince ginger root.

Cooking:

1.   In a heavy casserole, heat oil over high heat. Just before it begins to smoke, stir-fry beef until lightly browned.
2.   Add remaining ingredients and bring to a boil. Simmer over low heat uncovered for 2 hours, or until meat is very tender and all the liquid has evaporated. Add more water if necessary. Serve with rice.

Yield: 4–6 servings

Cooking time: 2 to 3 hours

Calories per serving: 308
Saturated fat: 5 g
Cholesterol: 105 mgs.

Total fat: 14 g
Polyunsaturated fat: 5.5 g
Sodium: 100 mg

Variation: Lamb may be substituted for beef.

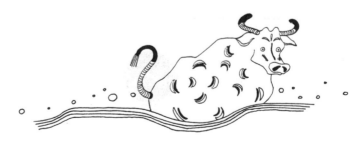

Soybean Curd
(Doufu)

Soybean curd, also known by its Japanese name (*tofu*), is very popular in the United States as a healthy alternative source of protein. It is available at most large supermarkets throughout the country. For information on how to buy and store soybean curd, please see p. 26. There is an enormous number of recipes using soybean curd, but I have given only four in this book. The most popular, Grandma Ma's Bean Curd (*Ma Po Doufu*), I have adapted it following the principles I have used in this book and create a tasty and healthy dish.

Soybean Curd
with Crabmeat and Snow Peas
(Xierou Doufu)

12 ounces firm soybean curd,
    cut into 1-inch cubes
3 large cloves garlic, minced
1 cup snow peas, or fresh
    green peas
4 ounces cooked crabmeat,
    flaked
1½ tablespoons safflower oil

Freshly ground pepper
1 teaspoon cornstarch,
    dissolved in 1 tablespoon
    water

Sauce:

1 tablespoon Chinese rice wine, or pale dry sherry	½–1 teaspoon oyster sauce
¼ teaspoon sugar	¼ cup unsalted chicken stock (p. 10)
½ teaspoon low-sodium soy sauce	1 teaspoon black pepper, or to taste

Preparation:

1.   Combine sauce ingredients in a bowl and set aside.
2.   Prepare remaining ingredients and place within easy reach of the stove.

Cooking:

1.   Heat a nonstick skillet over medium heat. Add half the oil and stir-fry garlic 10 seconds.
2.   Add soybean curd and gently brown on all sides. Sprinkle with freshly ground pepper. Remove from pan and drain on paper towels. Do not worry if some of the pieces fall apart.
3.   Wipe pan clean with paper towel. Heat pan again over high heat and add remaining oil. Add snow peas and stir-fry briskly for 30 seconds.
4.   Reduce heat and stir in crabmeat and cook 30 more seconds.
5.   Return soybean curd to pan and stir gently to reheat.
6.   Mix in sauce ingredients and cook until heated through.
7.   Mix in cornstarch mixture and cook until slightly thickened.

Yield: 4–6 servings	Cooking time: 7–10 minutes
Calories per serving: 180	Total fat: 9 g
Saturated fat: 1.5 g	Polyunsaturated fat: 6.5 g
Cholesterol: 25 mg	Sodium: 85 mg

Soybean Curd with Chicken and Mustard Greens
(*Doufugan Chao Jisi*)

Mustard greens offer a pungent contrast to the mild taste of soybean curd in this delicious dish from Shanghai.

1 ½ *tablespoons safflower oil*
  3 *large cloves garlic, minced*
12 *ounces firm soybean curd,*
    cut into 1-inch cubes
  6 *ounces boneless chicken (or*
    lean pork), all fat
    removed, cut into shreds
  3 *dried Chinese mushrooms,*
    or ½ *cup fresh mush-*
    rooms
  1 *pound (4 cups trimmed)*
    mustard greens, cut into
    2-inch lengths
  1 *teaspoon black pepper, or to*
    taste
  1 *teaspoon cornstarch,*
    dissolved in 1 tablespoon
    water

Sauce:

1 *teaspoon hoisin sauce*
1 *tablespoon Chinese rice wine,*
  or pale dry sherry

2–4 *tablespoons stock, or water*
  Dash of cayenne pepper
½ *teaspoon sugar*

Preparation:

1. Soak mushrooms in warm water for 30 minutes. Discard hard stems and slice.
2. Combine sauce ingredients in a bowl and set aside.
3. Prepare remaining ingredients and place within easy reach of the stove.

Cooking:

1. Heat a nonstick skillet over medium heat. Add 1 tablespoon oil. Swirl to coat the pan. Add garlic and stir-fry 10 seconds. Brown soybean curd on all sides. Sprinkle with freshly grated black pepper. Some of the pieces may fall apart no matter how careful you are. Don't worry about it. Remove and drain on paper towels.
2. Heat pan again over high heat and add remaining oil. Stir-fry chicken 1 minute. Sprinkle with black pepper. Remove from pan and set aside.
3. Add mushrooms and stir-fry 1 minute.
4. Add mustard greens and stir-fry until they are wilted but still green.

5.   Stir in combined sauce ingredients and cook over low heat until slightly thickened.
6.   Return soybean curd and chicken to pan, mix and cook until heated through.
7.   Stir in cornstarch mixture and cook until slightly thickened.

Yield: 4–6 servings

Cooking time: 12–15 minutes

Calories per serving: 225
Saturated fat: 2 g
Cholesterol: 40 mg

Total fat: 12 g
Polyunsaturated fat: 7 g
Sodium: 115 mg

Soybean Curd with Sliced Chicken and Chili Sauce
(*Jia Chang Doufu*)

Stephen Comee, a devotee of Asian foods (as well as the editor-designer of this book), has generously contributed this recipe. He tells me that the Chinese name for this dish means "home-style" soybean curd, and once you've tried it you'll know why it is such a perennial favorite, not only in its native Hunan but throughout China. It is also very popular in Japan. Although the original dish uses pork, I have suggested this variation with chicken as a healthier alternative. It is every bit as tasty.

1½ *tablespoons safflower oil*
3 *large cloves garlic, minced*
12 *ounces firm soybean curd,*
  cut into 1-inch cubes
8 *ounces boneless chicken (or*
  lean pork), all fat removed
4 *dried Chinese mushrooms,*
  or ¾ cup fresh
  mushrooms
1 *small carrot, sliced and par-*
  boiled
1 *green bell pepper, quartered*
  and seeded
1 *small piece of bamboo*
  shoot, sliced

Sauce:

1 teaspoon hoisin sauce
1 tablespoon Chinese rice
    wine, or pale dry sherry
½ teaspoon low-sodium soy
    sauce

1 teaspoon chopped red pepper,
    or cayenne pepper, to taste
½ teaspoon sugar

Preparation:

1.   Soak mushrooms in warm water for 30 minutes. Discard hard stems and slice.
2.   Boil chicken until cooked through but still tender let cool and slice thin. (If you prefer to use pork, boil it for 30 minutes, let cool, and slice thin.)
3.   Combine sauce ingredients in a bowl and set aside.
4.   Prepare remaining ingredients and place within easy reach of the stove.

Cooking:

1.   Heat a nonstick skillet over medium heat. Add 1 tablespoon oil. Swirl to coat the pan. Add garlic and stir-fry 10 seconds. Brown soybean curd on all sides. Some of the pieces may fall apart no matter how careful you are. Don't worry about it. Remove and drain on paper towels.
2.   Heat pan again over high heat and add remaining oil. Stir-fry green peppers, bamboo shoot, and carrot 1 minute.
3.   Add mushrooms and stir-fry 1 minute.
4.   Stir in combined sauce ingredients and cook over low heat until slightly thickened (about 3–5 minutes).
5.   Return soybean curd and chicken to pan, mix and cook until heated through.

Yield: 4–6 servings

Cooking time: 12–15 minutes

Calories per serving: 255
Saturated fat: 2 g
Cholesterol: 50 mg

Total fat: 13 g
Polyunsaturated fat: 7 g
Sodium: 130 mg

Soybean Curd with Chicken and Hot Bean Sauce
(*Mo Po Doufu*)

This is a highly adapted recipe for a very popular dish that is usually made with pork and a large quantity of hot bean sauce. Legend says it is named after its creator, a famous Chengdu chef's wife whose face was scarred with pockmarks. Thus, the name "Grandmother Pockmark's Soybean Curd."

1–2 teaspoons hot bean sauce	*3 large cloves garlic, minced*
6 ounces boneless ground chicken (or lean pork), all fat removed	*½ cup chicken stock (p. 10), or water*
½ teaspoon low-sodium soy sauce	*1 teaspoon ground Sichuan peppercorns, or black pepper*
½ teaspoon sugar	*1 teaspoon cornstarch, dissolved in 1 tablespoon water*
12 ounces firm soybean curd, cut into 1-inch cubes	*1 tablespoon sesame oil*
1½ tablespoons safflower oil	*Fresh coriander leaves, chopped for garnish*
2 tablespoons fresh ginger root, minced	

Preparation:

1. Mash the bean sauce with a fork. Combine in a bowl the bean sauce, ground chicken, soy sauce, and sugar and set aside
2. Prepare remaining ingredients and place within easy reach of the stove.

Cooking:

1. Heat a nonstick skillet over high heat. Add oil and swirl to coat the pan. Stir-fry the ginger and garlic for 10 seconds.
2. Add the chicken mixture and stir-fry for 30–60 seconds.
3. Stir in the chicken stock and cook for 3–4 minutes.
4. Add the soybean curd cubes and stir them gently so they will not fall apart too much. Cook for 2 or 3 minutes stirring now and then to prevent sticking.
5. Mix in the pepper, scallions, and cornstarch mixture and cook until slightly thickened, about 1 minute.
6. Remove from heat and stir in sesame oil. Garnish with chopped coriander leaves.

Yield: 4–6 servings

Cooking time: 10 minutes

Calories per serving: 250
Saturated fat: 2.5 g
Cholesterol: 40 mg

Total fat: 13.5 g
Polyunsaturated fat: 10 g
Sodium: 150 mg

◊  ◊

Vegetables
(*Su Cai*)

Contrary to the Western inclination to cook a vegetable until it is soft, the Chinese and other Far Eastern cuisines prefer to preserve its original character. The Chinese method of stir-frying in vegetable oil at high temperatures seals in the flavor and the color of the food; it also preserves crispness and nutrients. However, salt is added at the beginning of the stir-frying process, a step which for the purposes of this book must be left out. To make up for its absence, extra garlic, ginger, and pepper have been added. The cardinal rule when cooking vegetables the Chinese way is have the oil very hot and to stir-fry very briskly. However, the amount of oil that Chinese cooks use is much greater than that suggested in these recipes. When using less oil, it is necessary to steam some vegetables by covering the pan for part of the cooking time. Equally important to a successful stir-fry is freshness. This point cannot be over-stressed. If a vegetable is limp and tired, it may be good enough for a soup or stew but not for a stir-fry. Stay away from canned vegetables, with the exception of tomatoes and corn. Some Chinese vegetables are difficult to find fresh, and one must resort to a can to be authentic. But canned vegetables are notoriously high in sodium and usually do not remotely resemble the fresh original they once were. So don't be afraid to substitute. For example, carrots can stand in for bamboo shoots, and jicama roots for water chestnuts. Perhaps the best rule to follow is to use any fresh vegetables in season—the dish will not only taste better but will be better for you.

Stir-Fried Mixed Vegetables
(Shushijin)

To make a stir-fry of several vegetables it is important to choose them for their color and texture contrasts as well as for their taste. The amount of moisture that a vegetable possesses will also determine how long it needs to be cooked and whether water must be added to produce the steam some fibrous vegetables need to bring them to the desired tenderness. Decide which vegetable needs the longest cooking and stir-fry that one first, leaving the shortest-cooking vegetable to the end. Some cooks prefer to blanch or parboil a long-cooking vegetable first before stir-frying, but with rare exceptions I do not find this step necessary. The following recipe is one possible combination. Follow your own inclination for other combinations, depending on availability and freshness. I cannot over-emphasize the importance of a firm, lively looking plant to make a good-tasting dish.

1 ½ tablespoons safflower oil
1 tablespoon fresh ginger
    root, minced
3 large cloves garlic, minced
2 scallions, thinly sliced
2 small carrots, cut into
    matchstick lengths or into
    a very small dice
1 cup mushrooms, sliced

2 medium zucchini squashes,
    cut into thin 2-inch
    strips
½–1 teaspoon crushed or
    ground Sichuan pep-
    percorns
½–1 teaspoon freshly
    ground black pepper
½ teaspoon sugar
2–3 tablespoons water

1. Heat a wok or nonstick skillet over high heat. Add oil and swirl to coat the pan. Just before it begins to smoke, stir-fry ginger, garlic, and scallions 10 seconds.
2. First add carrots and stir-fry 1 minute. Add mushrooms and stir-fry 1 minute. Finally add zucchini and stir-fry 1 more minute.
3. Add peppers, sugar, and water. Mix well and cover for 30 seconds to 1 minute.
4. Remove lid and stir-fry until liquid evaporates. Transfer to a heated platter.

Yield: 4–6 servings

Cooking time: 5 minutes

Calories per serving: 105
Saturated fat: 0.5 g
Cholesterol: 0 mg

Total fat: 6 g
Polyunsaturated fat: 4.5 g
Sodium: 30 mg

Variations:

1.   One-quarter cup slivered almonds toasted in a dry skillet or toaster oven may be sprinkled on top of vegetables
2.   Fresh bean curd cut into small cubes may be browned and added to the stir-fry at the end.

Other suggested combinations:

1.   Broccoli and cauliflower cut into small flowerets
2.   Snow peas, or asparagus cut on the diagonal into 2-inch lengths
     Fresh water chestnuts thinly sliced, or try jicama roots if water chestnuts are not available
3.   Green and red bell peppers cut into ¼ inch strips
     Onions thinly sliced
4.   Eggplant cut into a small dice
     Tomatoes cut in wedges
     Green peppers cut into ¼ inch strips
5.   Cauliflower cut into flowerets
     Spinach leaves
     Mushrooms

Spicy Eggplant
(Hongshao Qiezi)

If you have a taste for eggplant and for spicy, tangy food, then this delicacy from Sichuan and Hunan is the dish for you. I strongly recommend, however, that you use a nonstick pan in which to cook the eggplant. Otherwise a large amount of oil will be necessary to cook this dish because of eggplant's blotter-like capacity to soak up oil. A Turkish dish called *Imam Bayildi* (literally, the Imam fainted), points up this fact in a delightful tale. One version of the story relates that the Imam, for whom this dish was created, was so fond of it that he had it prepared for him over and over, until one night it did not appear. When he learned that his favorite dish had exhausted his entire supply of olive oil, he fell into a faint. Another version tells us that he asked that his bride's dowry be the olive oil in which to cook this wonderful dish that she had created for him. Then she used it all up in less than a week. No wonder he fainted.

1 pound eggplant, preferably
  the small Chinese or
  Japanese variety
2 tablespoons safflower oil
4 large cloves garlic, minced
2 tablespoons fresh ginger
  root, minced
1–4 fresh or dried chili peppers,
  seeded and chopped, or
  cayenne pepper, to taste
1–2 teaspoons low-sodium soy
  sauce

½ teaspoon sugar
1 tablespoon Chinese rice
  vinegar, or other mild
  white vinegar
1 teaspoon Chinese rice
  wine, or pale dry sherry
¼–½ cup chicken stock
  (p. 10), or water
1 teaspoon sesame oil
  Chopped coriander leaves,
  or scallions, for garnish

Preparation:

1.   If using small Oriental eggplants, do not peel them. Large eggplants have tough skins and must be peeled. Whichever variety you use, cut them into thin 1-inch strips.
2.   In a small bowl combine soy sauce, sugar, vinegar, wine, and water. Set aside.
3.   Prepare remaining ingredients and place within easy reach of the stove.

Cooking:

1.   Heat a wok or a nonstick skillet over very high heat. Add oil and swirl to coat the pan. Just before it begins to smoke, stir-fry garlic and ginger 10 seconds.
2.   Add eggplant and chili peppers and stir-fry briskly 3–4 minutes.
3.   Add combined sauce ingredients and bring to a boil. Reduce heat, cover, and simmer 15–20 minutes, or until eggplant is very soft. Add more stock or water if mixture seems dry. Add sesame oil. May be made ahead and reheated.

Note: This dish makes an excellent appetizer either chilled or at room temperature, served on rounds of French bread.

Yield: 4–6 servings

Cooking time: 20–25 minutes

Calories per serving: 130
Saturated fat: 1 g
Cholesterol: 0 mg

Total fat: 7.5 g
Polyunsaturated fat: 6 g
Sodium: 50 mg

Variation: Some cooks include a small quantity of minced pork (but I recommend chicken) in this dish. About 3 ounces would be stir-fried separately with chopped scallions and added after step 3.

Stir-Fried Broccoli with Garlic
(*Qingchao Gailan*)

This is the standard, everyday way to cook a vegetable in the Chinese style. Garlic is the dominant seasoning, though ginger root may be substituted or used in addition. The amount of liquid you add at the end depends on how much moisture the vegetable contains. For example, a tender leafy vegetable like spinach will need less water than broccoli or string beans.

*4 cups broccoli, Chinese or
    American*
1 tablespoon safflower oil
4 cloves garlic, minced
*1 tablespoon fresh ginger root,
    minced (optional)*

¼ teaspoon sugar
*½–1 teaspoon freshly
    ground pepper*
2–4 tablespoons water

Preparation:

1.   Cut broccoli flowerets into 2-inch lengths.
2.   Cut the tender parts of the stems diagonally into strips ⅛ inch thick and place in a separate bowl from the flowerets.

Cooking:

1.   Heat a wok or nonstick skillet over very high heat. Add oil and swirl to coat the pan. Just before it begins to smoke, stir-fry the garlic for 10 seconds.
2.   Add broccoli stems and stir-fry briskly to coat pieces evenly, about 1 minute.
3.   Add flowerets and stir-fry another minute.
4.   Stir in sugar, pepper, and water. Cover and steam for 1–2 minutes. Uncover and stir-fry until liquid has evaporated. Vegetable should be green and crisp but not raw. Serve immediately.

Yield: 4–6 servings

Cooking time: 4–5 minutes

Calories per serving: 85
Saturated fat: 0.5 g
Cholesterol: 0 mg

Total fat: 4.5 g
Polyunsaturated fat: 3 g
Sodium: 20 mg

Hot-and-Sour Cabbage
(*Suanla Baicai*)

This is another tangy recipe from the Sichuan region. Chinese cabbage or Napa cabbage is best, but any cabbage may be substituted.

1½ pounds Chinese cabbage
1 tablespoon safflower oil
1–4 fresh or dried chili peppers,
   seeded and chopped, or
   cayenne pepper, to taste
½–1 teaspoon Sichuan peppercorns, or black peppercorns crushed or
   ground
3 tablespoons rice vinegar,
   or other mild white
   vinegar
1 tablespoon sugar, dissolved
   in 2 or 3 tablespoons
   water
½–1 teaspoon low-sodium soy
   sauce
½ teaspoon sesame oil

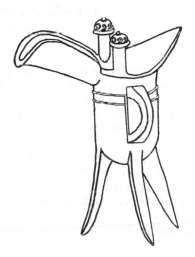

Preparation:

1.   Wash and cut Chinese cabbage in pieces 2 inches long and ½ to 1-inch wide. Use both leaves and stalks. Dry well on paper towels.
2.   In a small bowl combine vinegar, sugar, soy sauce, and sesame oil. Set aside.

Cooking:

1.   Heat a wok or nonstick skillet over high heat. Add oil. Just before it begins to smoke, stir-fry chili peppers 30 seconds.
2.   Add cabbage and Sichuan peppercorns and stir-fry 2–3 minutes or until cabbage wilts.
3.   Stir in combined sauce ingredients and cook until heated through. May be served hot or cold. May also be served as an appetizer.

Yield: 4–6 servings

Cooking time: 5–6 minutes

Calories per serving: 100
Saturated fat: 0.5 g
Cholesterol: 0 mg

Total fat: 6 g
Polyunsaturated fat: 5 g
Sodium: 50 mg

Dry-Cooked Green Beans
(*Ganshao Qingdou*)

A distinctive method of preparing non-leafy vegetables typical to Sichuan cooking is known as dry-cooking (*ganshao*), which leaves the vegetables dry, crunchy, and delicious. In this simplified recipe, the soy sauce and chili peppers are left out altogether, as well as the salty dried shrimps that some cooks add. The result is very low in sodium, fat, and calories.

*4 cups fresh green beans, or
    Chinese long beans, cut into
    2-inch lengths
1 tablespoon safflower oil*

*3 large cloves garlic, minced
1 tablespoon fresh ginger
    root, minced
½–1 teaspoon black pepper*

Preparation:

Wash and cut the beans into 2-inch lengths and dry thoroughly to minimize spattering.

Cooking:

1.   Heat a wok or nonstick skillet over high heat. Add oil and swirl to coat the pan. Just before it begins to smoke, add the beans and stir-fry briskly until they are wrinkled and lightly browned, about 4 or 5 minutes.
2.   Add the garlic, ginger, and pepper and stir-fry another minute. If beans are not tender enough, stir-fry a few seconds longer.

Yield: 4–6 servings

Cooking time: 7–10 minutes

Calories per serving: 70
Saturated fat: 0.3 g
Cholesterol: 0 mg

Total fat: 4 g
Polyunsaturated fat: 3 g
Sodium: 6 mg

String Bean and Red Pepper Salad
(*Sijidou Qiang Lajiao*)

Chinese do not eat their vegetables raw. Even lettuce is cooked. Therefore, the vegetables in this dish are blanched first.

8 ounces (3 cups) string beans, trimmed and cut into thin matchstick strips
2 large red bell peppers, deribbed and cut into thin strips

1 tablespoon fresh ginger root, minced
2 tablespoons Chinese rice vinegar, or mild white vinegar
2 tablespoons sugar

1.   Blanch beans and peppers separately in boiling water for 1–2 minutes. Drain and place in a serving bowl.
2.   Combine dressing ingredients and mix into the salad.

Yield: 4–6 servings

Cooking time: 2 minutes

Calories per serving: 50
Saturated fat: 0 g
Cholesterol: 0 mg

Total fat: 0 g
Polyunsaturated fat: 0 g
Sodium: 9 mg

Rice
(Fan)

Boiled Rice
(Damifan)

Cooking rice the Chinese way means cooking it without salt or fat. It also means that it must be washed in several changes of water before cooking. Chinese cooks say that washing rids the rice of excess starch and makes for fluffier grains. This appears to be true to some degree. But washing also removes many of the vitamins and minerals, and since the difference is hardly discernible, I prefer not to wash rice. If you decide to go the Chinese way, wash it in 2–3 changes of cold water and drain it well.

1 cup long-grain enriched rice   *1¾–2 cups cold water*

Note: Two cups of water will produce softer, moister rice.

1.   Place rice in a 2-quart pan. Add water and bring to a boil over high heat. Turn down heat to lowest point. Cover and cook 15 minutes.
2.   Without removing the lid, turn off heat and allow the rice to stand undisturbed 10–15 minutes. If necessary, rice may be kept warm in the oven until needed.

Variation: Another method is to bring rice to a boil and cook it for 15 minutes in an oven-proof dish on top of the stove. Then cover it tightly and bake it for 45 minutes or longer in a slow oven, about 250°F, until ready to serve. The most foolproof method is in an electric Japanese cooker.

Note: Glutinous rice should always be washed and soaked before cooking.

Yield: About 3 cups

Cooking time: 30 minutes

Calories per cup: 225
Saturated fat: Trace
Cholesterol: 0 mg

Total fat: 0.5 mg
Polyunsaturated fat: Trace
Sodium: 5 mg

Brown Rice
(*Xuanmifan*)

2 cups long-grain brown rice   *3 cups water*

1.   Combine rice and water in a medium-size saucepan. Bring to a boil. Reduce heat and simmer covered 40 minutes, or until moisture is absorbed.
2.   Remove from heat and let stand covered 10 minutes. Fluff with fork and serve.

Yield: About 5 cups

Calories per cup: 235
Saturated fat: 0.5 g
Cholesterol: 0 mg

Total fat: 1.5 g
Polyunsaturated fat: 1 g
Sodium: 5 g

Fried Rice
(*Chaofan*)

Preparing fried rice with less soy sauce makes it a more appealing dish both in taste and appearance. The recipe can be varied to include other meats and vegetables, but they must be stir-fried before being combined with the rice.

3 cups cold boiled rice (p. 148)
1 tablespoon safflower oil
2 large cloves garlic, minced
1 tablespoon fresh ginger root, minced
4 ounces raw chicken, cut into bite-sized pieces
4 scallions, thinly sliced
1 carrot, coarsely grated

1 green bell pepper, cut into ¼-inch strips
½ cup fresh mushrooms
1 teaspoon low-sodium soy sauce, mixed with 2 tablespoons chicken stock
1 tablespoon Sichuan peppercorns, crushed or coarsely ground, or freshly ground black pepper

Preparation:

1. To get the best results cook the rice the night before or early in the day and cool. Separate the grains and allow to dry.
2. Prepare remaining ingredients and place within easy reach of the stove.

Cooking:

1. Heat a wok or a large nonstick skillet over high heat until hot. Add oil and just before it begins to smoke, stir-fry garlic and ginger for 30 seconds.
2. Add chicken and stir-fry 1 minute.
3. Add scallions, carrot, green pepper, and mushrooms and stir-fry over high heat for 2 to 3 minutes.
4. Add rice and stir and toss until heated through.
5. Add soy sauce mixture and pepper and mix well.

Yield: 4 servings

Cooking time: 10 minutes

Calories per serving: 285
Saturated fat: 1 g
Cholesterol: 25 mg

Total fat: 5 g
Polyunsaturated fat: 3 g
Sodium: 85 mg

The Philippines

The Philippines

The Filipino Kitchen

Of all the countries of the Far East, the Philippines is the most Western-ized in customs and taste. Though the Malays and Chinese were among the earliest inhabitants, four hundred years of Spanish rule and fifty years of American occupation has had an overwhelming influence on these islands. More than 85 percent of the population is Roman Catholic and most Filipinos bear Spanish names. Not surprisingly, the average Filipino's taste in foods is not incompatible with a Westerner's. Though the origin of many Philippine dishes can be traced to Spain, some Filipino foods have been influenced by Chinese and Malay cooking styles. For ex-ample, there is a Filipino version of Chinese eggrolls, called *lumpia*, a salty fish sauce called *patis* that is similar to the Thai *nam pla* and the Viet-namese *nuoc mam*, and an equivalent to the *kapi* of Thailand and the *terasi* of Indonesia called *bagong*. Filipino cooking is marked by a few key preferences. One is a fondness for sour and salty tastes. The sour taste is achieved by the lavish use of vinegar, tamarind, and *calamansi*, a sour lime, and the salty taste, by the fish paste and fish sauce that is common to Southeast Asia. Filipinos also have a penchant for making stews in which a number of diverse foods are cooked together, as well as for saute-ing foods in olive oil, garlic, and onions, which they learned from the Spanish. But as in most countries of Southeast Asia, rice and fish are the mainstay of the diet for the majority of the people.

◊  ◊

Fish
(Pescado)

Pickled Fish
(Escabeche)

This dish is obviously of Spanish origin. It is a perfect way to cook fish, especially for summer months, because it can be prepared at leisure a few hours before it is needed. There are so many variations that the proportions are hardly sacred. The dressing can be as sour, as sweet, or as hot as you wish. It's also a perfect low-sodium recipe. This adaptation is simpler than the usual recipes that contain a much larger proportion of vinegar. The usual method is to simmer the fish in the dressing and then marinate it for 24 hours. The result is a bit strong for my taste, and I prefer this milder version.

1 ½ *pounds firm fish fillets*   1 *tablespoon olive oil*

Dressing:

½ *cup scallions, thinly chopped, or a mild onion*
1–2 *large cloves garlic, minced*
½ *green bell pepper, cut into thin short matchstick strips*
¼–½ *teaspoon freshly ground black pepper*
1 *small fresh or dried red chili pepper, seeded and finely chopped, or chili*

pepper flakes or cayenne pepper, to taste
¼–1 *teaspoon sugar*
1 *tablespoon olive oil*
2 *tablespoons white wine vinegar, or other mild vinegar*
3 *tablespoons lime or lemon juice*
Fresh chopped coriander or parsley leaves

1.   In a nonstick skillet, heat oil and saute fish fillets until lightly browned on both sides. Before removing from pan, sprinkle with chopped coriander leaves or parsley. Transfer to a serving platter.

2.   Mix dressing ingredients and pour over fish. Garnish with more coriander or parsley leaves

Yield: 6 servings   Cooking time: 5 minutes

Calories per serving: 155   Total fat: 6 g
Saturated fat: 1 g   Polyunsaturated fat: 1 g
Cholesterol: 60 mg   Sodium: 80 mg

Chicken
(Pollo)

Chicken Cooked in Vinegar
(Pollo Adobo)

If the Philippines can be said to have a national dish, *adobo* would be it. A method of cooking using vinegar, soy sauce, and garlic, *adobo* in its many variations turns up everywhere. Pork, seafood, and vegetables are also cooked in *adobo* style, and some versions contain coconut milk as well as fish sauce (*patis*). All of the recipes I have surveyed use a lot more soy sauce and an incredible amount of garlic—a whole head in one of them. This recipe has been highly adapted, but it remains just as sour—though not nearly as salty—as the original.

.1 *cup vinegar*
1 *cup water*
4 *large cloves garlic, minced*
1 *teaspoon black pepper*
4 *bay leaves*
1 *whole chicken breast and 2
    chicken legs (thigh and
    drumstick), cut into small
    serving pieces, fat and skin
    removed*
2 *teaspoons low-sodium soy
    sauce*
1 *tablespoon safflower oil
    Chopped parsley for garnish*

1.   In a large saucepan, combine vinegar, water, garlic, pepper, and bay leaves. Add chicken and bring to a boil. Turn chicken pieces to coat with sauce, cover and simmer over low heat for 15–20 minutes.

2.   Stir in soy sauce and simmer 5–10 minutes, or until chicken is tender.

3.   Remove chicken pieces and keep warm. Boil sauce uncovered until it is reduced to approximately half its original volume.

4.   In the meantime, heat oil and brown chicken pieces on both sides. This step is optional. Fat content will be reduced further without it. Place on a serving platter and pour sauce on top. Garnish with parsley.

Yield: 4 servings

Cooking time: 35–45 minutes

Calories per serving: 260
Saturated fat: 2.5 g
Cholesterol: 100 mg

Total fat: 10 g
Polyunsaturated fat: 4.5 g
Sodium: 170 mg

◇  ◇

Vegetables
(Verduras)

Spinach Sauteed in Olive Oil
(Espinaca en Aceite del Oliva)

Saute, from the French *sauter*, meaning to jump, refers to a method of cooking using so little fat that food is constantly stirred or made to "jump" in the pan to prevent sticking. Sauteing vegetables and meats in olive oil, onions, and garlic is the preferred cooking method in Mediterranean countries, and the Filipinos learned it from the Spanish. Similiar to stir-frying, though slower and on a lower fire, its main drawback is that many cooks use too much oil and foods are allowed to sit in it too long. Olive oil has a fine flavor and almost any vegetable can be cooked this way.

1 ½ *pounds fresh spinach*	*2 large cloves garlic, minced*
(*about 6 cups*)	¼–½ *teaspoon freshly ground*
1 *tablespoon olive oil*	*black pepper*
½ *cup onion, finely chopped*	*4 large lemon wedges*

1.   Wash and dry spinach. Remove stems.
2.   In a large saucepan, heat oil and saute onions and garlic until transparent but not brown.
3.   Add spinach and cook 2–4 minutes, turning leaves over in oil until wilted but still very green. Serve with lemon wedges.

Yield: 4 servings   Cooking time: 8-10 minutes

Calories per serving: 65   Total fat: 3.5 g
Saturated fat: 0.5 g   Polyunsaturated fat: 0.5 g
Cholesterol: 0 mg   Sodium: 40 mg

Note: Olive oil, which is a monounsaturated fat, was thought to be neutral so far as its effect on the heart and arteries, but some studies indicate that it may be as beneficial as polyunsaturated fats.

Vietnam

◊  ◊

The Vietnamese Kitchen

Of all the countries in Southeast Asia, Vietnam is the most familiar to the world at large because of the long tragic war that was fought there. Descendants of Chinese and Indonesian migrations, the Vietnamese have been struggling to maintain their independence for more than 2,000 years. Until the fifteenth century, this small kingdom was dominated by China. A century later, the Portuguese entered the area, followed by the French in the nineteenth century. France maintained a strong foothold until 1954, when the country was arbitrarily divided. War and escalating American involvement resulted in untold tragedy few can forget. More than a decade has passed since then. Thousands of refugees have made their homes in the United States and their number is growing. In the last few years Chinese grocery stores have begun to stock Vietnamese ingredients, and dozens of Vietnamese restaurants have sprung up in metropolitan areas. For Americans who have an insatiable appetite for ethnic food this is very good news.

The cuisine of Vietnam offers a fascinating contrast with that of its near neighbors to the north and to the west. Although it owes a great deal to the example of China, Vietnamese sauces are not as rich as their Chinese counterparts. A variety of fresh raw herbs and vegetables—lettuce, cucumber, coriander, and mint—that never appear in Chinese cooking are used in abundance in Vietnamese dishes. Shallots, also absent from Chinese cooking but common to Indonesian cooking, also appear frequently in Vietnamese dishes. Borrowing hot chili peppers, lemon grass, coconut, and tamarind from Thailand and Indonesia, Vietnamese cooks succeed in combining these flavors in a style that is lighter and more subtle than those seen in these neighboring countries.

Perhaps the most important difference between Chinese and Vietnamese cuisine is the absence of soy sauce, the universal Chinese seasoning. In its place is *nuoc mam,* a clear amber-colored liquid made from layers of salted and fermented anchovies. *Nuoc mam,* which is similar to the *nam pla* of Thailand, is present in just about every dish and on almost every table, where it takes the place of salt in Western cooking and soy sauce in Chinese. Diluted with lemon juice and water, and flavored with garlic, sugar, and chili peppers, it becomes the dipping sauce *nuoc cham,* which accompanies almost all Vietnamese dishes. It is important to know that there are varying qualities of this fish sauce. The first pressing is the best. It is lighter in color and very clear. The second and third pressings are considered less desirable. When Vietnamese fish sauce is not available, Thai fish sauce (*nam pla*) is an excellent substitute. If neither is available, low-sodium soy sauce may be used, though without fish sauce the characteristic flavor of Vietnamese food will be missed.

Generally speaking, the Chinese influence is strongest in the cooler temperatures of North Vietnam. Dishes tend to be least spicy, and fish and seafood are prominent, with stir-frying being the favored cooking technique. Northerners, like their Chinese neighbors, prefer their vegetables cooked. Southerners, on the other hand, though they also rely on fish as their main source of protein, like their food to be spicier and some of their vegetables raw. The French, who ruled Vietnam for a good part of this century, have also had an influence on Vietnamese cooking. In the hot, humid South with its abundance of fresh fruits and vegetables, their influence was the greatest. Beef, as well as asparagus, tomatoes, and potatoes—which were introduced by the French—are frequently seen. While many well-to-do Vietnamese have cultivated a taste for French dishes and especially French bread, the staple starches remain rice and noodles.

Though the historical influence of China is substantial, Vietnamese cookery retains its own distinct character and would never be mistaken for Chinese food. Perhaps the most important similarity is in the Vietnamese and Chinese manner of eating. Vietnam is the only Southeast Asian nation that uses chopsticks. Like the chopstick users of China and Japan, Vietnamese tend to eat their rice plain or after other dishes, unlike the finger-eaters of Thailand and Indonesia, who mix rice with other foods. Another similarity is the use of the stir-frying technique in a wok-shaped utensil.

Preparing and serving a Vietnamese meal is very similar to preparing a Chinese meal. Plain white rice, cooked, firm, separate, and without salt, is the basis of most meals, except breakfast, which consists of a very hearty noodle soup. Besides rice, a typical meal would consist of a soup, vegetables or salad, and a fish or meat dish. The table is set with small bowls and chopsticks, and all the dishes are served at once. A meal usually concludes with fruit, while sweets are taken during the day as between-meal snacks. No special utensils are required besides a wok or a teflon coated, nonstick skillet and one or two saucepans, which are usually available in any kitchen. For tips on stir-frying and using a wok see pages xxxiii–xxxiv.

Vietnamese cooks stir-fry vegetables in much the same way as Chinese cooks do. Please refer to pages 140–47 in the Chinese section for vegetable recipes to serve with Vietnamese dishes. As in the beef fondue recipe on page 186, the Vietnamese also commonly serve a platter of fresh herbs and vegetables, consisting of lettuce leaves, fresh mint and coriander leaves, and sliced cucumber and tomato.

Boiled rice is cooked by the absorption method without salt, and fluffy firm grains are preferred by most Vietnamese. The recipe in the Chinese chapter on page 148 is recommended. Stir-fried rice is also a staple dish. Please refer to the Chinese recipe on page 150.

Adapting Vietnamese Food to a Low-Sodium, Low-Cholesterol Diet

All in all, the deemphasis on fats and thickening agents, as well as the use of fresh uncooked salads and vegetables, makes Vietnamese cuisine ideal for low-fat, low-calorie diets. As for the sodium component, *that* is another story. Vietnamese fish sauce (*nuoc mam*), is the main seasoning ingredient in Vietnamese cooking, and it is a very salty product. It is not standardized as is Japan's soy sauce, and to the best of my knowledge no food chemists have measured its sodium content. To arrive at an approximate sodium count, I have assumed that there is about the same amount of sodium in fish sauce as there is in regular soy sauce: 320 mg per teaspoon, not 170 mg, which the low-sodium product contains. Insofar as the recipes in this book are concerned, far less fish sauce is added than Vietnamese cooks would use, while more of other assertive seasonings are relied upon to add distinctly pronounced flavors.

◊  ◊

Appetizers
(Mon An Choi)

Vietnamese Spring Rolls
(Cha Gio)

If Vietnam has a national dish it is *cha gio*. These crisp and delicate deep-fried spring rolls are similiar to the Chinese egg rolls that everyone is familiar with, but the wrapper is quite different. It is a very thin, brittle, translucent sheet made of rice flour that miraculously transforms to a soft tissue-like dough when it is dipped into warm water. These rice papers are available at most Asian groceries and some large supermakets. My favorite is the brand made in Thailand, which is about 9 inches in diameter. The words Banh Trang appear on the wrapper. Some brands should be avoided because they are too salty. Making these rolls is quite simple, and the rice papers though fragile are not at all difficult to manage if you moisten only two at a time. Once rolled, the rice sheet sticks to itself, making the finished rolls very easy to handle. Every Vietnamese cook has a favorite way of making *cha gio*. The filling may contain ground pork, salted shrimp, crabmeat, and some form of mushroom. Some cooks make them large and flat, while others make a very long roll that is cut into small serving pieces. *Cha gio* are perfect for hors d'oeuvres because they can be made tiny enough to be eaten in one bite. Of course, my original impulse was to leave the recipe out of the book, since deep-fried dishes should be avoided in a low-fat diet. But the rolls are so delicious that I could not abandon the recipe. After several trials, I succeeded in adapting it so that they could be cooked either in the oven or in a nonstick frying pan with only 1 tablespoon of oil. So please feel free to try these tasty tidbits—but then go on to try the Salad Wraps (*Goi Cun*; p. 169), which are succulent pieces of boiled shrimp and chicken wrapped in lettuce leaves.

32–40 rice paper wrappers
  1 tablespoon safflower oil
  Fresh coriander or mint
    leaves

Lettuce leaves
Cucumber slices

Filling:

1 pound ground chicken, or a
  mixture of ground chicken,
  lean pork, and finely
  chopped shrimp or crab-
  meat
5 large cloves garlic, minced
¼ cup onions, finely chopped
¼ cup scallions, both white and
  green parts, finely chopped

About 10 tree ears, or ½
  cup fresh mushrooms,
  finely chopped
1 teaspoon Vietnamese fish
  sauce (nuoc mam), or
  Thai fish sauce (nam pla),
  or low-sodium soy sauce
1½ teaspoons freshly ground
  black pepper

1.   Soak tree ears in warm water to soften. Drain and chop finely. There should be about ½ cup.

2.   Combine filling ingredients and mix well with hands. If mixture does not seem to adhere, add a teaspoon of cornstarch or a slightly beaten egg white. Mix thoroughly.

3.   Put warm water in a bowl wide and deep enough for one rice paper to fit comfortably. Spread a dry towel over a cutting board.

4.   To make the rolls, work with only 2 sheets of rice paper at a time. Immerse the first sheet of rice paper in the warm water and quickly remove it. Lay it flat on the dry towel. Repeat with the second sheet and lay it next to the first. Wait 3–5 seconds for the paper to soften. Fold over the bottom third of each paper.

5.   Put 2 to 3 teaspoons of filling in the center of the folded-over portion. Shape it into a compact rectangle. Fold one side of the paper over the meat mixture, then fold over the other side. Roll securely from bottom to top to enclose the filling. You should have a firm, compact cylinder. Repeat until all the sheets are filled. As you work, keep the rolls covered with plastic wrap or a damp towel to keep them from drying out. It may be helpful to evenly divide the filling into equal portions before you begin filling the rolls.

6.   Brown the rolls, preferably in 2 nonstick skillets. Heat ½ tablespoon of oil in each. Add the rolls and cook over low heat 30 minutes, turning them often until they are crisp and brown on all sides. To be sure that the filling cooks completely, add a teaspoon or two of water and cover the pan to steam the rolls about 1 minute. Uncover and brown again. Alternatively, they may be baked in a 350°F oven in a lightly greased baking dish for about 20–25 minutes on each side, or until they are brown. Brush with a little oil from time to time.

7. Drain on paper towels and serve with *nuoc cham* dipping sauce (p. 168), and a platter of lettuce, coriander, or mint leaves, and strips of cucumbers. If desired, diners may wrap each roll in a lettuce leaf including a sprig of coriander or mint and a strip of cucumber.

Note: To make hors d'oeuvre-size rolls, cut the rice papers into quarters and fill them as directed above, making 4 small rolls with each sheet instead of 1 large one.

Yield: 32 rolls   Cooking time: 30 minutes

Nutrient analysis does not include rice papers.

Calories per roll: 35   Total fat: 1.5 g
Saturated fat: 0.5 g   Polyunsaturated fat: 0.5 g
Cholesterol: 15 mg   Sodium: 25 mg

Garlic-and-Chili Fish Sauce
(*Nuoc Cham*)

3 tablespoons fish sauce   2 teaspoons sugar
  (nuoc mam), *or Thai fish*   2 tablespoons lemon or lime
  sauce (nam pla)   juice
5 tablespoons water   Fresh or dried chili pepper,
1–2 large cloves garlic, minced   chopped, or cayenne pepper,
                                      to taste

Combine all ingredients and mix well.

Note: Since the sodium content of fish sauce is unknown, the sodium count for this Garlic-and-Chili Fish Sauce (*Nuoc Cham*) is only approximate. I have assumed that a teaspoon of fish sauce contains about the same amount of sodium as regular soy sauce (not the low-sodium variety), 320 mg.

Yield: About 10 tablespoons

Calories per tablespoon: 8   Total fat: 0 g
Saturated fat: 0 g   Polyunsaturated fat: 0 g
Cholesterol: 0 mg   Sodium: 290 mg

Salad Wraps
(*Goi Cun*)

This recipe was given to me by Stephen Comee, who says that in the three most popular Vietnamese restaurants in Tokyo this dish is the main attraction. It is the raw version of *Cha Gio*. These little salad "wraps" are like lettuce rolls—each "wrap" is a small bundle. Each diner wraps a little filling in lettuce and dips the "wrap" in a piquant sauce. The dish is a perfect appetizer as well as picnic food; it can also be a complete meal if served with soup. It can be prepared far in advance of serving time, too, as it is basically a cold platter from which diners take the ingredients and fashion their own little salad wraps, *chacun à son goût!*

2 pounds leaf lettuce   Nuoc Cham *sauce (p. 168)*

Fillings:

¼ pound rice sticks (rice   *Fresh coriander (Chinese*
vermicelli)   *parsley) leaves*
¾ pounds boiled shrimp   *Fresh mint leaves*
½ pound boiled white
chicken meat
1 scallion, cut into
matchsticks 2–3 inches
long

1.   Prepare rice sticks according to directions on the package. Drain and rinse under cold water. Place on a bed of lettuce leaves to serve.
2.   Boil shrimp and chicken separately until cooked through but tender. It should take about 15 minutes for the chicken and 2–3 minutes for the shrimp. Drain and rinse under cold water. Slice the shrimp into 2 or 3 lengthwise slices; slice chicken into small slices. Arrange on a bed of lettuce leaves with the chicken around the edges of the serving plate and the shrimp in the middle.
3.   Wash and drain all the vegetables. Serve on a large plate or in separate bowls.
4.   Be sure to make enough *Nuoc Cham* sauce so that each person can have about half a cupful of it, served in individual cups.

To serve:

1.   Let each person assemble his own "wrap" by taking a lettuce leaf and placing in it any of the above ingredients desired except the sauce. Then wrap the lettuce firmly around the fillings.

2. Diners should dip their Salad Wraps in the *Nuoc Cham* sauce. If they fall apart, they can be fished out with chopsticks or with a fork.

Yield: 5 servings	Cooking time: 20 minutes

Calories per serving: 205	Total fat: 4 g
Saturated fat: 1 g	Polyunsaturated fat: 0.5 g
Cholesterol: 145 mg	Sodium: 140 mg

Variation: To serve these little Salad Wraps as one of many types of hors d'oeuvres, make many small rolls ahead of time to your own preference, and set aside in a cool place covered with plastic wrap. Serve chilled, with *Nuoc Cham* sauce.

Chicken Salad with Fresh Mint
(*Ga Xe Phay*)

This unusual chicken salad is suitable as an appetizer or as part of a meal. The mint that is used in Vietnamese cooking is a milder, smaller leafed variety than the spearmint which is common in Western cooking. Choose the young tender leaves of the plant and use less than the recipe calls for if you prefer a milder salad.

1 whole chicken breast and 1 chicken leg and thigh, skin and fat removed
¼ cup shallots sliced paper thin, or substitute the white part of scallions or a mild onion

½ small carrot grated or finely chopped (about ½ cup)
¼ cup finely chopped mint leaves
Lettuce leaves to be used as wrappers

Dressing:

2 tablespoons mild white vinegar
1 teaspoon fish sauce (nuoc mam) or substitute Thai fish sauce (nam pla) or low-sodium soy sauce
½ teaspoon sugar dissolved in 1 tablespoon water

1 large clove garlic minced
¼–½ teaspoon black pepper
Finely chopped fresh or dried chili pepper, or cayenne pepper, to taste

1. Cover chicken with boiling water and simmer 15–20 minutes or until tender. Cool. Bone and shred into thin strips.

2. While chicken is cooking combine dressing ingredients and pour over shallots, carrots, and mint leaves. Let stand 15 minutes. Add chicken shreds and mix thoroughly. Drain.

3. If serving as an appetizer place on a platter surrounded by lettuce leaves. Diners may use lettuce leaves as wrappers if they wish.

Yield: 6 servings   Cooking time: 20 minutes

Calories per serving: 120   Total fat: 3.5 g
Saturated fat: 1 g   Polyunsaturated fat: 1 g
Cholesterol: 50 mg   Sodium: 100 mg

Soups
(Canh)

Fish Stock
(Nuoc Canh Ca Mon)

1 ½–2 *pounds fish collars*
    (salmon is best but
    other available fish will
    do)
4 *cups water*

2–3 *bay leaves, or kaffir lime*
    leaves, if available
1 *onion, quartered*

Put all ingredients in a large saucepan and bring to a boil. Simmer 30 minutes and strain. Discard collars.

Crabmeat and Asparagus Soup
(Man Tay Cua)

Asparagus, introduced by the French, is called Western bamboo by the Vietnamese. This is a beautiful soup happily combining East and West.

2 *teaspoons safflower oil*
¼ *cup chopped shallots, or white*
    part of scallions, or onions
1 *small clove garlic, minced*

½ cup fresh mushrooms, thinly
    sliced, or Chinese
    mushrooms soaked in
    warm water to cover for 30
    minutes, then thinly sliced
6 ounces cooked crabmeat
4 cups unsalted chicken stock
    (p. 10)
1 teaspoon fish sauce (nuoc
    mam) or Thai fish sauce
    (nam pla), or low-sodium
    soy sauce

8–12 asparagus spears, cut
    diagonally into 1½-inch
    lengths
¼–½ teaspoon freshly
    ground black pepper
1 teaspoon cornstarch,
    dissolved in 2 table-
    spoons water
2 egg whites, beaten until
    frothy but not stiff
Chopped watercress for
    garnish

1.   In a skillet, heat oil over medium heat and saute shallots and garlic until transparent. Add mushrooms and saute 2 or 3 minutes.

2.   Add crabmeat and saute 1 minute, stirring constantly. Remove from heat and set aside.

3.   In a soup kettle, bring chicken stock to a boil. Add the fish sauce. Drop in asparagus spears and cook 1 minute, or until barely tender.

4.   Add pepper and cornstarch mixture and stir for a few seconds.

5.   Place ingredients from skillet into stock and cook until heated through.

6.   Gently fold in beaten egg white. Garnish with watercress and serve immediately.

Yield: 4–6 servings

Cooking time: 10–15 minutes

Calories per serving: 130
Saturated fat: 1 g
Cholesterol: 35 mg

Total fat: 4 g
Polyunsaturated fat: 2.5 g
Sodium: 160 mg

Sour Fish Soup with Tomatoes
(Canh Chua Ca)

A particularly delicious fish chowder with the flavors of pineapple, tomatoes, and tamarind subtly blended and nicely tart.

1 tablespoon safflower oil
¼ cup shallots, or onion, finely
    chopped

2 large cloves garlic, minced
4 tomatoes, cut into thin wed-
    ges, or 1 can tomatoes

1 cup fresh or canned
  pineapple, cut into thin 1-
  inch slices
1 teaspoon fish sauce (nuoc
  mam), or Thai fish sauce
  (nam pla) or low-sodium soy
  sauce
4 cups unsalted chicken stock
  (p. 9), or fish stock (p. 172)
4 tablespoons tamarind water
  (p. xxxii), or 4 tablespoons
  lemon juice and grated rind
  from 1 lemon

1½ cups mung bean sprouts,
  trimmed
12 ounces firm fish fillets,
  cut into 1-inch slices
¼–½ teaspoon black pepper
  Fresh or dried chili pepper,
  chopped, or cayenne
  pepper, to taste
Lemon wedges
Chopped fresh coriander
  leaves for garnish

1.   In a soup kettle, heat oil over high heat. Add onions and garlic and cook until transparent.
2.   Add tomatoes and pineapple and saute 2 or 3 minutes.
3.   Add fish sauce and chicken stock and bring to a boil.
4.   Add tamarind water, bean sprouts, fish fillets, and pepper, and cook 2 or 3 minutes, or until fish is tender. Do not overcook fish.
5.   Serve with lemon wedges and garnish with coriander leaves.

Yield: 4–6 servings

Cooking time: 45 minutes

Calories per serving: 235
Saturated fat: 1 g
Cholesterol: 45 mg

Total fat: 6 g
Polyunsaturated fat: 3.5 g
Sodium: 165 mg

Variations: For a more substantial soup, ½ pound shrimp, shelled and deveined, may be added with the fish in step 3. The soup may also be made with shrimp alone, or with just beef.

Beef-and-Pineapple Soup
(Canh Ca Chua Thom Thit Bo)

The combination of beef and pineapple with tomatoes is unusual and exciting. The soup is equally flavorful made with shrimp. Note that although canned pineapple will do, it is too sweet, and fresh pineapple will make a much tangier soup.

1 tablespoon oil
¼ cup chopped shallots, or
    white part of scallion, or
    onion
1 large clove garlic, minced
6 ounces very lean beef, cut
    into thin 1-inch-square
    slices
1 cup fresh or canned pineap-
    ple, cut into thin 1-inch
    slices
1 tomato, cut into thin wedges

4 cups unsalted beef stock
    (p. 176)
1 teaspoon fish sauce (nuoc
    mam), or Thai fish sauce
    (nam pla), or low-sodium
    soy sauce
½–1 teaspoon freshly ground
    black pepper
Chopped coriander leaves
    or scallion greens for gar-
    nish

1. In a saucepan, heat 2 teaspoons oil over high heat and saute shallots and garlic until transparent.
2. Add beef and saute, turning frequently until it changes color. Remove from pan and set aside.
3. Heat remaining oil and saute pineapple and tomato 2–3 minutes stirring constantly.
4. Add stock, beef mixture, fish sauce and pepper and bring to a boil.
5. Cook until heated through. Serve immediately, garnished with coriander leaves.

Yield: 4–6 servings

Cooking time: 20 minutes

Calories per serving: 170
Saturated fat: 2 g
Cholesterol: 40 mg

Total fat:7 g
Polyunsaturated fat: 4 g
Sodium: 110 mg

Variation: Substitute ½ pound shrimps, shelled and deveined, for the beef. Be sure not to overcook shrimps or they will toughen.

Hanoi Beef Soup
(Pho Bo)

Pho Bo is a north Vietnamese specialty, though it is eaten in various forms throughout Vietnam. Basically, it is a sort of soup-salad. A rich beef broth is ladled over noodles and paper-thin slices of beef, then garnished with bean sprouts, chopped scallions, and coriander leaves, and seasoned with *nuoc mam* (fish sauce). A fast-food favorite, it was traditionally eaten for breakfast as well as all day long (and probably still is), in the market food stalls of Hanoi and Saigon, now called Ho Chi Minh City. Huge steaming cauldrons of soup simmer from dawn to sunset, ready to serve in seconds to workers and shoppers walking through the market. The stock is supposed to cook for hours—the longer the better—since a very rich broth is the essence of the dish. The noodles and "salad" ingredients are added just before serving. To remove the fat, the broth is best made a day or so ahead and refrigerated so that it can be skimmed off the surface. *Pho Bo* constitutes a complete meal.

Stock:

1 tablespoon oil	2 carrots, peeled and sliced
2–3 pounds meaty beef bones	2 teaspoons fish sauce (nuoc
½ pound boneless lean beef	mam), or Thai fish sauce
shank, well trimmed	(nam pla), or low-sodium
3 slices (½-inch long) fresh	soy sauce
ginger root	3 star anise
1 large onion, sliced	2-inch stick cinnamon
	4 quarts water

1.   Combine all the stock ingredients in a large soup kettle and bring to a boil. Skim off the froth. Simmer uncovered for at least 3 hours. Add more water if much of it boils away.

2.   Strain and measure stock. Adjust yield to 6 cups, either by adding water or boiling down excess stock. Refrigerate overnight. When chilled, discard layer of fat that congeals on the surface.

3.   Remove the cooked meat from the bones and discard all fat. Cut into bite-sized pieces and refrigerate.

½ pound rice sticks (rice vermi-	Chopped scallions and fresh
celli)	coriander leaves for garnish
3 cups bean sprouts, trimmed	2 lemons or limes, quartered
6 scallions, chopped	Black pepper to taste
1 onion, quartered and thinly	Fresh chili peppers, seeded,
sliced	chopped, and cut into very
½ pound lean beef fillet or	thin slices, or hot red pepper
other tender beef, sliced	or cayenne pepper, to taste
thin against the grain	

1.   Bring skimmed stock to a boil. Add cut cooked beef reserved from night before.

2.   Soak rice sticks in hot water for 10–15 minutes to soften. (It is wise to follow directions on package.) Drain, rinse with cold water, and set aside.

3. Arrange bean sprouts, scallions, onion, and beef slices in separate mounds.

To serve:

1. You will need 1 or 2 wire strainers with handles, and large soup bowls. Place bowls next to the simmering kettle.
2. Place soaked noodles in wire strainer and submerge in boiling broth for 1 or 2 minutes, or until hot and tender. Divide among soup bowls.
3. Put vegetables in wire strainer and submerge in broth for a few seconds. Place some on top of noodles in soup bowls.
4. Place slices of raw meat in strainer. Submerge and cook until meat changes color. Add a few pieces to each bowl.
5. Now ladle some simmering broth and reserved cooked meat in each bowl. Garnish with chopped scallions and coriander leaves. Serve with freshly ground black pepper, chilies, onion slices, and lemon wedges for each person to add according to taste.

Yield: 6–8 servings

Cooking time: 3–4 hours
(some say 8 hours or more)

Calories per serving: 325
Saturated fat: 5 g
Cholesterol: 105 mg

Total fat: 11 g
Polyunsaturated fat: 2.5 g
Sodium: 195 mg

◊  ◊

Seafood
(Hai-vi)

Steamed Fish
(Ca Hap)

Fish fillets are heaped with a fragrant pile of vegetables, noodles, and seasonings, and then steamed on the serving platter from which they will be served. Simple to prepare and elegant to serve, this dish is also delicious to eat.

1 pound firm fish fillets, or a 2-pound whole fish	2 tablespoons fresh ginger root, grated
1 ounce cellophane noodles (bean threads)	1 teaspoon fish sauce (nuoc mam), or Thai fish sauce (nam pla), or low-sodium soy sauce
3 dried Chinese mushrooms, or ½ cup fresh mushrooms	½–1 teaspoon black pepper
2 shallots, or white part of 2 scallions, chopped	1 tomato, thinly sliced Fresh coriander leaves, chopped, for garnish
1 large clove garlic, minced	

1.   Place fish fillets on a heat-proof serving platter. If using a whole fish, make diagonal cuts in it to allow the seasonings to penetrate.
2.   Soak the cellophane noodles in warm water for 30 minutes.
3.   Soak the dried mushrooms for 30 minutes. Discard tough stems and slice.
4.   Combine all ingredients except the tomatoes and coriander. Spread over fish. Arrange tomatoes attractively on top.
5.   Bring water in a steamer (pp. xxxii–xxxiii) to a boil. Steam fish fillets on the serving platter for 15 to 20 minutes. A whole fish will take up to 30

minutes. Do not overcook. Garnish with coriander leaves and serve with rice.

Yield: 4–6 servings

Cooking time: 20 minutes

Calories per serving: 135
Saturated fat: 0.5 g
Cholesterol: 60 mg

Total fat: 1.5 g
Polyunsaturated fat: 0.5 g
Sodium: 160 mg

Sweet-and-Sour Fish
(Ca Chien Chua Ngot)

It was difficult to decide whether to place this recipe in the Vietnamese or the Thai chapter. It's a favorite in both countries with very little variation. The origin, of course, is Chinese. The fish is usually deep fried and the sweet-and-sour sauce poured on top. To avoid the large amount of fat used in the deep frying process, I recommend pan browning, or better still, steaming. The sauce contains a variety of assertive flavors that make up for the absence of the crispy feature that is so mouth-wateringly good when the fish is deep fried.

A whole snapper, sea bass, salmon, or other firm-fleshed fish weighing about 2 pounds

Black pepper
1 tablespoon safflower oil

Sauce:

1 teaspoon safflower oil
2 large cloves garlic, minced
1 small onion, cut into thin slices
1 carrot, cut into thin matchstick strips
2 scallions, finely chopped
2 small tomatoes, quartered and cut into thin slices
3 dried Chinese mushrooms, or ½ cup fresh mushrooms
¼ cup vinegar
3 tablespoons sugar

¼ cup unsalted chicken stock (p. 10), or water
1 teaspoon fish sauce (nuoc mam), or Thai fish sauce (nam pla), or low-sodium soy sauce
1–2 fresh or dried chili peppers, chopped, or cayenne pepper, to taste
1 teaspoon cornstarch, dissolved in 2 tablespoons water
Fresh coriander leaves, chopped, for garnish

Preparation:

1.   Make 3 or 4 deep diagonal cuts on each side of the fish. Sprinkle with pepper and dredge very lightly inside and out with cornstarch. Set it aside.

2.   Soak mushrooms in hot water for 30 minutes. Discard tough stems and cut into thin small slices.

3.   Prepare remaining ingredients.

Cooking:

1.   Prepare sauce first and keep warm until fish is done. To make sauce, heat oil in a small saucepan and stir-fry garlic for 10 seconds. Add onions, carrots, scallions, tomatoes, and mushrooms and stir-fry 2 or 3 minutes.

2.   Stir in vinegar, sugar, stock, fish sauce, and chilies. Bring to a boil and cook 5 minutes. Add cornstarch mixture and cook until sauce thickens.

3.   To cook fish, heat a large nonstick skillet until very hot. Add oil and brown the fish on one side over high heat for about 1 or 2 minutes. Reduce heat and continue cooking 2 or 3 minutes longer. Gently turn the fish over and brown the other side. Cover pan for 1 or 2 minutes to steam the fish briefly. Keep in mind that as the fish cooks it becomes increasingly fragile. Use wide sturdy spatulas and an extra pair of hands to help you if necessary. Test for doneness. Do not overcook the fish. Remove to paper towels to drain fat, then place on a heated platter and keep warm. (Alternatively, the fish may be steamed.)

4.   Pour sauce over fish and garnish with coriander leaves.

Yield: 4–6 servings   Cooking time: 20 minutes

Calories per serving: 225   Total fat: 7 g
Saturated fat: 0.5 g   Polyunsaturated fat: 3.5 g
Cholesterol: 60 mg   Sodium: 180 mg

Stuffed Squid
(*Muc Don Thit*)

Squid must be very fresh to be good. Before attempting this dish, please read about squid on page xxv. Pork is usually used for the filling in this recipe, but chicken makes a nice, healthier substitute.

12 small whole squids (1 pound uncleaned squid yields about 11–12 ounces edible meat)

1 tablespoon safflower oil

Stuffing:

12 ounces ground or finely minced chicken meat, all fat and skin removed, or ground chicken mixed with very lean ground pork
2 shallots, or white part of 2 scallions, finely chopped
½ cup mushrooms, finely chopped

1 large clove garlic, minced
½–1 teaspoon black pepper
1 teaspoon fish sauce (nuoc mam), or Thai fish sauce (nam pla), or low-sodium soy sauce
¼ teaspoon sugar
2 tablespoons fresh coriander leaves, finely chopped

1.   Clean and wash the squids, removing the transparent center bone, purple spotted skin, and inner matter. Cut off tentacles, chop finely and reserve.

2.   Combine filling ingredients, adding chopped tentacles, and knead well with hands.

3.   Pat squids dry with paper towels. Stuff each with the meat mixture about three quarters full or less. Sew the opening with a coarse needle and thread or close end with a toothpick.

4.   In a nonstick frying pan, heat oil and saute squids over medium heat until brown on all sides. Add a tablespoon or two of water to the pan, cover, and steam 2–3 minutes to be sure chicken is thoroughly cooked. Uncover and brown again. Do not overcook or squid will toughen.

5.   Serve with *Nuoc Cham* sauce (p. 168).

Yield: 4–6 servings

Cooking time: 5–10 minutes

Calories per serving: 270
Saturated fat: 2 g
Cholesterol: 270 mg

Total fat: 9.5 g
Polyunsaturated fat: 4 g
Sodium: 205 mg

◊  ◊

Chicken
(Thit Ga)

Chicken with Lemon Grass
(Ga Xao Sa Ot)

The use of lemon grass and chilies links this dish to Vietnam's Thai neighbor to the west. The method of cooking, however, is Chinese, and the result is tangy-hot and marvelous.

1 pound boneless chicken
  meat, all fat and skin
  removed, cut into ½-inch
  cubes
4 stalks fresh or dried lemon
  grass, or grated rind of 1
  large lemon and 4 tablespoons lemon juice
1–2 teaspoons fish sauce (nuoc
  mam), or Thai fish sauce
  (nam pla), or low-sodium
  soy sauce
3 scallions, finely chopped

¼–½ teaspoon black
  pepper
1 teaspoon sugar
4 cloves garlic, minced
1 tablespoon safflower oil
1–2 fresh or dried chili
  peppers, seeded and
  chopped, or cayenne
  pepper to taste
Fresh coriander leaves,
  chopped, for garnish
Lemon wedges

Preparation:

1. If using fresh lemon grass, discard outer leaves and finely chop the tender white parts at the base of the stalk.
2. Combine the lemon grass, fish sauce, scallions, pepper, sugar, and half the garlic and mix with chicken cubes. Let stand 30 minutes.

Cooking:

1.   Heat a wok or nonstick skillet over high heat. Add oil and swirl to coat the pan evenly. Just before it begins to smoke, add garlic and stir-fry 30 seconds.

2.   Add the chicken pieces with seasonings and stir-fry until chicken changes color. Add 2 or 3 tablespoons water and more black pepper, to taste. Turn heat down and keep stirring until chicken is tender and flavors blend. Garnish with coriander leaves and lemon wedges. Serve with rice.

Yield: 4–6 servings

Cooking time: 5 minutes

Calories per serving: 262
Saturated fat: 2.5 g
Cholesterol: 100 mg

Total fat: 10 g
Polyunsaturated fat: 4.5 g
Sodium: 170 mg

Chicken with Mushrooms
(Ga Xao Nam Rom)

Quick and easy, this dish is another exceptional stir-fry.

1 pound boneless, skinless
     chicken meat, cut into
     1/2-inch cubes
8 dried Chinese mushrooms, or
     1 1/2 cups fresh mushrooms,
     sliced
1 teaspoon fish sauce (nuoc
     mam), or Thai fish sauce
     (nam pla), or low-sodium
     soy sauce
2 tablespoons Chinese rice
     wine, or pale dry sherry

2 large cloves garlic, minced
2 tablespoons fresh ginger
     root, minced
1 teaspoon sugar
1/2 teaspoon black pepper
     Fresh or dried chili
     peppers, seeded and
     chopped, or cayenne
     pepper, to taste
1 1/2 tablespoons safflower oil
2 scallions, chopped

Preparation:

1.   Soak mushrooms in warm water for 30 minutes. Discard tough stems and slice.

2.   Combine fish sauce, wine, garlic, ginger, sugar, and peppers. Mix thoroughly with chicken and let stand 30 minutes.

3.   Arrange remaining ingredients within easy reach of the stove.

Cooking:

1.   Heat a wok or nonstick pan over high heat. Add half the oil and swirl to coat the pan. Just before it begins to smoke, stir-fry seasoned chicken pieces 1–2 minutes, or until they change color. Remove from pan.

2.   Add remainder of the oil and stir-fry mushrooms 1–2 minutes.

3.   Return chicken to pan. Add scallions, 2 or 3 tablespoons of water, and another teaspoon of fish sauce (if desired), and stir and toss until well blended and heated through. Add more black pepper and serve with rice.

Yield: 4–6 servings

Cooking time: 5–7 minutes

Calories per serving: 285
Saturated fat: 2.5 g
Cholesterol: 100 mg

Total fat: 12 g
Polyunsaturated fat: 6 g
Sodium: 175 mg

Variation: Add 1 cup cauliflower or broccoli flowerets with mushrooms in step 2 and stir-fry until tender but still crisp.

Stir-Fried Chicken with Cellophane Noodles
(Ga Xao Bun Tao)

This chicken-and-noodle dish makes a satisfying all-in-one main course similar to fried rice. Some cooks use a greater proportion of noodles to meat, but, like fried rice, the proportions and ingredients are variable. Some form of this dish is eaten all over the Far East with minor differences in seasonings. Best of all, the cooking is quick and easy.

8 ounces cellophane noodles
1 pound chicken meat, cut into
   ½ inch cubes
1 tablespoon safflower oil
¼ cup shallots, or onions,
   chopped
2 scallions, chopped

½–1 teaspoon black pepper
1 teaspoon fish sauce (nuoc
   mam), or Thai fish sauce
   (nam pla), or low-sodium
   soy sauce

Salad:

3 tomatoes, cut into thin slices
1 cucumber, thinly sliced
1 carrot, cut into matchstick
    pieces

Watercress or fresh
    coriander leaves,
    chopped, for garnish

1.   Soak noodles in a bowl of warm water to cover for 30 minutes. Rinse, drain, and cut into 4-inch lengths.

2.   Heat a wok or nonstick pan over high heat. Add oil and swirl to coat the pan. Just before it begins to smoke, stir-fry chicken for 1 to 2 minutes.

3.   Add onions, scallions, and pepper and stir-fry 1 more minute.

4.   Add fish sauce and ¼ cup water and bring to a boil. Simmer 1 to 2 minutes.

5.   Add noodles and stir constantly until they are heated through. Serve hot with a grinding of black pepper and a garnish of chopped coriander leaves.

6.   Prepare a side dish of sliced tomatoes and cucumber and carrot sticks dressed with a mixture of vinegar, sugar, and black pepper.

Yield: 4–6 servings

Cooking time: 5–7 minutes

Calories per serving: 360
Saturated fat: 2.5 g
Cholesterol: 100 mg

Total fat: 10.5 g
Polyunsaturated fat: 4.5 g
Sodium: 190 mg

◇   ◇

Beef
(Thit Bo)

Beef Fondue
(Bo Nhung Dam)

Lean and very thin slices of beef are cooked at the table in a vinegary broth, then wrapped in rice papers and eaten with dipping sauce. A carrot-and-turnip salad and an herb-and-vegetable platter usually go with this fondue.

> 1 *pound very lean beef fillet,*
>   *or other tender beef*
> 16 *rice papers* (Banh Trang, if
>   available)

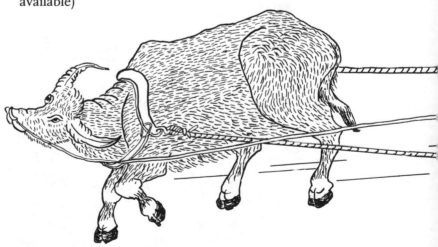

Broth:

2 *cups water*	2 *cloves garlic, minced*
½ *cup white vinegar*	2 *scallions, chopped*
2 *teaspoons sugar*	

1.   Cut meat into paper-thin slices and arrange in overlapping slices on a serving platter. If the meat is slightly frozen, it is easier to cut neater slices.
2.   Combine broth ingredients in a fondue pot or other heat-proof pan that can be placed over a hot plate at the table.

Carrot-and-Turnip Salad:

2 *carrots and 3 small turnips,*
    peeled and cut into thin
    matchstick strips (1
    Japanese white radish, or
    daikon *may be substituted*
    for the turnips)
1 *small onion, cut into paper-*
    thin slices
¼ *cup white vinegar, diluted*
    with ¼ *cup water*
1 *tablespoon sugar*

1.   Prepare vegetables and place into a bowl.
2.   Combine dressing ingredients and pour over vegetables.

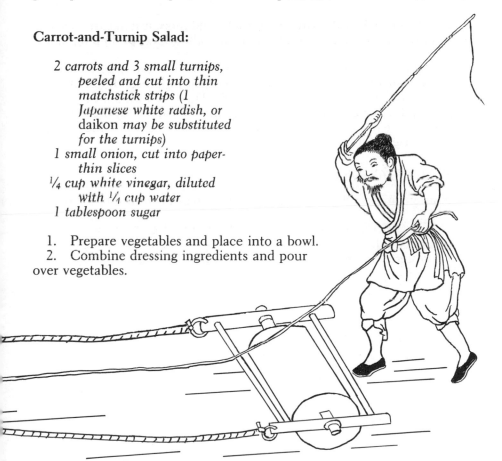

Herb-and-Vegetable Platter:

Lettuce leaves   *Fresh coriander leaves*
Fresh mint leaves   *1 cucumber*

1. Arrange greens attractively on a platter.
2. Peel cucumber lengthwise, leaving 2 or 3 green strips for color. Cut in half lengthwise, then slice into thin half-moon slices.
3. Arrange on platter with greens.

To serve:

1. Set the table with plates, chopsticks (and forks, just in case), a small bowl of water for each diner, and a small shallow bowl of dipping sauce (*Nuoc Cham*; p. 168).
2. All diners take a rice paper, which they must dip briefly into the water bowl to soften. They then take some meat with their chopsticks and place it in the boiling broth for 30 seconds. They then wrap it in the rice paper, dip the bundle into the dipping sauce and eat it with the hands. If rice papers are not available, meat may be dipped directly into the dipping sauce by itself and then eaten.

Yield: 4 to 6 servings

Nutrient analysis does not include the rice papers or the dipping sauce.

Calories per serving: 340   Total fat: 11 g
Saturated fat: 5 g   Polyunsaturated fat: 2.5 g
Cholesterol: 105 mg   Sodium: 140 mg

Indonesia, Malaysia, and Singapore

◊  ◊

The Indonesian, Malaysian, and Singaporean Kitchens

To understand and appreciate Indonesian, Malaysian, and Singaporean food, it is important to have some idea of the geography and history of the area. Indonesia, the fifth most populous country in the world, with an area only about three times that of Texas, consists of more than 13,000 islands, strung like a necklace along the equator. Located south of the Malay Peninsula and the Philippines, this island nation stretching for more than 3,000 miles between the Asian mainland and Australia is a land of superlatives and contrasts. In the coastal areas, there are thriving cosmopolitan cities, bustling seaports, and countless terraced rice fields. A backbone of mountain ranges extends throughout the main islands, including over 100 active volcanoes.

Malaysia is divided into two parts—West Malaysia (on the Malay Peninsula) and East Malaysia (which comprises Sabah and Sarawak on the island of Borneo). Thus, Malaysia has a diverse population and a rich cultural heritage based on the traditions of its many inhabitants—Chinese, Indians, Ceylonese, Eurasians, Portuguese, hill tribesmen, and aborigines. Because of its strategic geographic position, Malaysia has long maintained close ties with both China and India; and although the present population of Malaysia is predominantly Chinese, the culture of Malaysia was mostly influenced by India.

Singapore, the largest port in Southeast Asia and the fourth largest in the world, is a cosmopolitan metropolis. For centuries this sparsely populated, remote tropical island located at the southern tip of the Malay Peninsula—between Malaysia and Indonesia's Sumatra—was occupied only by native Malay fisherman. In 1819 Sir Stamford Raffles of the British East India Trading Company saw in Singapore the potential for a great trading port and founded a trading post on the island. It is the only nation in the world with a population made up primarily of overseas Chinese.

Much of this vast area, including the Indonesian archipelago, Malaysia, and, originally, Singapore, is covered by dense jungle, and in some remote areas primitive, almost stone-age tribes (such as the Ibans and Dyaks) exist untouched by the modern world. Blessed with abundant—almost daily— rainfall, rich soil, and seas teeming with edible life, this tropical paradise is home to more than 173 million people. Rubber, rice, coconuts, sugar cane, coffee, tea, tobacco, and spices are among the area's most valuable crops. In terms of natural resources potential, the area is one of the wealthiest of the world, rich in oil, tin, rubber, and timber. Its extraordinary animal life roughly forms a connecting link between the fauna of Asia and that of Australia. Elephants are found in Sumatra and Borneo, tigers as far south as Java and Bali, and marsupials in Timor and Irian. Crocodiles, snakes, and brilliantly colored birds are everywhere.

The complex ethnic structure of Indonesia—which dominates the region in terms of tradition and language as well as cuisine—is the result of great migrations from Asia and the Pacific. More than 250 mutually unintelligible languages are spoken in Indonesia, but an official language, Bahasa Indonesia, regarded as the purest Malay, has been adopted throughout the area. It has spread rapidly and is now understood in all but the most remote villages. English is the official foreign language. Close to 90% of the population is Muslim. Hindus comprise less than 5% of Indonesia's people and are concentrated mainly on Bali, which is known for its unique Hindu-based culture. There are also Christian and Buddhist minorities.

Early in the Christian Era, Indonesia came under the influence of the Indian civilization through the influx of Indian traders and Buddhist and Hindu monks, and by the ninth century the spectacular Buddhist temples of Borobudur had been built. But in the fourteenth and fifteenth centuries, with the arrival of Arab missionaries and traders in search of spices, Islam replaced Buddhism and Hinduism as the dominant religion. However, the cultural heritage of the Hindus is still preserved in the life and art of Bali, the majority of whose people still retain their Hindu heritage.

The Malaccas, or the Spice Islands as they were called, were for thousands of years the only source of the world's nutmeg and cloves, and the trade for these and other spices made Sumatra and Malaysia the crossroads of Asia. Marco Polo wrote in the thirteenth century that Java "abounds with rich commodities. . . . Pepper, nutmegs, spikenard, galangal, cubebs, cloves, and all the other valuable spices . . . are the produce of the island. The quantity of gold collected there exceeds all calculation and belief."* But the Arabs held a tight monopoly over these spices and could command fantastic prices for them. So high was the price of pepper that it was used as currency to pay taxes in England. By the fifteenth century, spices had become such an indispensable ingredient in the West that European states striving to break the Arab monopoly began to look for ocean routes to the places where spices grew. Spices were what Columbus was looking for when he set out to find a shortcut to the East by sailing west. The Portuguese came in the sixteenth century also in pursuit of the spice trade, followed by the Dutch and the English. But it was the Dutch who by brute force finally gained a political and economic foothold and stayed for nearly three centuries, until they were forcibly ejected in a bitter and bloody war. In addition to Indian, Muslim, Arab, and European influences, the Chinese, who have been settling in Indonesia in large numbers since the eighteenth century, have also had considerable impact on Indonesian life.

Not surprisingly, the cuisine that emerges from this rich cultural diversity is a varied and complex one that offers much to the adventurous eater. Taste buds will awaken to sauces that vary from sweet soy sauces to fiery, lemony, and spicy chili sauces. Flour or cornstarch is never used to thicken them. Instead, coconut milk and other thickening agents, such as ground peanuts or candlenuts (kemiri), very oily nuts much like macadamias, are used. Because they are lower in fat and commonly available in local markets, almonds replace candlenuts in these recipes. Shallots, the most delicate of the onion family, are as common as coconuts in Indonesia. Long a hallmark of fine French cooking, they are difficult to find in American markets and are usually very expensive. Onions, or the white portion of scallions, may be substituted. Indonesians, as do most Southeast Asians, use the leaves of spice trees, fruit trees, and grasses to season their food. The ultimate must among these is lemon grass. Laos and kencur, both in the ginger family, are also used in some dishes. Many of the seasonings native to the country are available only in stores specializing in Asian ingredients. However, the three most commonly used spices—turmeric, coriander, and cumin—can be purchased in any grocery store. Ironically, Indonesians use very little clove or nutmeg in their cooking. Most of the cloves they grow are mixed with tobacco to make Kretek, the nation's most popular cigarette. Indian-style dishes, however, do contain cloves, as well as other spice combinations for curries.

As in most Asian countries, rice is the foundation of every meal. With rice there could be as few as one and as many as six or even twenty-six dishes, if one has a battery of servants as the Dutch colonial rulers did when they served their rijsstafel, or Rice Table, as it was called. There is no more vivid description of this sumptuous eating ritual than Aldous Huxley's in this passage about his travels in Java.

A waiter appears at your elbow with an enormous cauldron of rice; you heap your plate with it. He moves away. Immediately another takes his place, offering fish soup. You dampen your rice; the soup man goes. A dish of chops at once replaces the tureen. Looking around, you see that the chop carrier is standing at the head of a long procession of Javanese waiters, extending in unbroken line from your table right across the dining room to the kitchen door. Each time you help yourself, the procession advances a step, and a new dish is presented. I took the trouble one

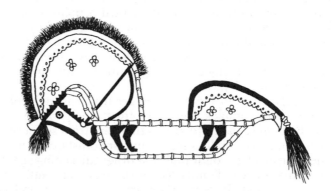

day to count the number of dishes offered to me. Twenty-six actually appeared before me; but it was a busy day for the waiters, and I do not think I got all the dishes I was entitled to. They included after the chops two other kinds of meat; two kinds of birds; a species of sausage; fish, both fresh and dried; roast bananas; several kinds of vegetables, plain and curried; two varieties of salad; fried nuts; numerous pickles and jam; a queer kind of unleavened bread, and various other things which I cannot at the moment remember.*

This ostentatious display could not have been possible without dozens of servants and limitless amounts of money and leisure. In the contemporary servantless household, for an average family or a dinner party, a typical menu might include one chicken or fish dish, a meat dish, two vegetable dishes, and of course a *sambal*. But for everyday fare, just one chicken, fish, or meat dish served together with a vegetable dish would be sufficient. Many dishes such as curries are better the second day, so they may be made ahead and reheated. If you decide to make vegetable dishes ahead, be sure to undercook them, or they will be limp and grey when they are reheated. The cooking of all of these dishes is quick and easy, but, as with Chinese dishes, preparation is as important as cooking. Serving is not difficult since everything is put on the table at the same time. Traditionally, Indonesians eat with the fingers of the right hand. However, the use of a soup spoon and fork is common now. No knife is needed since everything is usually cut into bite-sized pieces.

As with Chinese and Southeast Asian cooking, the wok is the pan most commonly used in Indonesia, but a teflon-coated nonstick skillet may be used in its place. Besides a saucepan or two, and a mortar and pestle or electric blender, no other special equipment is necessary. For tips on stir-frying and using a wok, see pages xxxiii–xxxiv.

Naturally, since the Chinese seem to predominate in Singapore, it should be no surprise that Chinese-style cuisine is the most popular. But the Malays, Indonesians, Indians, and Pakistanis remain dominant ethnic groups in Singapore, and their cuisines are all richly represented. The city-state, often called a gourmet's paradise, teems with restaurants offering not only all these ethnic styles but other Asian and Western cuisines as well. One cuisine peculiar to Singapore and not readily found in restaurants is a cooking style known as *Nonya*. It is the result of the inter-marriage of early Chinese settlers with Malay women. Hot, spicy, and sometimes sour, Nonya cuisine is an interesting mixture of Chinese ingredients combined with Malay spices. The dishes chosen here, readily available from itinerant and outdoor vendors, are not only popular in Singapore; some version of them is well known all over Southeast Asia.

Adapting Indonesian, Malaysian, and Singaporean Food to a Low-Sodium, Low-Cholesterol Diet

The question to be asked is whether foods from these countries can be adapted to a low-fat, low-sodium diet. The answer is definitely affirmative. Much of Indonesian, Malaysian, and Singaporean food is easily adaptable, precisely because all of it is so highly seasoned with a variety of spices and seasonings all low in fat and sodium. But, as in most Asian countries, fish sauces and soy sauces, which are astronomically high in sodium, are also used liberally. Shrimp paste (*terasi*), as well as soy sauce, both sweet (*kecap manis*) and salty (*kecap asin*), are very high in sodium, and to my knowledge there is no published source that tells how much they contain. They are used sparingly in these recipes, while other assertive seasonings are increased to take their place.

Coconut milk, another essential ingredient in Indonesian cooking, is high in saturated fat, and wherever possible it is replaced by yogurt or chicken stock. How to make coconut milk and what to substitute for it can be found on page xxviii.

Though hot chili peppers are added to almost every recipe, it would be a mistake to think that every dish must be hot. Food is seasoned to suit individual tastes, and the quantity of chilies and spices used in any one dish varies widely. Unlike the chopstick users of China and Japan, who generally eat rice separately or after other dishes, Indonesians like to mix their rice with other cooked foods before eating it, making a hotter dish easier to tolerate. For diners who prefer food with even more fire, the *sambal*, equivalent to our bottled chili condiments, contains large quantities of chilies and is always served with every meal.

---

*   *References*: *The Travels of Marco Polo* (*The Venetian*). Introduction by Manuel Komroff (New York: Liveright Publishing Corp., 1930); Huxley is quoted by Yohanni Johns in *Dishes from Indonesia* (Australia:Thomas Nelson, Ltd., 1971).

◊  ◊

Appetizers
(*Sesuap*)

Pancakes with Savory Chicken-and-Shrimp Filling
(*Poh Piah*)

This snack is best known when it is deep fried and called a spring roll. In the United States it is often called an egg roll. It is of Chinese origin and is probably on the menu of every Chinese restaurant around the world. There are many versions, and each country in Southeast Asia has its own name for it. In this version, no frying is required. The filling and garnishes are prepared ahead of time and brought separately to the table, where all diners take a fresh pancake and roll up whatever combination suits their tastes. Pork is usually the meat that goes into *Poh Piah*, but any kind of cooked or raw meat may be used for the filling, as well as any crispy vegetable. The wrapper comes in many versions too. Some have no eggs in them at all, and others have a large proportion of eggs. The low-cholesterol recipe used for the pancakes in the Korean chapter is recommended here. They're a bit of trouble to make but so tasty that they're worth it.

Pancake wrappers:

Prepare pancake recipe for Nine Delicacies Hors d'Oeuvres (p. 78). While batter rests, prepare filling and sauces.

Filling:

1 tablespoon safflower oil	3 large cloves garlic, minced
6 ounces firm bean curd, cut into 1-inch slices	½ cup onions, finely chopped
	8 ounces chicken breast meat, cut into fine shreds

8 ounces shrimp, shelled,
   deveined, and cut into
   small pieces
½ cup fresh mushrooms, cut
   into thin strips

2 cups Chinese (Napa)
   cabbage, finely shredded
1 teaspoon black pepper

1.   Heat half the oil in a wok or a nonstick skillet. Brown bean curd on all sides. Drain on paper towels and cut into very thin matchstick strips.
2.   Heat pan on high heat, add more oil and stir-fry garlic and onions 10 seconds.
3.   Add the chicken shreds and stir-fry for 1 minute. Add shrimp pieces and stir-fry 30 seconds. Remove from pan.
4.   Stir-fry mushrooms, cabbage, and pepper and cook until wilted.
5.   Return bean curd, chicken, and shrimps to pan. Cook 1 minute, stirring constantly. Mixture should be dry. Drain if necessary. Keep warm.

Garnishes and sauces:

Lettuce leaves, ribs removed, cut into 2-inch strips
1 small cucumber, peeled, quartered, and very thinly sliced
1 cup bean sprouts, blanched for 30 seconds
1 cup fresh coriander leaves, trimmed and cut into small sprigs
Any or all of the following sauces:
   Sambal Ulek,   (p. 232)
   Sambal Kecap, (p. 234)
   Kecap Manis, (p. 233)

1.   Arrange the lettuce, cucumbers, and coriander leaves on a plate.
2.   Place whatever sauces you decide to serve in separate shallow bowls.

Cooking and Assembling the Pancakes:

1.   Heat a griddle or nonstick frying pan hot enough so that a drop of water sputters on contact. Lightly grease it. (It is best to make one trial cake first. If batter is too thick, dilute with a little water; if too thin, add some flour.) Pour 1 to 2 tablespoons of batter into the pan to make a very thin pancake about 5–6 inches in diameter. Cook until barely golden. Turn and cook the other side. Do not allow the pancakes to brown beyond the very pale stage. Stack them on top of each other and keep warm.
2.   Place stacked warm pancakes, bowl of hot filling, and garnishes in center of table. Put a pancake on each plate. To eat, place a lettuce leaf, coriander sprig, a sauce of one's choice, and some filling in the center of the pancake. Fold edges over to enclose filling securely and enjoy.

Yield: 6 servings,   Cooking time: About 1 hour
    about 24 pancakes

Nutrient analysis does not include garnishes and sauces.

Calories per serving: 360   Total fat: 8.5 g
Saturated fat: 1.5 g   Polyunsaturated fat: 5.5 g
Cholesterol: 75 mg   Sodium: 155 mg

Pancakes (*Rotis*) with Spiced Meat Filling
(*Murtaba*)

Of Indian origin, this popular Singaporean snack is served in outdoor eating stalls. With quick deft movements, large parchment-thin pancakes are magically produced in no time at all from a small lump of dough by flinging it into the air and patting it from one hand to the other. It is then cooked on a griddle and filled with a savory meat filling. The filling is easy to make, but the trick is to make the pancake thin enough.

Pancakes (Rotis):

2 cups white or whole wheat
    flour
2 tablespoons safflower oil
⅔ cup warm water

1 or 2 tablespoons safflower oil,
    for coating dough

Filling:

1 tablespoon safflower oil
1 cup onions, finely sliced
2 large cloves garlic, finely
    minced
1 teaspoon fresh ginger root,
    minced
½ teaspoon black pepper
½ teaspoon each ground
    coriander, cumin, and
    cinnamon

¼ teaspoon cayenne pepper, or
    to taste
1¼ pounds very lean ground
    beef
¼ cup green peas
1 medium tomato, finely
    chopped
2–4 tablespoons plain low-fat
    yogurt

Garnishes:

Chopped coriander leaves　　　　　*1 onion, finely sliced*

To make the pancakes:

1.   Combine flour and oil until thoroughly mixed.
2.   Add water and knead 15 minutes.
3.   Divide dough into 12 balls of equal size and coat with oil. Cover tightly with plastic wrap and let them rest for 2 hours.

To cook the filling:

1.   In a nonstick skillet, heat oil and saute onion, garlic, and ginger until soft and golden.
2.   Add spices and stir for a few seconds.
3.   Add ground beef and stir and turn for 10 minutes, separating meat into the smallest morsels possible. Add green peas and cook until done.
4.   Stir in yogurt. Mixture should be quite dry; set aside and keep warm while you cook the *rotis*.

Cooking and assembling the pancakes:

1.   Preheat griddle.
2.   The dough should be at room temperature before rolling out. Brush a bit of oil on a board or other flat surface. Press out one of the balls with the fingers, then with a rolling pin. The pancake should be rolled out as thinly as possible. Some cooks find it easier to roll the dough between two sheets of waxed paper.
3.   Grease a moderately heated griddle lightly and cook the pancake on one side. It will take less than a minute. Turn over and cook the other side. Spoon some filling in the center of the pancake.
4.   Place a few chopped coriander leaves and a little sliced onion on top of the filling. Fold one edge over the other into a neat package, completely enclosing the filling. Brown the filled *rotis* on both sides. Serve hot.

Yield: 6 servings　　　　　　　　Cooking time: 1 hour

Calories per serving: 450　　　　Total fat: 18 g
Saturated fat: 5 g　　　　　　　　Polyunsaturated fat: 10 g
Cholesterol: 90 mg　　　　　　　Sodium: 75 mg

Note: This recipe is rather high in fat and should be served only on occasion.

◊  ◊

Soups
(*Sop*)

Indonesian Chicken Soup
(*Soto Ayam*)

This is one of the great soups of the Indonesian archipelago. There are many versions, some more highly seasoned than others. All are served with a variety of garnishes that provide interesting contrasts in flavors and textures. *Soto ayam* is substantial enough to feed four as a main dish.

One 2½ *pound chicken,*
cut into pieces (Yield:
about 24 ounces boneless,
skinless meat)
2 *quarts water*
1 *cup onions, coarsely*
chopped
4 *large cloves garlic, minced*
2 *tablespoons fresh ginger*
root, minced
½ *teaspoon turmeric*
1½ *tablespoons ground*
coriander

½–1 *teaspoon black pepper*
1 *teaspoon ground cumin*
2 *small pieces of galanga*
(laos), or ½ *teaspoon*
ground ginger
1 *teaspoon safflower oil*
2 *stalks fresh or dried lemon*
grass, or 1 *teaspoon*
grated lemon rind and 2
to 4 tablespoons fresh
lemon or lime juice

1. This step is best done the day before. Place the chicken and water in a soup kettle and bring to a boil. Reduce heat and simmer 15–20 minutes. Remove the breasts when no longer pink. Continue to simmer until dark meat of the chicken is done. Remove from heat. When cool, skin and bone chicken. Discard all fat and cut meat into bite-sized pieces. Set aside. Return bones to stock and simmer 45 minutes longer. Strain

and discard bones. There should be about 8 cups of stock. Adjust yield to 8 cups by adding water or cooking down excess broth. Cover and refrigerate overnight or until cold. Discard the fat that congeals on the surface.

2.   Pulverize in an electric blender, or pound with a mortar and pestle, onions, garlic, ginger, and spices.

3.   Heat oil in a small skillet and add spice mixture. Rinse out blender with a little water and add it to the skillet. Stir and cook 1 minute. Add the lemon grass. Cook spice mixture 3 or 4 minutes and add it to the stock. Bring to a boil and simmer 20 minutes.

4.   Meanwhile prepare the garnishes in separate bowls. The chicken pieces should be in the center of a platter surrounded by the other garnishes. If desired, all the chicken pieces and half the garnishes (except the *sambal*) may be added to the soup before serving.

Garnishes:

4 scallions, thinly sliced
2 cups bean sprouts blanched in
   boiling water for 30 seconds
2 cups Chinese (Napa) cabbage,
   thinly sliced and blanched
   in boiling water for 2 or 3
   minutes
1 ounce cellophane noodles,
   soaked in boiling water for
   10 minutes and drained

1 cup shallot flakes (Baweng
   Goreng, p. 000; optional)
3 small new potatoes, boiled in
   their jackets and sliced
2 lemons or limes, cut into
   quarters
Sambal Ulek (*p. 232*), or
   Sambal Iris (*p. 233*)

Yield: 6–8 servings   Cooking time: About 1 hour

Nutrient analysis includes all garnishes except shallot flakes and *sambal*.

Calories per serving: 300   Total fat: 8 g
Saturated fat: 2 g   Polyunsaturated fat: 2 mg
Cholesterol: 100 mg   Sodium: 95 mg

Rice Noodles, Chicken, and Seafood in Spicy Broth
(Laksa)

This soup, a lunch or snack of Chinese origin popular all over Southeast Asia, has many versions. Some are rich in coconut milk, others leave it out completely. It may be prepared using seafood alone or a combination of fish and chicken. Squid is especially good in it. In this recipe from Singapore, the shrimp paste and fish sauce (that would be essential in Thailand) have been left out and the spices increased.

½ pound Chinese rice vermicelli (rice sticks)
3 cups bean sprouts
8 ounces boneless chicken, skin and fat removed, cut into bite-sized cubes

8 ounces shrimps, shelled and deveined
8 ounces firm fish fillets, cut into bite-sized cubes
6 ounces soybean curd, cut into bite-sized cubes

Broth:

1 tablespoon safflower oil
3 large cloves garlic, finely minced
1 cup onions, finely minced
1 cup mushrooms, sliced
1 stalk lemon grass cut into 1-inch lengths, or grated rind from ½ lemon
1½ teaspoons ground turmeric
1 teaspoon paprika
2 tablespoons ground coriander

1 teaspoon ground cumin
2 teaspoons sugar
½–1 teaspoon black pepper
2 or 3 dried chilies, crumbled
8 cups unsalted chicken stock (p. 10), or a combination of coconut milk (p. xxviii) and chicken stock
3 cups spinach, or Chinese (Napa) cabbage, coarsely chopped

Garnish:

1 medium cucumber, scored, quartered, and thinly sliced
6 scallions, thinly sliced

Fresh mint or basil leaves
Lemon or lime quarters

Cooking:

1.   Pour boiling water over rice sticks and soak 10 minutes until softened or follow directions on package. Drain well and keep hot.
2.   Blanch bean sprouts in boiling water for 30 seconds and drain immediately.

3.   In a soup kettle heat oil and saute garlic and onions until soft and golden. Add mushrooms and saute 1 more minute.
4.   Add the seasonings and chicken stock, bring to a boil and simmer 15 minutes.
5.   Add chicken, shrimp, and fish and simmer for 2 minutes.
6.   Add bean curd and spinach and cook another 2 minutes.

To serve:

Place a generous helping of rice noodles in a large soup bowl. Add some bean sprouts on top. Ladle the steaming hot soup on top with the seafood and chicken pieces. Garnish generously with mint or basil leaves and squeeze a few drops of lemon juice over all.

Yield: 6–8 servings   Cooking time: 35 minutes

Calories per serving: 320   Total fat: 8 g
Saturated fat: 2 g   Polyunsaturated fat: 4 g
Cholesterol: 75 mg   Sodium: 140 mg

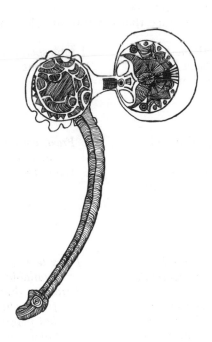

Seafoods
(Ikan Laut)

Broiled Whole Fish with Coconut-Almond Sauce
(Tjolo-Tjolo)

A fish served whole always makes an impressive presentation. This Indonesian recipe uses a sauce that is white in color and very rich.

A 3-pound firm fleshed fish,
with tail and head left on
(Yield: 24 ounces meat)

1 tablespoons safflower oil, for
basting

Garnish:

1 large tomato, peeled and
sliced
1 medium cucumber, scored
lengthwise and cut into
¼-inch slices

Fresh coriander, parsley, or
watercress leaves
Lemon slices

Sauce:

⅔ cup blanched almonds, or
kemiri nuts, if available
¾ cup water
1 tablespoon safflower oil
3 large cloves garlic, minced
1 cup shallots, or onions, finely
chopped

1 bay leaf, or djeruk leaf, if
available
2 fresh or dried chili peppers,
finely chopped, or ground
hot pepper, to taste
Grated rind of ½ lemon
½ teaspoon cumin

½ teaspoon low-sodium soy
    sauce, or terasi (shrimp
    paste)
¼ cup coconut milk (p. xxviii)

2 tablespoons tamarind water
    (p. xxxii), or lemon or lime
    juice

1.   Combine nuts and water and puree in an electric blender, or pound nuts with a mortar and pestle or nut grinder. Set aside.

2.   In a small saucepan, heat oil and saute garlic and shallots until golden.

3.   Add remaining ingredients, stirring constantly. Simmer 5 minutes but do not boil. Add more water, stock, or coconut milk if sauce is too thick. Remove bay leaf. Serve in a separate bowl.

4.   Broil the fish in a preheated broiler for about 10 minutes on each side. Remove to heated platter and arrange garnishes decoratively around fish. Serve with the coconut-almond sauce and with Sambal Ulek (p. 232), if desired.

Note: For ease of preparation, the fish may be placed in a lightly greased baking dish with the sauce poured on top and baked in a moderate oven for 20 minutes or until done.

Yield: 6 servings

Cooking time: 30 minutes

Calories per serving: 275
Saturated fat: 2 g
Cholesterol: 60 mg

Total fat: 9 g
Polyunsaturated fat: 6 g
Sodium: 95 mg

Spiced Fish Fillets
(Ikan Rica-Rica)

In Indonesia, this fish would normally be broiled or grilled. Baking is simpler, though, and produces results that are just as tasty.

1 ½ pounds thick fish fillets

Marinade:

¼ cup shallots, or onions,
    chopped
3 large cloves garlic, minced

2 tablespoons fresh ginger root,
    minced
2 teaspoons cumin

¼ teaspoon turmeric

½–1 teaspoon black pepper

2 tablespoons lemon juice

1.   In a mortar or electric blender, puree all marinade ingredients into a smooth paste.

2.   Place the fish in a lightly greased baking dish and spread the paste on top. Let stand for 30 minutes to an hour in the refrigerator.

3.   Preheat oven to 350°F. Bake in the marinade for 10–20 minutes or until fish is done. Do not overcook.

Yield: 6 servings

Cooking time: 10–20 minutes

Calories per serving: 120
Saturated fat: 0.5 g
Cholesterol: 60 mg

Total fat: 1.5 g
Polyunsaturated fat: 0.5 g
Sodium: 80 mg

Spicy Fish Steamed in Banana Leaves
(Otak-Otak)

Banana leaves are cooking utensils in Southeast Asia and their obvious counterpart in the West is aluminum foil. Of course it is not the same, since the banana leaf supplies moisture as well as some flavor and aroma. In this recipe, thin slices of onion are included in the bundle to add extra moisture for the steaming process, and yogurt is substituted for coconut milk.

1 pound fish fillets
8 small shrimps, shelled and
    deveined (optional)

8 thin onion slices
4 pieces of alumimum foil
    (8 × 10 inches)

Sauce:

3 large cloves garlic, minced
½ cup onions, coarsely chopped
1 or 2 dried chili peppers,
    seeded and chopped or
    cayenne pepper, to taste
1 teaspoon ground cumin

2–4 tablespoons plain low-
    fat yogurt, or coconut milk
    (p. xxviii)
¼ teaspoon ground turmeric
1½ tablespoons ground
    coriander

1. In a mortar or electric blender, puree the sauce ingredients to a smooth paste. Add more yogurt if needed to keep mass moving.

2. Coat the fish and shrimps with the sauce. Divide the fish into 4 servings and lay on aluminum foil. Place 2 shrimps on top. Fold into a neat package and steam (pp. xxxii–xxxiii) for 20 minutes or until fish is tender. Do not overcook.

Note: If banana leaves are used, wash, and scald them first. Secure the package with toothpicks.

Yield: 4 servings	Cooking time: 20 minutes
Calories per serving: 160	Total fat: 2 g
Saturated fat: 0.5 g	Polyunsaturated fat: 0.5 g
Cholesterol: 105 mg	Sodium: 125 mg

Broiled Skewered Shrimps
(*Saté Udang*)

Recent studies indicate that prohibition of shellfish from diets designed to lower blood cholesterol is no longer necessary. Please read about protective oils in fish and seafood on page xxiv. Yogurt substitutes for coconut milk in this Malaysian recipe for delicious shrimps. May be served as an appetizer.

1 ⅓ pounds large green shrimps (Yield is about 1 pound without shells)

Marinade:

¼ cup plain low-fat yogurt
¼ cup lemon or lime juice
    Cayenne pepper, to taste
½ teaspoon low-sodium soy
    sauce

1–2 teaspoons brown sugar, or
    palm sugar, if available
3 large cloves garlic, minced
8–10 bamboo skewers at least 6
    inches long

1. Soak bamboo skewers in water for at least one hour before using.

2. Combine marinade ingredients and marinate shrimp 30 minutes in refrigerator.

3.   Thread 3 or 4 shrimps on skewers. Large shrimps may be straightened and threaded lengthwise. Grill over hot coals or under a broiler, turning over after 1 minute or less. Do not overcook.

4.   If any marinade remains, cook for 1–2 minutes and serve as a dipping sauce, if desired, or serve shrimps with peanut sauce (p. 218).

Yield: 4–6 servings   Cooking time: 2–3 minutes

Nutrient analysis does not include peanut sauce.

Calories per serving: 115   Total fat: 2 g
Saturated fat: 0.5 g   Polyunsaturated fat: 1 g
Cholesterol: 115 mg   Sodium: 195 mg

Squid Curry
(*Gulai Cumi-Cumi*)

This Malaysian curry is usually prepared with coconut milk, which lends a distinctive flavor and texture to the dish, but to reduce fat content, yogurt or milk is substituted for coconut milk in this recipe. To make this curry a success, please read about squid in the ingredients section on page xxv.

1 pound squid (Yield is about
    ⅔ pound edible meat)
1 tablespoon safflower oil
1 cup onions, finely chopped
3 large cloves garlic, minced
1 tablespoon fresh ginger
    root, minced
1–2 fresh or dried chili peppers,
    seeded and chopped, or
    cayenne pepper, to taste
2 tablespoons ground
    coriander
2 teaspoons ground cumin

1 teaspoon paprika
1 cup plain low-fat yogurt,
    or milk; coconut milk
    may be used if more
    authentic taste is desired
    (p. xxviii)
1 stalk lemon grass, or grated
    rind of 1 lemon
½–1 teaspoon brown sugar, or
    palm sugar, if available
2–4 tablespoons tamarind
    liquid (p. xxxii), or lemon
    juice

1.   Clean squid, discarding ink sac, head, cuttlebone, and everything inside body cavity. Cut off tentacles and reserve. Wash squid thoroughly, and cut across into narrow rings.

2.   In a wok or a nonstick pan, heat oil and saute onions, garlic, ginger root, and peppers until onions are soft and golden.

3.   Add spices and cook 1 minute.
4.   Add squid slices and cook over low heat for 1 minute, turning them frequently.
5.   Add yogurt, lemon grass, and sugar. Bring to a simmer and cook gently for 2 minutes. Do not overcook, or squid will toughen. If mixture seems dry, add more yogurt, stock, or a little water.
6.   Add tamarind liquid, or lemon juice, and serve with rice, a *sambal* (pp. 232–34), and one or two condiments for curries (pp. 309–10), if desired.

Yield: 4–6 servings

Cooking time: 10 minutes

Calories per serving: 205
Saturated fat: 1 g
Cholesterol: 200 mg

Total fat: 6 g
Polyunsaturated fat: 3 g
Sodium: 115 mg

Stuffed Squid Cooked in Yogurt
(*Sotong Ayam*)

This very unusual dish obtainable in Singapore from outdoor vendors is normally cooked in coconut milk. Substituting yogurt reduces the saturated fat content and gives it a delicious tang. Please read about squid in the ingredients section on p. xxv before attempting to make this dish.

12 small squids (1 pound uncleaned squid yields about ⅔ pound of edible meat)
12 ounces chicken meat, ground, or chopped into very small pieces
2 teaspoons safflower oil
2 scallions, white portion only, finely chopped

⅓ cup green bell pepper, finely chopped
½–1 teaspoon black pepper
⅔ cup plain low-fat yogurt
2 teaspoons ground coriander
½ teaspoon ground cumin
1–3 chopped fresh or dried red chili peppers
3 tablespoons chopped coriander leaves

1.   Wash squid, discarding ink sac, head, cuttlebone, and everything inside body cavity. Cut off tentacles and reserve. Wash thoroughly and set aside.
2.   In a nonstick pan, heat oil and stir-fry chicken pieces until they change color.
3.   Add scallions, green pepper, and black pepper and cook until

vegetables are soft and wilted. Mix in tentacles and 2 tablespoons yogurt.

4.   Stuff squid ¾ full or less with chicken mixture and secure with a toothpick or sew together with a coarse needle and thread.

5.   In a large saucepan, combine yogurt, coriander, cumin, and chilies and cook for 2–3 minutes. Do not boil. Place the stuffed squid in the pan, being sure they are well coated with the yogurt mixture. Sprinkle with half the coriander leaves and simmer gently for 10 minutes. Do not overcook or squid will toughen. Serve garnished with remaining leaves.

Yield: 4–6 servings   Cooking time: 20 minutes

Calories per serving: 275   Total fat: 9 g
Saturated fat: 2 g   Polyunsaturated fat: 3 g
Cholesterol: 270 mg   Sodium: 165 mg

◇  ◇

Chicken
(*Ayam*)

Chicken-Tomato Curry
(*Ayam Kari*)

This Straits Indian curry is a tangy, lightly spiced Nonya dish that is easy to prepare. Some cooks use coconut milk, the preferred ingredient of the area, instead of yogurt, which is favored by many Indian cooks.

One 2½ pound chicken, cut
   into serving pieces, fat and
   skin removed
1 tablespoon safflower oil
3 large cloves garlic, minced
2 tablespoons fresh ginger root,
   minced
2 cups onions, thinly sliced
2-inch stick cinnamon
2 tablespoons ground coriander
½ teaspoon ground cloves
½ teaspoon cardamom
½ teaspoon turmeric

1–2 chili peppers, seeded and
   chopped, or cayenne
   pepper, to taste
1 teaspoon low-sodium
   tomato paste, or 1 tablespoon low-sodium
   tomato puree
4 medium fresh tomatoes,
   peeled and chopped, or 1
   can low-sodium
   tomatoes
2 tablespoons lemon juice
¼–½ cup plain low-fat yogurt
   Fresh coriander or mint
   leaves for garnish

1.   In a heavy saucepan, heat oil over medium heat and saute garlic, ginger, and onions until soft and golden.
2.   Stir in spices and tomate paste and cook 2 to 3 minutes
3.   Add chicken pieces, turning them over frequently to coat them with mixture.

4.   Add tomatoes and lemon juice and mix well. Cover and cook over low heat 30 minutes, or until chicken is tender.

5.   Stir in yogurt and cook until heated. Do not boil. Garnish with coriander or mint leaves. Serve with white rice and any *sambal* (p. 232–34).

Yield: 6 servings	Cooking time: 40 minutes
Calories per serving: 295	Total fat: 9.5 g
Saturated fat: 2.5 g	Polyunsaturated fat: 4 g
Cholesterol: 100 mg	Sodium: 100 mg

Grilled Flattened Chicken with Spicy Coconut Sauce
(*Singgang Ayam*)

A whole chicken is split down the back, flattened with a cleaver, cooked briefly in a skillet with its seasonings, and then grilled on charcoal or under the broiler. This makes an unusual dish for outdoor cooking. Cut the chicken in half if your pan is too narrow to accommodate the whole bird. Yogurt is substituted for coconut milk in this recipe.

One 2½ pound broiler, split and flattened, with skin left on
1½ cups plain low-fat yogurt, or 1½ cups coconut milk (p. xxviii)
4 large cloves garlic, minced
1 cup onions, coarsely chopped
1–3 fresh or dried red chili peppers, seeded and chopped, or ground hot pepper, to taste

1 tablespoon fresh ginger root, minced
½ teaspoon turmeric
1 tablespoon ground coriander
1 tablespoon black pepper
1 stalk lemon grass, cut into 3-inch lengths, or grated rind from ½ lemon
2 djeruk or bay leaves

1.   Light a charcoal fire or preheat oven broiler.

2.   In an electric blender, or a mortar and pestle, puree garlic, onions, chilies, ginger, and spices into a smooth paste. Two or 3 tablespoons water may be needed in blender to keep mass moving.

3.   Spread half the mixture over the chicken and put the remainder of

the paste in a large frying pan or wok. Add the lemon grass, bay leaves, and yogurt. Bring to a slow simmer, stirring constantly.

4.   Place the flattened chicken in the pan skin side up and cook uncovered for 5 minutes, ladling the sauce over the chicken. Turn chicken over and cook 5 more minutes. Remove to a platter.

5.   Grill chicken on both sides over coals, or under the broiler, until brown. Transfer to a heated serving platter.

6.   Continue cooking sauce. Ladle some over the chicken and serve the remainder separately if desired. Do not eat the skin, since most of the fat is there.

Yield: 6 servings   Cooking time: 50 minutes

Nutrient analysis is for the chicken without skin.

Calories per serving: 185   Total fat: 7 g
Saturated fat: 5 g   Polyunsaturated fat: 1.5 g
Cholesterol: 75 mg   Sodium: 75 mg

Chicken in Coconut Milk and Almond Sauce
(*Opor Ayam*)

Though the amount of coconut milk in this recipe from Singapore has been reduced to cut down on saturated fat, it remains quite delicious with a most exciting flavor.

3 *half chicken breasts and 3*
   whole legs, all skin and
   fat removed
½ *cup coconut milk (p. xxviii),*
   mixed with ½ *cup un-*
   salted chicken stock (p.
   10)
¼ *cup unsalted blanched*
   almonds, or candlenuts
   (kemiri)
2 *teaspoons safflower oil*
1 *cup onions, finely chopped*
3 *large cloves garlic, minced*
1½ *tablespoons ground*
   coriander

1 *teaspoon ground cumin*
¼ *teaspoon mace*
2 *small pieces galanga* (laos),
   or ½ *teaspoon ground*
   ginger
½–1 *teaspoon black pepper*
1 *teaspoon brown sugar, or*
   palm sugar, if available
1 *stalk lemon grass cut into*
   2-inch lengths, or 1 tea-
   spoon grated lemon peel
2–3 *tablespoons tamarind*
   water (p. xxxii), or lemon
   juice
2-inch *piece cinnamon stick*

1. Prepare coconut milk mixture and set aside.
2. Pulverize the nuts in a nut grinder or puree them in an electric blender with a little water to keep the mass moving. Set aside.
3. In a large heavy pot, heat oil over moderate heat and cook onions and garlic for 5 minutes until soft but not brown. Stir in spices and cook 1 or 2 minutes.
4. Add the brown sugar and lemon grass. Cook 2 minutes, or until well blended.
5. Add the chicken. Cook for 10 minutes, turning the pieces until they are evenly coated with the spice mixture. Add the cinnamon stick.
6. Combine the coconut milk mixture and almonds and pour over the chicken. Simmer over low heat for 30 minutes. Do not allow to boil, or the coconut milk may curdle. If mixture seems dry, add more stock.
7. Stir in tamarind water or lemon juice.
8. Remove lemon grass and cinnamon stick and serve with white rice and a *sambal* (pp. 232–34).

Yield: 6 servings

Cooking time: 50 minutes

Calories per serving: 310
Saturated fat: 4.5 g
Cholesterol: 100 mg

Total fat: 11.5 g
Polyunsaturated fat: 3.5 g
Sodium: 95 mg

Roasted Chicken Pieces in Spicy Marinade
(*Ayam Panggang*)

Indonesian cooks would start the chicken in this dish in a wok or large frying pan and finish it over glowing coals. The recipe has been adapted for oven roasting and is very good this way. Yogurt is substituted for coconut milk.

3 half chicken breasts and 3 whole legs, all skin and fat removed

Marinade:

1 cup onions, coarsely chopped
4 large cloves garlic, minced
1 tablespoon fresh ginger root, minced
1 tablespoon safflower oil

½ teaspoon low-sodium soy sauce
2 tablespoons lemon or lime juice
½ cup plain low-fat yogurt

2 tablespoons brown sugar
1–2 fresh or dried chili peppers,
  seeded and chopped, or
  cayenne pepper, to taste
½–1 teaspoon black pepper

1 teaspoon ground caraway
  seeds
1 tablespoon ground
  coriander
¼ teaspoon turmeric

1.   In a mortar or electric blender, puree onion, garlic, and ginger into a smooth paste. Add a little water if needed to keep mass moving.

2.   In a saucepan or small skillet, heat oil and cook mixture for 1 minute, stirring constantly. Add remaining ingredients and blend over low heat for 2 to 3 minutes.

3.   Coat both sides of chicken pieces with marinade and refrigerate for 1 to 2 hours, or overnight for stronger flavor.

4.   Place chicken pieces with the marinade in a lightly greased baking pan. Cover and cook in a 375°F oven for 40–50 minutes, or until done.

Yield: 6 servings

Cooking time: 50 minutes

Calories per serving: 280
Saturated fat: 2.5 g
Cholesterol: 100 mg

Total fat: 9 g
Polyunsaturated fat: 3.5 g
Sodium: 100 mg

Balinese Chicken
(*Ayam Bumbu Bali*)

The Balinese season their food with liberal amounts of soy sauce. They are also fond of mixtures that are not only sweet, but hot and sour as well. In this recipe, a combination of brown sugar, chilies, and tamarind achieve this effect.

2 whole chicken breasts,
  skinned and cut in half
2 fresh or dried chili peppers,
  seeded and chopped, or
  cayenne pepper, to taste
1 cup onions, coarsely chopped
3 tablespoons fresh ginger root,
  minced
2 tablespoons blanched
  almonds, or kemiri nuts

2 teaspoons safflower oil
2 teaspoons brown sugar, or
  palm sugar, if available
1 teaspoon low-sodium soy
  sauce
¼ cup coconut milk (*p. xxviii*)
2–4 tablespoons tamarind water
  (*p. xxxii*), or lemon juice

1.   In a mortar or electric blender, puree peppers, onions, ginger, and almonds. If needed add 2 or 3 tablespoons of water to blender to keep mass moving.

2.   In a wok or nonstick skillet, heat oil and cook blended ingredients for 1 minute.

3.   Add chicken pieces and coat with mixture. Cook over moderate heat until chicken is lightly colored.

4.   Mix in sugar, soy sauce, coconut milk, and tamarind water. Turn heat down and simmer covered for 20–25 minutes, or until chicken is done. Do not allow to boil. Add a little water if mixture seems dry.

Yield: 4 servings	Cooking time: 30 minutes
Calories per serving: 300	Total fat: 10.5 g
Saturated fat: 4 g	Polyunsaturated fat: 4 g
Cholesterol: 90 mg	Sodium: 125 mg

Chicken Minahassa Style
(Ayam Masak Di Buluh)

This dish from the Celebes is simplicity itself. Prepared with plump, ripe tomatoes, lemons, and chilies, it has a hot, lemony flavor. It is usually cooked in a bamboo container (*buluh* is the Indonesian word for bamboo) over a charcoal fire with an incredibly large quantity of chili peppers. Tame the fire to suit your own taste.

One 2½ pound chicken, cut into serving pieces, skin and fat removed
6 medium ripe tomatoes, cut into thin wedges
4 cups onions, thinly sliced
1–4 green chili peppers, coarsely chopped, or to taste

1 green bell pepper, cut into thin strips
1 stalk lemon grass, or grated peel from ½ lemon
¼ cup lemon juice
1 cup unsalted chicken stock (p. 10)
4 scallions, both green and white parts, thinly sliced

1.   Place the chicken into a heavy saucepan. Add all the ingredients except scallions.

2.   Cover and bring to a boil. Reduce heat to very low and simmer until chicken is tender, about 30 minutes.

3.   Serve with chopped scallions sprinkled on top.

Yield: 6 servings

Cooking time: 30 minutes

Calories per serving: 225
Saturated fat: 2 g
Cholesterol: 75 mg

Total fat: 4 g
Polyunsaturated fat: 1 g
Sodium: 90 mg

Broiled Skewered Marinated Chicken
(Saté Ayam)

Saté, a method of grilling meat on skewers, originated in Java but has spread all over Indonesia, Singapore, Malaysia, and Thailand. Bite-sized pieces of meat are marinated and grilled, then dipped in a peanut sauce before eating. *Saté* is eaten as part of a meal or as a snack, and can be had not only in restaurants but at any time of day or night from the itinerant *saté* vendors. There are probably as many *saté* recipes as there are cooks. Chicken, beef, lamb, pork, goat, and even turtle meat are all prepared this way. Yogurt substitutes for coconut milk in this recipe. May be served as an appetizer.

*1 ½ pounds boneless, skinless
    chicken breast meat, cut
    into 1-inch cubes*

*18–24 bamboo skewers, at least
    6 inches long*

Marinade:

*3 large cloves garlic, minced
¼ cup onions, finely chopped
¼ cup lime or lemon juice
1 tablespoon fresh ginger
    root, minced (optional)
1 ½ tablespoons ground
    coriander
½ teaspoon ground cumin*

*½–1 teaspoon black pepper
    Cayenne pepper, to taste
½ cup plain low-fat yogurt
1 teaspoon low-sodium soy
    sauce, mixed with 1 tea-
    spoon brown sugar or 3
    teaspoons* Kecap Manis
(p. 233)

1.   Soak bamboo skewers in water for at least one hour before using.
2.   Mix the marinade ingredients together and coat chicken pieces on all sides. Marinate for at least 30 minutes.
3.   Light a charcoal fire or preheat the broiler to high.
4.   Thread the chicken pieces on the skewers and grill 3 or 4 inches

from the heat, turning skewers until chicken is crisp and brown, about 5 minutes. Baste with marinade as needed.

5.   Serve directly from skewers with peanut sauce (*Bumbu Kacang*, p. 218).

Note: Lean beef, lamb, or pork, cut into ½-inch cubes, may be substituted for chicken. May also be served with *Sambal Kecap* (p. 233).

Yield: 6 servings   Cooking time: 5–10 minutes

Nutrient analysis does not include peanut sauce.

Calories per serving: 235   Total fat: 7 g
Saturated fat: 2 g   Polyunsaturated fat: 1.5 g
Cholesterol: 90 mg   Sodium: 115 mg

Peanut Sauce
(*Bumbu Kacang*)

Processed peanut butter has approximately 80 mg of sodium in one tablespoon, or 1,280 mg in one cup. If you can't find the unprocessed kind, I recommend that you grind your own peanuts.

1 teaspoon safflower oil
2 large cloves garlic, minced
2 tablespoons shallots, or
   onions, finely chopped (optional)
⅔ cup unprocessed creamy
   peanut butter
2 teaspoons lemon juice

2 teaspoons Kecap Manis (p.
   233), or substitute 1 teaspoon low-sodium soy
   sauce mixed with 1 teaspoon brown sugar
Cayenne pepper, to taste,
   or a drop or two of
   Tabasco sauce
½–1 cup water, for thinning

1.   Heat the oil over moderate heat and cook the garlic and onions for 5 minutes, stirring frequently until lightly browned.

2.   Stir in the peanut butter, lemon juice, *Kecap Manis,* and pepper, adding water to thin the mixture. Cook 10 minutes, stirring and adding more water as needed to thin to desired consistency. Sauce should be thick enough to coat the spoon heavily.

Note: The sauce will thicken as it cools. Reheat it just before serving, thinning with more water if necessary.

Yield: About 1 cup

Cooking time: 15 minutes

Calories per tablespoon: 65
Saturated fat: 1 g
Cholesterol: 0 mg

Total fat: 3.5 g
Polyunsaturated fat: 1.5 g
Sodium: 20 mg

◊  ◊

Beef
(Daging Sapi)

Broiled Skewered Beef (or Chicken) in Spicy Coconut-Milk Marinade
(Saté Padang)

Sumatrans like their *saté* highly seasoned and fiery hot. Adjust the heat of this recipe popular in Padang (West Sumatra) to suit your own taste. Everybody will love this wonderful *saté*.

1 pound lean tender beef, all fat removed	*15–20 bamboo skewers, at least 6 inches long*

Marinade:

3 large cloves garlic, minced	*1 tablespoon ground coriander*
1 cup onions, finely chopped	*½ teaspoon ground cumin*
1 tablespoon fresh or dried chilies, chopped, or ground hot pepper, to taste	*1 teaspoon turmeric*
	¼ cup water
2 teaspoons fresh ginger root, minced	*¼ cup coconut milk (p. xxviii)*
1 tablespoon safflower oil	

1. Soak bamboo skewers in water for 1 hour or longer.
2. Cut meat into strips approximately 3 inches long, 1 inch wide, and ¼ inch thick.
3. Pulverize in a blender, or pound with a mortar and pestle, garlic, onions, chilies, ginger root, oil, and spices until mixture is smooth. Add

water if needed to keep mass moving. Spoon into a bowl and stir in coconut milk.

4. Add beef strips and mix well, making sure meat is well coated. Set aside for 30 minutes.

5. Light charcoal fire, or preheat broiler to highest temperature. Thread beef on skewers like a ribbon and cook quickly 3 or 4 inches from the heat, turning skewers when meat is brown.

6. Cook remaining marinade for 1 or 2 minutes and serve with *saté*, if desired. Peanut Sauce (*Bumbu Kacang*; p. 218) may also be served with this beef *saté* for a less fiery version.

Yield: 4–6 servings

Cooking time: 5–10 minutes

Calories per serving: 315
Saturated fat: 7 g
Cholesterol: 105 mg

Total fat: 14 g
Polyunsaturated fat: 5.5 g
Sodium: 80 mg

Note: Chicken breast meat cut into ½-inch cubes may be used instead of beef.

Beef Curry
(*Daging Sapi Kalio* and *Daging Sapi Rendang*)

The cooking of Sumatra and Malaysia is heavily influenced by Arab and Indian styles. One of the best known ethnic groups from this region is made up of the Menangkabau, who come from the mountains of West Sumatra. They are noted for their trading and culinary talents. This Menangkabau dish, though usually far richer—since it uses a copious amount of thick coconut cream—improves its flavor so much with each reheating that it is worth making a lot of it. Yogurt substitutes for coconut milk in this recipe. Although this recipe is for the dry curry (*rendang*), it can also be served—and is delicious as—a sauce curry (*kalio*) if served before the liquid has been cooked away.

2 pounds lean beef, all fat
  removed, cut into 1½-inch
  cubes
2 cups plain low-fat yogurt
  or milk; or, if a more authentic taste is desired, use
  coconut milk mixed with
  stock (p. xxviii)
3 cups onions, coarsely chopped
1 tablespoon fresh ginger root,
  coarsely chopped
4 large cloves garlic, minced
2 tablespoons ground coriander

1 teaspoon turmeric
1 stalk lemon grass, or grated
  rind of ½ lemon
1 teaspoon ground cumin
1 teaspoon ground cloves
½–1 tablespoon ground
  black pepper
1–3 fresh or dried hot chilies,
  seeded and chopped, or
  cayenne pepper, to taste
2–4 tablespoons tamarind water
  (p. xxxii), or lemon juice

1.   In a mortar or electric blender, puree onions, ginger root, garlic, spices, and chilies. Add a little water if necessary to keep the mass moving.

2.   Pour spice mixture in a heavy casserole. Add yogurt and bring to the boiling point, stirring constantly. Turn heat down and add meat cubes. Bring to a boil again, then turn heat to lowest setting and simmer until meat is tender, about 1 hour. If the curry seems dry, add a little more yogurt.

3.   If the curry is served at this stage, with its sauce, it is called *kalio*. To become *rendang*, a dry curry, it must be cooked until most of the liquid has evaporated. Add 1 teaspoon of sugar and stir gently as you cook the meat over moderate heat on top of the stove. The casserole may be placed uncovered in a 300° oven at this point to prevent the meat from sticking to the bottom of the pan. Serve with rice, a *sambal* (pp. 232–34), and one or two accompaniments to curry (pp. 309–10), if desired.

Yield: 8 servings

Cooking time: 1¼ to 2 hours

Calories per serving: 310
Saturated fat: 5.5 g
Cholesterol: 110 mg

Total fat: 12 g
Polyunsaturated fat: 2.5 g
Sodium: 110 mg

Vegetables
(Sayuran)

Vegetable Salad with Peanut Sauce
(Gado-Gado)

This salad is well known all over the islands. The robust flavor of the peanut sauce makes a fine contrast to the fresh crisp vegetables. It can be served either as an appetizer or as a vegetable to accompany a fish or meat course. When it includes bean curd it can be a meal in itself. Any raw or blanched vegetable is suitable for this dish and may be served as an appetizer with the sauce as a dip.

3 small new potatoes
8 ounces firm soybean curd, cut
   into ½-inch cubes
1 tablespoon safflower oil
1 cup green beans, cut into
   3-inch lengths
1 cup cauliflower or broccoli
   flowerets
1 cup bean sprouts

4 cups spinach, washed and
   trimmed
2 cups Chinese (Napa)
   cabbage, shredded
½ recipe shallot flakes (Baweng
   Goreng, p. 230)
   Cucumber slices and fresh
   coriander leaves or watercress, for garnish
1 recipe Peanut Sauce (p. 218)

1.   Boil unpeeled potatoes until tender. Cool, peel, and slice. Set aside.
2.   Heat oil and brown bean curd cubes lightly on all sides. Drain on paper towels.
3.   Steam or boil the string beans and cauliflower separately in rapidly boiling water until barely tender and very crisp. Rinse with cold water to stop cooking process. Drain.

4.   Blanch the bean sprouts, spinach, and cabbage separately for 30 seconds. Drain immediately.

5.   Prepare the shallot flakes.

6.   Arrange the vegetables decoratively in separate piles on a large platter. Garnish with shallot flakes, cucumber slices, and coriander leaves. Serve with Peanut Sauce.

Yield: 6–8 servings   Cooking time: 45 minutes to 1 hour

Nutrient analysis includes shallot flakes but not peanut sauce.

Calories per serving: 135   Total fat: 4.5 g
Saturated fat: 0.5 g   Polyunsaturated fat: 3.5 g
Cholesterol: 0 mg   Sodium: 30 mg

Raw Vegetables and Soybean Curd
(Asinan)

Bean sprouts, cabbage, and radishes are mixed in a sweet-and-sour dressing and topped with crunchy peanuts.

3 cups bean sprouts
4 ounces very fresh soybean
    curd, cut into 1/2-inch cubes
1 medium cucumber, scored
    lengthwise and thinly sliced

3 cups cabbage, shredded
12 radishes, thinly sliced
1/4 cup unsalted, dry roasted
    peanuts

Dressing:

1 teaspoon fresh ginger root,
    minced
2 large cloves garlic, minced
1/4 cup vinegar
1/2 cup water

2–4 fresh or dried red chili
    peppers, seeded and finely
    chopped, or cayenne pep-
    per, to taste
2 tablespoons sugar

1.   Blanch bean sprouts, cabbage, and bean curd in boiling water for 30 seconds. Rinse with cold water to stop cooking process. Drain.

2.   Combine cut vegetables and bean curd in a salad bowl.

3.   Thoroughly mix dressing ingredients. Pour over salad and toss. Top with peanuts. Some prefer a sweeter dressing. Add more sugar if desired.

Yield: 6–8 servings

Preparation time: 15 minutes

Calories per serving: 105
Saturated fat: 1 g
Cholesterol: 0 mg

Total fat: 5 g
Polyunsaturated fat: 1.5 g
Sodium: 10 mg

Tossed Cooked Vegetable Salad
with Coconut Dressing
(Urap)

If you like fresh coconut, you will like this dressing on almost any cooked vegetable. It is especially good on broccoli.

4 cups spinach, trimmed and
   coarsely chopped
3 cups bean sprouts
2 cups Chinese cabbage,
   coarsely chopped
1 cup green beans, cut into bite-
   sized lengths

1 sweet bell pepper, green or red,
   cut lengthwise into ½-inch
   strips
1 small carrot, peeled and cut
   into thin bite-sized lengths.

Dressing:

1 tablespoon safflower oil
1 large clove garlic, finely
   minced
¼ cup onions, finely chopped
½ teaspoon Sambal Ulek (p.
   232), or crushed or ground
   hot pepper, to taste

½ cup tamarind water (p. xxxii),
   or lemon or lime juice
½ cup grated fresh or dessicated
   unsweetened coconut
2 tablespoons hot water

1.   Steam the vegetables briefly (see pp. xxxii–xxxiii) one at a time until they are barely tender. They should retain their color and be crisp to the bite. Transfer them to a large serving bowl.

2.   In a nonstick pan, heat the oil and saute the garlic and onions until golden. Add the *sambal* or hot pepper to taste. Remove from the fire and cool.

3.   Add lemon juice, water, and coconut. Stir until the coconut absorbs the liquid.

4.   Sprinkle the coconut mixture over the vegetables and toss gently un-

til they are thoroughly combined. The salad may be served at room temperature or chilled.

Yield: 6–8 servings

Calories per serving: 100
Saturated fat: 2.5 g
Cholesterol: 0 mg

Cooking time: 20 minutes

Total fat: 4 g
Polyunsaturated fat: 1.5 g
Sodium: 5 mg

Vegetables Cooked in Coconut Milk
(Sayur Lodeh)

A *sayur* is a dish generally made of combinations of crisp vegetables cooked in a spiced, thin, coconut-milk sauce and eaten like every other dish, spooned on rice. It is often mistaken for a soup, but, strictly speaking, soups as we know them do not exist in Indonesian cookery, although *Soto Ayam* (p. 200) is classified as a soup. Any combination of vegetables in season may be used in this *sayur*. Bean curd makes it a complete meal, perfect for lunch or a light dinner. To reduce fat, more stock and less coconut milk is used in this recipe than in the original version, but this one is just as tasty.

2 teaspoons safflower oil
½ cup shallots, or onions, finely chopped
3 large cloves garlic, minced
½ to 1 teaspoon Sambal Ulek (p. 232), or cayenne pepper, to taste
1 tablespoon ground coriander
1 teaspoon ground cumin
2 salem leaves, or bay leaves
1 stalk lemon grass, or grated peel from ½ lemon
2 medium ripe tomatoes, peeled and chopped
2 cups unsalted chicken stock (p. 10)

1 cup string beans, cut into thin bite-sized lengths
1 cup eggplant, cut into bite-sized cubes
2 cups spinach, or Chinese cabbage, coarsely shredded
1 zucchini, cut into bite-sized pieces
4 ounces soybean curd, cut into ½-inch cubes
1 cup coconut milk (p. xxviii)
Lemon quarters and fresh coriander leaves

1.   Prepare vegetables and coconut milk and set aside.

2.   Heat oil in a soup kettle and saute onions and garlic until golden. Blend in *Sambal Ulek*, spices, and leaves, and stir for 1 or 2 minutes.

3.   Add lemon grass (or lemon peel), tomatoes, and chicken stock, and bring to a boil.

4.   Add vegetables according to the time they take to cook. In this selection, begin with the green beans. Altogether, the vegetables should cook about 3 minutes. At this point they should remain underdone.

5.   Mix in the coconut milk and cook until heated through.

6.   Add the bean curd last and cook 1 to 2 minutes. Remove lemon grass and leaves before serving. Place a lemon quarter beside each bowl and garnish with coriander leaves. Serve with boiled rice.

Yield: 6–8 servings   Cooking time: 15–20 minutes

Calories per serving: 135   Total fat: 8 g
Saturated fat: 4.5 g   Polyunsaturated fat: 2 g
Cholesterol: 0 mg   Sodium: 20 mg

Spiced Carrots
(Bortol Dibumbui)

Indonesian cooks usually cook vegetables as *sayurs* in a spicy coconut sauce. In this highly adapted recipe, I have eliminated the coconut milk to cut down on fat and used only the spices. If you are missing your salt, you won't notice its absence in this dish. Almost any vegetable can be prepared this way.

6 medium carrots
1 tablespoon safflower oil
½ cup shallots, or onions,
    coarsely chopped
1 large clove garlic, minced
1 teaspoon fresh ginger root,
    minced

½ teaspoon ground cumin
1 tablespoon ground coriander
¼ teaspoon black pepper
3 tablespoons lemon juice
½ teaspoon brown sugar
2 tablespoons fresh coriander,
    or watercress, chopped for
    garnish

1.   Scrape and cut carrots into thin slices. Steam for 3 or 4 minutes or boil until tender but still crisp. Drain and place in a serving bowl.

2.   Heat oil in a small skillet and saute the shallots, garlic, and ginger root for 2 or 3 minutes. Add remaining ingredients and cook another 2 minutes. Add 1 or 2 tablespoons chicken stock or water if mixture becomes too dry. Combine with carrots and serve at room temperature.

Yield: 4–6 servings   Cooking time: 10 minutes

Calories per serving: 75   Total fat: 2.5 g
Saturated fat: 0.5 g   Polyunsaturated fat: 2 g
Cholesterol: 0 mg   Sodium: 50 mg

◊  ◊

Pickles, Garnishes, and Condiments
(Atjar, Hiasi, and Sambal)

Pickled Mixed Vegetables with Spices
(Atjar Kuning)

Pickles are forbidden if you are on a low-sodium diet. But if you make your own, you can leave the salt out and rely on all the other interesting flavors, along with vinegar, to make quite an acceptable pickle. This "yellow pickle" (which is what *Atjar Kuning* means) is lovely to look at and delightful to eat.

2 tablespoons safflower oil
3 large cloves garlic, minced
½ cup onions, thinly sliced
1 tablespoon fresh ginger root, minced
½ teaspoon turmeric
1 tablespoon ground coriander
½ teaspoon ground cumin
½–1 tablespoon black pepper
4 or 5 whole cloves
½ cup white vinegar, mixed with ¼ cup of water

1 tablespoon sugar
1 small cucumber, cut into thin 1½ inch lengths
1 cup cauliflower or broccoli flowerets
1 sweet red or green bell pepper, seeded, deribbed, and cut lengthwise into ¼-inch strips
1 cup string beans, cut into 1-inch lengths

1.   Heat the oil in a large saucepan and cook the garlic, onions, and ginger root 1–2 minutes, or until wilted.
2.   Mix in the spices, vinegar, and sugar. Simmer over low heat for 2 minutes, stirring constantly.
3.   Add the vegetables. Stir and toss them to be sure they are completely coated with the spice mixture. Cover and cook over low heat until

tender but crisp. Serve at room temperature. May be kept in the refrigerator for 3 or 4 days.

Yield: About 4 cups   Cooking time: 15 minutes

Calories per ½ cup: 60   Total fat: 4 g
Saturated fat: 0.5 g   Polyunsaturated fat: 3 g
Cholesterol: 0 mg   Sodium: 10 mg

Shallot Flakes
(*Baweng Goreng*)

Indonesian and Malaysian cooks sprinkle golden brown toasted shallot flakes over rice or vegetables. The flakes are deep fried and kept on hand, then salted just before using. In this adapted recipe, to lessen the fat content, they are cooked in a nonstick pan with only a small amount of oil. The result is very light, and, of course, no salt is added to them.

1 cup shallots (*mild onions may*   2 teaspoons vegetable oil
   be substituted)

1. Cut shallots in half (onions in quarters), then cut into very thin slices.
2. Spread slices in a single layer on paper towels to dry for at least 1 hour. For busy people this step is optional.
3. In a nonstick pan, heat oil over moderate heat and saute shallots, turning frequently until they are uniformly very crisp and brown. Drain on paper towels.

Note: Bottled dried onion flakes take only a few seconds to brown. Some brands, however, may contain too much salt.

Yield: 1 cup   Cooking time: 20 minutes

Calories per tablespoon: 15   Total fat: 1 g
Saturated fat: 0 g   Polyunsaturated fat: 0.5 g
Cholesterol: 0 mg   Sodium: 1 mg

Thin Omelet Garnish
(*Dadar Hiasi*)

This is a popular garnish all over Southeast Asia. Indonesian cooks use an equal number of yolks and whites. However, since the yolk of an egg contains 274 mg of cholesterol, I discard every other yolk when making omelets.

1 whole egg and 1 egg white   Black pepper
½ tablespoon safflower oil

1. Beat eggs and season with pepper, to taste.
2. Heat a nonstick skillet and grease lightly with oil. Fry the eggs a little at a time to make 5 thin omelets. Do not fold them. When cool, roll up the omelets and cut into thin strips.

Yield: 5 thin omelets   Cooking time: 5–10 minutes

Calories per omelet: 31   Total fat: 3 g
Saturated fat: 0.5 g   Polyunsaturated fat: 1.5 g
Cholesterol: 55 mg   Sodium: 25 mg

Spiced Coconut and Peanut Condiment
(*Serundeng Kacang*)

What a delicious concoction this is! I just couldn't leave it out, even though it is high in calories and fat. That is, it's high if you're like me and want to eat the whole recipe. Remember that it's a condiment, so eat sparingly of it. Traditionally served with *Nasi Kuning* (p. 236), it is good any time to accompany any Indonesian meal.

1 tablespoon safflower oil
¼ cup shallots, or the white part
 of scallions, or mild onions,
 finely chopped
1 small clove garlic, minced
1 teaspoon ground coriander
½ teaspoon ground cumin

1 cup shredded unsweetened
 coconut
½ cup dry roasted unsalted
 peanuts
1 tablespoon brown sugar
1 tablespoon lemon juice

1.   In a wide nonstick skillet, heat oil over low heat and cook shallots and garlic until wilted.

2.   Turn heat down to lowest possible setting and stir in remaining ingredients. Cook mixture, stirring frequently, until it is lightly browned and crisp. This may take 30 minutes or more. Do not hurry it by raising heat or it will scorch.

Yield: 1 ½ cups	Cooking time: 30 minutes
Calories per tablespoon: 40	Total fat: 3.5 g
Saturated fat: 1.5 g	Polyunsaturated fat: 5 g
Cholesterol: 0 mg	Sodium: 5 mg

Hot Red Chili Condiment
(*Sambal Ulek*)

Sambals are fiery hot condiments and relishes that accompany Indonesian dishes much the way chutneys accompany Indian foods. Some of them are commercially available in jars, but it is unknown how much sodium is contained in these products. In the recipes that follow, the salt and shrimp paste have been left out. *Sambal Ulek* is used both as a seasoning and as a condiment. Take care. It is fiery hot.

Caution: Wear gloves when handling chilies and keep hands away from face.

1 cup fresh red chili peppers, seeded and finely chopped	2 tablespoons sugar
2 cloves garlic, minced	2 tablespoons lemon or lime juice
¼ cup onions, finely chopped	2–3 tablespoons water

Pulverize all ingredients in a blender, or pound with a mortar and pestle to a smooth paste. Cook for 10 minutes. Cool.

Yield: About ¾ cup	Cooking time: 10 minutes
Calories per tablespoon: 15	Total fat: 0 g
Saturated fat: 0 g	Polyunsaturated fat: 0 g
Cholesterol: 0 mg	Sodium: 5 mg

Fresh Onion, Tomato, and Chili Condiment
(Sambal Iris)

1 medium onion, quartered and
  sliced into thin ¼-inch
  strips
1 large tomato, cut into very
  small pieces
1 cucumber, peeled and cut into
  thin bite-sized strips

1–2 small red chili peppers,
  seeded and cut into very
  thin matchstick strips
⅓ cup lemon or lime juice
2 tablespoons fresh cori-
  ander, or fresh basil,
  chopped

Thoroughly combine all the ingredients in a bowl and serve as a relish or
condiment with any Indonesian or Malaysian meal.

Yield: About 1¼ cups

Calories per ¼ cup: 30
Saturated fat: 0 g
Cholesterol: 0 mg

Preparation time: 10 minutes

Total fat: 0.5 g
Polyunsaturated fat: 0 g
Sodium: 10 mg

Indonesian Sweet Soy Sauce
(Kecap Manis)

The most commonly used soy-sauce product used in Indonesia is known
as kecap manis. It has a thick consistency and a sweet molasses flavor,
which comes from the large amount of palm sugar in it. It is fermented
longer than Japanese soy sauce and does not contain as much salt. There
is a saltier version, too, known as kecap asin. It intrigued me to discover
that the American-English word "ketchup," or "catsup," as well as the Indonesian word kecap, are believed to have come from the Malay kecop.
The original source of these words is said to have derived from the
Chinese ketsiap. Both kecop and ketsiap, however, are fish sauces. How
tomato ketchup came to be identified with fish sauce is a mystery. The
only thing they have in common is that they are both bottled seasonings.
The following recipe is an approximation of the commercially prepared
one, but contains less soy sauce, and is therefore lower in sodium. Nevertheless, those who should restrict their sodium intake should use it sparingly.

½ cup dark brown sugar, or
palm sugar, if available
¼ cup water
3 tablespoons dark molasses

6 tablespoons low-sodium soy
sauce
¼ teaspoon ground coriander
¼ teaspoon ground black
pepper

1. Combine sugar, water, and molasses. Bring to a boil and cook 5 minutes, stirring constantly, until sugar dissolves.
2. Stir in soy sauce, coriander, and pepper, and simmer for 3 or 4 minutes, stirring constantly. Will keep for a few days in the refrigerator in an airtight jar.

Yield: About ½ cup

Cooking time: 10 minutes

Calories per teaspoon: 25
Saturated fat: 0 g
Cholesterol: 0 mg

Total fat: 0 g
Polyunsaturated fat: 0 g
Sodium: 135 mg

Chili Sweet Soy-Sauce Condiment
(Sambal Kecap)

1 recipe Kecap Manis (p. 233)
2–3 tablespoons lemon or lime
juice

2 fresh hot chili peppers, seeded
and cut into very thin
matchstick strips

Mix all the ingredients in a bowl and serve as a condiment.

Yield: About ¾ cup

Cooking time: 10 minutes

Calories per teaspoon: 10
Saturated fat: 0 g
Cholesterol: 0 mg

Total fat: 0 g
Polyunsaturated fat: 0 g
Sodium: 45 mg

Pineapple Relish
(Petjili Nenas)

1 small pineapple, cut into
   ½-inch wedges (2½
   cups) or one 20-ounce
   can pineapple chunks,
   drained
1 teaspoon safflower oil
¼ cup shallots, or white
   portion of scallions,
   thinly sliced
1 red chili pepper, thinly
   sliced, or ½ sweet red
   bell pepper and cayenne
   pepper, to taste
6 whole cloves
¼–½ teaspoon ground
   cinnamon
3 tablespoons sugar, or ¼
   cup pineapple juice (if
   using canned pineapple)

1.   In a nonstick pan, heat oil and saute shallots and red pepper 2 or 3 minutes.

2.   Add remaining ingredients and cook 10 more minutes, stirring frequently. Pineapple should be soft but not mushy.

Yield: About 3 cups

Cooking time: 15 minutes

Calories per ½ cup: 70
Saturated fat: 0 g
Cholesterol: 0 mg

Total fat: 1.5 g
Polyunsaturated fat: 1 g
Sodium: 5 mg

◊  ◊

Rice and Noodles
(*Beras* and *Bakin Mi*)

White Rice
(*Nasi Putih*)

Boiled white rice is central to all Indonesian meals. The recipe on page 148 of the Chinese section is recommended.

Yellow Rice
(*Nasi Kuning*)

The *Bruwah Slametan* (Breaking of the Fast), a ritual feast combining pagan, Hindu, and Islamic elements, is said to be the precursor of the *rijsstafel*. The feast was held to commemorate a joyous happening, such as the rice harvest, a wedding, or the birth of a child. Its purpose was to ward off evil spirits, and it usually began with prayers, with only the men taking part, and was followed by a sumptuous feast that included the women and children. Today, the *Slametan* may be held solely as a way for family and friends to have a party and to enjoy an extensive selection of Indonesian dishes. Whatever its purpose, the *nasi tumpeng*, a tall cone of yellow rice, is the centerpiece of the *Slametan*. Decorated with morsels of meat, eggs, vegetables, and nuts, and capped at the peak with a fresh red chili pepper decoratively cut to look like a flower, the rice is served buffet-style with a variety of poultry, fish, and vegetable dishes. *Nasi Kuning* is usually cooked in coconut milk. In the recipe offered here, however, chicken stock is substituted in order to cut down on saturated fat. If more authentic taste is desired, some coconut milk may be mixed with the stock. Directions for making coconut milk will be found on page xxviii. Keep in mind that there are 277 calories and 25 mg of saturated fat in 1 cup of coconut milk.

2 tablespoons safflower margarine or oil	1-inch slice fresh ginger or galanga root (laos)
3 large cloves garlic, minced	2 salem, or bay leaves
½ cup onions, finely chopped	2 cups long-grain rice
1 teaspoon turmeric	3⅔ cups unsalted chicken stock (p. 10)
2 stalks fresh or dried lemon grass, or grated peel from ½ lemon	

Suggested garnishes: A fresh chili pepper for the top of the cone, cucumber slices, tomato wedges, strips of green and red pepper, scallions, coriander or watercress sprigs, nuts, and raisins.

1. In a heavy casserole dish, heat oil over medium heat and cook garlic and onions, until soft.

2. Add tumeric, lemon grass, ginger, and bay leaf and cook 1 minute.

3. Add the rice and cook 4 to 5 minutes, stirring constantly, until all the grains are evenly coated with the oil.

4. Pour in the stock, stir briefly, and bring to a boil. Quickly reduce heat and cover. Cook over very low heat on top of the stove without disturbing for 25–30 minutes, or bake in a moderate oven for 35 minutes, until the rice is tender and all the liquid is absorbed. If rice needs more cooking, add 2 or 3 tablespoons water around the edge of the casserole, cover, and cook a few minutes longer. May be kept hot in a warm oven for 15–20 minutes until ready to serve.

5. In the absence of the traditional mold to shape the rice cone, simply fluff the rice and transfer it to a large platter. Discard the lemon grass stalks and ginger.

6. Garnish the mound with some of the vegetables suggested. If using a fresh red chili pepper, cut off stem end of chili. Make several slits from one inch below the tip to the cut end of stem. Place in the center of the fluffed rice and decorate the mound with some of the other garnishes suggested.

Yield: 6–8 servings   Cooking time: 40 minutes

Nutrient analysis does not include garnishes.

Calories per serving: 300   Total fat: 5 g
Saturated fat: 0.5 g   Polyunsaturated fat: 4 g
Cholesterol: 0 mg   Sodium: 20 mg

Fried Noodles, Singapore Style
(*Kway Teow Goreng*)

This is another dish common in Southeast Asia. Meat and seasonings are stir-fried separately and then combined with boiled noodles and stir-fried together, much as fried rice is prepared.

1 pound fresh noodles, rice or
   wheat (kway teow, hokkien
   mee, or bakin mi), or dried
   noodles, if fresh noodles are
   not available
2 tablespoons safflower oil
½ cup shallots, or onions,
   thinly sliced
3 large cloves garlic, finely
   minced
½ pound cooked or raw chicken
   or pork cut into bite-sized
   pieces

½ pound shrimps, shelled,
   deveined, and cut into
   small pieces
1½ teaspoons hoisin sauce
½ teaspoon sugar
¼ cup water
1 cup bean sprouts, washed
   and trimmed
1 tablespoon black pepper

Garnish:

1 cucumber, peeled and sliced
1 recipe thin omelet (p. 231;
   optional)
6 scallions, finely minced

2 red chili peppers, seeded and
   cut into thin matchstick
   strips (optional)
Fresh coriander leaves,
   coarsely chopped

1. Prepare garnishes and set aside.
2. Cook noodles according to directions on package in a large quantity of boiling water. Drain. They should be underdone and offer slight resistance to the bite.

3.   In a wok or nonstick skillet, heat oil and stir-fry onions and garlic until soft.

4.   Add chicken and shrimps, and stir-fry 2 or 3 minutes.

5.   Stir in hoisin sauce, sugar, and water, and boil 1 minute. Mix in bean sprouts and cook for 30 seconds, stirring constantly.

6.   Add noodles, and stir and toss gently, until well mixed and heated through. Serve hot with garnishes arranged on top.

Yield: 6 servings   Cooking time: 30 minutes

Nutrient count does not include garnishes.

Calories per serving: 320   Total fat: 7 g
Saturated fat: 1 g   Polyunsaturated fat: 4.5 g
Cholesterol: 50 mg   Sodium: 100 mg

Thailand

Thailand

The Thai Kitchen

Thailand occupies a central position on the Southeast Asian peninsula. What sets it apart from other countries of the area is its ability, throughout its history, to escape extended foreign domination. Even during the century of unbridled European imperialism in that part of the globe, of all the nations of Southeast Asia, Thailand was the only one that retained its sovereignty. Historians attribute this long heritage of independence to the cohesive rule of an extraordinary succession of scholar-innovator-warrior kings. This powerful monarchy traces its history to the kingdom of Sukhothai, founded in 1238. By that time, the Khmer empire and the great temples at Angkor Wat in Cambodia were well established. The Sukhothai dynasty reached its zenith under King Ramkambaeng, whose exploits on war elephants gained him a fearsome reputation, as he expanded his territory by conquering rival kingdoms. He established trade treaties with India and Burma and made close contact with Ceylon and China. Chinese artisans were imported to produce celadon pottery, internationally prized as *Suwankaloke* celadon, and Ceylonese monks were invited to teach their form of Buddhism. In the most far-reaching achievement of his 40-year reign, King Ramkambaeng created an alphabet—based on a Sanskritic script—that is still in use today, and in one stroke formed the tool for uniting the country's scattered tribes into a nation with an identity of its own.

In the nineteenth century, Thailand's ability to resist European imperialism was largely a credit to the diplomacy of three kings, Rama IV, V, and VI, during the years of their combined reigns (1851–1925). Rama IV, King Mongut, is the monarch familiar in the West through the grossly inaccurate depiction of him in the American musical *The King and I*. Before he ascended the throne at the age of 46, he had been a scholarly Buddhist monk and a student of European languages and science, as well as a devotee of Buddhism and the traditional culture of Thailand. To maintain the independence of the kingdom, the policy followed by King Mongut and his successors was one of yielding the necessary concessions while at the same time reorganizing and consolidating what remained. Undefendable territory was ceded to the British and the French. Western advisors were employed to reorganize government services, and young Thais were sent to Europe to be educated. Treaties were signed with European powers, which opened the kingdom to international trade. Under these three kings, the modernization of the country proceeded at a rapid rate, propelling Thailand into the twentieth century. But the rise of a Western-educated professional group and a series of financial crises causing unemployment and dissent diminished the psychological power of the monarchy. The culmination was the *coup d'état* of 1932, which ended 700 years of absolute monarchy and established a parliamentary constitution. However, the reverence felt by the Thai people for their king has been in no way diminished by the curtailment of his political power. The monarchy remains as strongly as ever the central, unifying element in the Thai triad of nation, king, and religion.

The heart of the country, the fertile and thickly populated central plain, is a vast expanse of rice paddies that is entirely flat and rarely more than a few feet above sea level. From the air, when the Chao Phraya River is high, one can see this splendid checkerboard of ricelands, veined by a system of canals, shimmering and unobstructed for miles. Rice forms the core of the Thai economic system. The staple food of the nation, it has been the country's largest single foreign-exchange earner. In recent years, however, as a result of modern technology, the Northeast and Southeast, which were previously considered two of the least fertile areas, are now producing tapioca in such quantities that the starchy root has surpassed rice in economic importance. As in the rest of Southeast Asia, rice is the mainstay of the Thai diet. For most of the people who live along the banks of the rivers and canals, freshwater fish is the principal addition to that diet. *Pla tu*, a small mackerel, is fried and eaten with a bowl of rice and a fiery hot sauce called *nam prik*. Glutinous or sticky rice is preferred in northeastern Thailand, whose people have more in common with Laotians than with the Thais of the central plain. Their dishes are cooked dry, and the sticky rice is rolled into balls and used in place of an eating utensil to scoop up the food. In the South, glutinous rice, sometimes called sweet rice, is used exclusively for sweets and little snacks that are often prepared with coconut milk.

Thai cuisine is a blend of Chinese and Indian cooking, with a predominance of stir-fried dishes and hot curries. This is not surprising, since Thai culture has been shaped by both of these influences, which remain conspicuously present in Thailand today. Overseas Chinese comprise by far the largest minority and their cuisine has been incorporated almost unchanged. One example is whole fish cooked with a sweet-and-sour sauce, also very popular in Vietnam and included in the Vietnamese section (p. 179). India exerted its culinary influence as a result of the trade with the spice islands of Indonesia and other countries of Southeast Asia, but Indian curries underwent gradual alteration to meet local tastes. Thai adaptations, obviously derived from Indian sources, add aromatic leaves to the spices and mix them with *kapi*, a salty, pungent paste made from fermented shrimp, similar to the Indonesian *terasi*. It is available commercially both in jars and in a dry form. Anchovy paste makes a good substitute, but all of these condiments are very high in sodium and are not used in the recipes selected for this book.

Stir-frying is the dominant cooking method in Thailand, but the seasoning is *nam pla*, a sauce made from salted and fermented fish or shrimp. It is so similar to the Vietnamese *nuoc mam* that they may be used interchangeably. *Nam pla* is used as frequently as soy sauce is used in Japanese and Chinese cooking. Also essential to Thai cuisine are lemon grass (*bai takrai*) and fresh kaffir lime leaves (*bai makrut*), which are used to achieve the sour, lemony flavor unique to Thai cuisine; fresh coriander leaves (*bai pak chi*), which are sprinkled lavishly on just about everything; garlic, which is used in astonishingly large quantities; and the world's smallest but hottest chili peppers (*prik khi nu*), the most celebrated of Thai seasonings. Another important ingredient in Thai cooking is coconut milk, which is used in curries as well as in sweets. In recent years, Thai food has been enjoying an international vogue, and many Thai restaurants have sprung up in large cities in the United States, especially in California and New York. With them, many Thai ingredients, such as *nam pla* or powdered lemon grass (*serai*) have become readily available in supermarkets as well as in Asian food shops.

Serving a Thai meal is very much like serving a Chinese family meal. Rice and all the dishes that go with it are brought to the table at the same time. A typical meal consists of soup, curry, and two or three side dishes, usually served at room temperature. Rice, however, is always served hot. Thais like their food to please the eye as well as the tastebuds, and a great deal of attention is given to serving food beautifully and creating elaborate garnishes. On special occasions, the art of fruit and vegetable carving comes into its own and exquisite flowers are sculpted from melons, rose-apples, and other edibles. No special cooking utensils are required to make Thai food. A nonstick pan or a wok and a saucepan or two will easily cope with any of these recipes. For tips on stir-frying and using a wok, see pages xxxiii–xxxiv. Modern Thais eat mostly with spoons and forks, though in the northeast and in rural areas food is eaten with the fingers.

Adapting Thai Food to a Low-Sodium, Low-Cholesterol Diet

To adapt Thai food to a low-sodium, low-cholesterol diet, fish sauce (*nam pla*), shrimp paste (*kapi*), and coconut milk (*nam gati*) are the ingredients that must be used sparingly if the sodium and saturated fat levels are to be kept reasonably low. As far as the recipes in this book are concerned, shrimp paste has been left out altogether and fish sauce is added in very small amounts. As with so many Asian condiments, the sodium content in fish sauce is unknown and probably varies from batch to batch. Since some estimate had to be made to arrive at an approximate sodium calculation for these recipes, it has been assumed that the amount in *nam pla* is about the same as for standard soy sauce, 320 mg per teaspoon, not the low-sodium variety, which has only 170 mg per teaspoon. If an exact count is required for your diet, substitute Kikkoman's low-sodium soy sauce, which is a highly standardized product.

As for coconut milk, it is so high in saturated fat and calories that wherever possible low-fat yogurt or milk has been substituted in these recipes. However, if more authentic taste is desired, some coconut milk ought to be used, preferably mixed with stock, nonfat milk, or water. How to make coconut milk and what to substitute for it will be found on page xxviii. Remember there are 277 calories and 25 mg of saturated fat in 1 cup of coconut milk.

Though these recipes contain far less fish or soy sauce than would normally be used, other seasonings are assertive enough to compensate for their omission. Among these are garlic, ginger root (although the Thais would use galanga, which they call *kha*), tamarind (*mak kham*), ground coriander, fresh coriander leaves (*pak chi*), spices used in curry pastes, lemon juice, lemon grass, black pepper, and, of course, chilies. Though Thais use chilies lavishly in almost every recipe, it would be a mistake to think that every dish must be hot. That is always a matter of individual taste. Thai foods contain so many other seasonings that they are flavorful even without chilies. Yet even when a dish is very hot, it must be remembered that it is never eaten alone but always with large quantities of unsalted boiled rice.

Soups and Curries
(Kaeng)

Soups
(Kaeng Chut)

Kaeng, meaning liquid, refers to any cooked food that has a great deal of liquid or sauce, such as a soup or curry. *Kaeng chut* is a bland *kaeng*, and *kaeng phet* is a spicy, peppery *kaeng*.

No typical Thai meal would be complete without soup, which is usually served with rice and other dishes; it never appears alone as a first course as in Western cooking. Soup is also eaten for breakfast. Rice soup (*khao dom*), which is equivalent to porridge but savory rather than sweet, is rice boiled in chicken stock and may be flavored with fish sauce, bits of meat, garlic, coriander leaves, onions, and chilies, as one wishes. A bland version of *khao dom* is fed to children. Another favorite soup eaten for lunch or a snack is *guwaytio*, a dish of Chinese origin. A favorite fast food of Bangkok, it is sold by itinerant food vendors or in food stalls in the market. In a base of strong pork or chicken stock you will find noodles, meat, fish balls, spiced pork bits, innards, mushrooms, and various vegetables all flavored with the ubiquitous fish sauce, *nam pla*, and garnished with fresh coriander leaves, peanuts, fried garlic, and, of course, fiery bits of chili peppers. No one manufactures a *guwaytio* at home because it would have to be made in enormous quantities, cooked for many hours, and contain more ingredients than one cook would care to bother with.

Hot-and-Sour Shrimp Soup
(Dom Yam Kung)

I have never met anyone, Thai or foreigner alike, who didn't love this soup. Succulent shrimps are cooked in a lemony-hot broth and seasoned with garlic, coriander, lemon grass, and peppers.

3 *large cloves garlic, minced*
1 *teaspoon safflower oil*
5 *cups unsalted chicken stock*
   (p. 10)
4 *stalks fresh or dried lemon*
   grass (bai takrai), cut into 1-
   inch lengths, or 2 table-
   spoons grated lemon peel
4 *lemon, kaffir lime (bai*
   makrut), or other citrus
   leaves (Bay leaves may be
   substituted, but the flavor
   will be different.)
8 *dried Chinese mushrooms,*
   soaked in warm
   water for 30 minutes to
   soften, or fresh mushrooms,
   sliced

1 ⅓ *pounds shrimp,*
   shelled and deveined
⅓–½ *cup fresh lime juice*
1 *teaspoon fish sauce*
   (nam pla), or Viet-
   namese fish sauce (nuoc
   mam), or low-sodium
   soy sauce
½–1 *teaspoon freshly*
   ground pepper
1–4 *fresh or dried chili*
   peppers, seeded and
   chopped, or cayenne pep-
   per, to taste
2 *scallions, cut into 1-inch*
   lengths
   Fresh coriander leaves,
   chopped, for garnish

1.   In a large saucepan, heat the oil and cook the garlic for 30 seconds.
2.   Add the stock, lemon grass, and citrus leaves, and boil 20 minutes. Remove and discard leaves with slotted spoon, or strain stock. For deeper flavor, some cooks leave the leaves in the soup.
3.   Bring the stock back to a boil. Add the mushrooms and cook 2–3 minutes.
4.   Add the shrimps and cook 2–5 minutes, depending on their size, or until they turn pink. Do not overcook them or they will toughen.
5.   Stir in the lime juice, fish sauce, peppers, and scallions, and simmer 1 minute.
6.   Transfer to a heated soup tureen and garnish with coriander leaves. Soup should have a peppery, lemony flavor. Add more of both to taste.

Yield: 6 servings

Cooking time: 30 minutes

Calories per serving: 125
Saturated fat: 0.5 g
Cholesterol: 80 mg

Total fat: 2 g
Polyunsaturated fat: 1.0 g
Sodium: 155 mg

Variations:

1. One pound boned chicken, all fat and skin removed, may be substituted for the shrimp.
2. A mix of bite-sized chunks of fish, crabmeat, and squid may be added in step 4 at the same time as the shrimps to make a sort of Thai bouillabaisse. For 4 servings, allow 4 ounces each of fish fillets, crabmeat, squid, and shrimps.

Chicken Soup with Coconut Milk
(Dom Kha Kai)

Kha (galanga, which is called laos in Indonesian), is a member of the ginger family that is very subtle in flavor and aroma. There is really no substitute for it, but fresh ginger root may be used in its place; even though the taste is not the same, the dish is outstanding anyway. This is a substantial soup and could be a main dish for four people.

6 pieces dried galanga (kha), or 4 teaspoons laos powder, or 3 tablespoons fresh ginger root, finely minced
3 large cloves garlic, minced
One 2½ pound chicken, skinned with all fat removed and cut into small serving pieces
2 cups coconut milk (p. xxviii), mixed with 4 cups unsalted chicken stock (Please read about coconut milk on pp. xxvii–xxix. Usually all the liquid in this soup is coconut milk.)
3 stalks lemon grass, cut into 1-inch pieces, or 2 tablespoons grated lime or lemon rind

2 lemon or citrus leaves (bai makrut), or bay leaves
1 tablespoon ground coriander
½–1 teaspoon black pepper
1–3 fresh or dried chili peppers, seeded and chopped, or cayenne pepper, to taste
1 teaspoon fish sauce (nam pla), or Vietnamese fish sauce (nuoc mam), or low-sodium soy sauce
3–4 tablespoons lime or lemon juice
Fresh coriander leaves, chopped, for garnish

1. If using dried kha, soak it in hot water for 30 minutes.
2. In a soup kettle, combine chicken pieces with kha or ginger root,

garlic, one-half the coconut milk mixture, lemon grass, citrus leaves, coriander, and peppers, and bring to a slow boil. Turn heat to lowest setting and simmer gently uncovered, 20–25 minutes or until chicken is tender, stirring occasionally and skimming off froth.

3.   Add remainder of coconut milk and cook until heated through, but do not boil.

4.   Remove from heat and add fish sauce and lemon juice. Garnish with coriander leaves and serve in shallow soup bowls with rice.

Yield: 6 servings   Cooking time: 30 minutes

Note: This is a dish that ought to be on your menu very rarely. As you can see from the nutrient analysis below, the coconut milk adds a lot of saturated fat.

Calories per serving: 270   Total fat: 15 g
Saturated fat: 9.5 g   Polyunsaturated fat: 1 g
Cholesterol: 65 mg   Sodium: 130 mg

Variation: Fish fillets cut into small chunks may be substituted for the chicken. First bring coconut milk mixture to a boil, then add fish and cook only 3 or 4 minutes.

Stuffed Squid Soup
(*Kaeng Chut Pla Muk*)

Please read about squid in the ingredients section on page xxv. Chicken has been substituted for pork in the filling.

12 small whole squids (1
    pound uncleaned squid
    yields 11–12 ounces edible meat)
2 large cloves garlic, minced
½–1 teaspoon black pepper
12 ounces ground chicken, no
    fat or skin included
1 teaspoon fish sauce (nam
    pla), or Vietnamese fish
    sauce (nuoc mam), or
    low-sodium soy sauce

6 cups unsalted chicken stock
    (p. 10)
3 scallions, cut into 1-inch
    pieces
1 fresh or dried chili pepper,
    seeded and finely chopped,
    or cayenne pepper, to taste
Fresh coriander leaves,
    chopped, for garnish

1.   Clean and wash squid, removing the transparent center bone, purple spotted skin, and inner matter. Cut off tentacles and reserve.
2.   To make stuffing, chop the tentacles finely and mix with black pepper, chicken, and fish sauce. Mix thoroughly and knead well with hands.
3.   Stuff each squid about ¾ full or less. Sew the opening with a coarse needle and thread or use toothpicks to hold the opening closed. If any filling remains, make tiny meatballs with it.
4.   In a large saucepan, bring stock to a boil. Drop in the squid and meatballs and simmer 5–10 minutes, depending on size of squid, over low heat. Skim off froth that rises to the surface. Do not overcook, or squid will toughen.
5.   Stir in scallions and chili pepper and remove from heat. Serve garnished with fresh coriander leaves.

Yield: 6 servings

Cooking time: 15 minutes

Calories per serving: 195
Saturated fat: 1.5 g
Cholesterol: 180 mg

Total fat: 4 g
Polyunsaturated fat: 1 g
Sodium: 120 mg

Shrimp, Chicken, and Cellophane-Noodle Soup
(*Kaeng Ron*)

This is another soup which is substantial enough to serve four people as a main lunch or supper dish. Only chicken is used in this recipe. The Thai meat of preference is pork, or half pork and half chicken.

4 ounces cellophane noodles
2 tablespoons tiger lily buds
*   (optional)*
1 tablespoon safflower oil
2 large cloves garlic, finely
*   minced*
8 ounces boneless chicken, all
*   skin and fat removed, cut*
*   into bite-sized pieces*
½ cup onions, coarsely chopped
1 cup mushrooms, sliced
6 cups unsalted chicken stock
*   (p. 10)*

⅓ pound shrimp, shelled and
deveined, and cut into
small pieces
1 cucumber unpeeled, scored
and cut lengthwise, then
cut crosswise into thin
slices
1 teaspoon fish sauce (nam
pla), or Vietnamese fish
sauce (nuoc mam), or low-
sodium sauce

1 tablespoon ground cori-
ander
½–1 teaspoon black pepper
1–4 fresh or dried chili
peppers, seeded and chop-
ped, or cayenne pepper,
to taste
2 egg whites, slightly beaten
Fresh coriander leaves,
chopped, for garnish

Preparation:

1. Soak noodles in warm water to cover for 15 minutes. Rinse, drain, and cut into short lengths. Set aside.
2. Soak tiger lily buds in warm water for 30 minutes. Wash and drain. Discard hard ends and cut into small pieces.
3. Cut meat and vegetables and place within easy reach of the stove.

Cooking:

1. Heat oil in a large saucepan over high heat. Stir-fry onions for 2 minutes or until translucent.
2. Add garlic and stir-fry for 10 seconds.
3. Add chicken and stir-fry briskly 1 minute or until lightly browned.
4. Stir in mushrooms and cook another minute.
5. Add stock and bring to a boil. Turn heat down to low and simmer 4–5 minutes.
6. Add shrimp, cucumber, fish sauce, coriander, pepper, and chili peppers, and cook 2–3 more minutes.
7. Pour slightly beaten egg whites into the boiling soup, stirring constantly.
8. Transfer to a heated soup tureen and garnish with coriander leaves.

Yield: 6 servings

Cooking time: 15-20 minutes

Calories per serving: 200
Saturated fat: 1 g
Cholesterol: 50 mg

Total fat: 5 g
Polyunsaturated fat: 2.5 g
Sodium: 155 mg

Curries
(*Kaeng Phet*)

Kaeng phet, the curries so beloved by the Thais, were developed from Indian sources, but they have been so adapted and blended that they are truly Thai in character as well as in flavor now. The suffix *phet* means hot, and Thai curries can be very hot indeed. Similar to the wet *masalas* of India, the Thai curry pastes are made of spices that are usually pounded together in a mortar with garlic, shallots or onions, and shrimp paste (*kapi*), a salty, pungent condiment. Anchovy paste makes a good substitute, but since it contains too much sodium for the purposes of this book I have substituted safflower oil and vinegar. Most Thai curries contain coconut milk, which makes a rich gravy and smoothes out the raw heat of the spices and peppers. Since coconut is very high in saturated fat, low-fat yogurt or milk has been substituted in these recipes. More about coconut milk will be found on pagse xxvii–xxix.

In Thai cooking, curry pastes are often referred to by color. The color means simply that the base is either red chilies, which give the sauce a ruddy cast, or fresh green ones, the most incendiary, which tint the sauce green. Indian–style curries, called Muslim or Masaman curries, contain more aromatic spices such as cloves, cinnamon, or nutmeg. There is also a yellow curry paste that results in a *kaeng* that is similiar to a Masaman curry but that includes turmeric. Other ingredients are likely to include cumin, caraway and coriander seeds, lemon grass, galanga (a relative of ginger called *kha* in Thai and *laos* in Indonesian), garlic, shallots, shrimp paste, and, in green curry paste, fresh coriander.

Once the paste is made, preparing a Thai curry is easy. Just 20 to 30 minutes is all it takes. In recent years, curry pastes have been available in jars or packets in stores specializing in Asian foods. In Thailand, there is no such thing as "curry powder" in the Western sense, and a discussion of our misconceptions about curries in general will be found in the India section on page 279.

Curry Pastes
(Khrung Kaeng)

It is easier though not as flavorful to use already ground spices to make curry pastes, but if whole spices are available, a mortar and pestle, a pepper grinder, an electric coffee mill (used only for spices), or an electric blender will do the job. Usually onion and garlic are pounded with the spices, but some cooks prefer to add them fresh when they make the curry. Either way produces good results.

Red Curry Paste
(Khrung Kaeng Daeng)

1. To make Red Curry Paste, pound spices to a fine powder using the utensil of your choice. Mince onions and garlic and mix with spices. Add oil and vinegar and blend into a fine paste. If you decide to combine all these ingredients in an electric blender, more liquid may be needed to keep the mass going.

2. This paste may be kept in the refrigerator in a small airtight jar for a few days but not much longer because of the absence of salt and the salty shrimp paste (kapi), which function as preservatives.

2 teaspoons nutmeg, freshly grated
1 teaspoon whole or ground cloves (optional)
10 cardamom pods (remove seeds and grind), or 1 teaspoon cardamom powder
1 tablespoon fresh or dried lemon grass, finely chopped
2 tablespoons coriander seeds
2 teaspoons ground caraway seeds
3 pieces dried galanga (kha or laos), or ½ teaspoon ground ginger

1 tablespoon paprika
1 teaspoon freshly ground black pepper
4–6 fresh or dried hot red chili peppers, seeds removed, or ½–3 teaspoons cayenne pepper, to taste
1 small onion, coarsely chopped (about ½ cup)
4 large cloves garlic, minced
Grated peel of 1 lime
2 tablespoons safflower oil
1 tablespoon vinegar

Yellow Curry Paste
(Khrung Kaeng Leuang)

To make Yellow Curry Paste, leave out the paprika in the above recipe and add 2 teaspoons turmeric and 1 teaspoon ground cumin.

Green Curry Paste
(*Khrung Kaeng Kheeo*)

To make Green Curry Paste, leave out the paprika in the recipe for Red Curry Paste and substitute green chilies for the red ones. Add 1 cup fresh coriander leaves, chopped, and pound or pulverize with the spice mixture.

The nutrient analysis of these curry pastes is based on the estimate that most spices on the average contain 5 calories and 1 mg of sodium per teaspoon.

Yield: About ½ cup

Preparation time: 10 minutes

Calories per tablespoon: 50
Saturated fat: 0.5 g
Cholesterol: 0 mg

Total fat: 3.5 g
Polyunsaturated fat: 1 g
Sodium: 5 mg

Chicken in Green Curry Paste
(*Kaeng Kheeo Wan Kai*)

To make an authentic Thai curry, rich coconut cream is simmered until it is reduced to one quarter of its original volume before it is mixed with the curry paste. Then the meat and more coconut milk are added. The result is very rich and very tasty but the amount of saturated fat in the coconut milk is just too much to be included in a recipe in this sort of book. The recipes offered here substitute low-fat yogurt or milk, though instructions for using coconut milk are also included for those wishing to use it. Before making a curry with coconut milk, please read about it on pages xxvii–xxix.

Note: Any leftover cooked meat or chicken may be used in these curry recipes.

1 teaspoon safflower oil
2 large cloves garlic, minced
1½ cups plain low-fat yogurt or milk
3–4 tablespoons Green Curry Paste (p. 255)
3 chicken legs and 3 half breasts, cut into small serving pieces

½ cup or more unsalted chicken stock (p. 10)
2 lemon or citrus leaves (bai makrut), or bay leaves
2 fresh green chilies, chopped (optional)
¼ cup fresh basil leaves (bai horapa), finely chopped

1. In a heavy saucepan, heat oil and saute garlic. Add 1 cup yogurt and heat until it comes to a boil. Reduce heat, add curry paste, and cook 3–4 minutes, stirring constantly.

2. Add chicken, turning pieces to coat with sauce. Cook over medium heat until chicken changes color.

3. Add the rest of the yogurt and all other ingredients, except for chilies and basil. Stir well and bring to a boil. Turn heat down to lowest setting and simmer uncovered for 15–20 minutes, or until chicken is tender.

4. Add chilies and basil leaves, and simmer 4 to 5 minutes longer. Add more yogurt or stock if curry seems dry. Serve with rice and 2 or 3 condiments for curry (pp. 309–10).

Yield: 6 servings

Cooking time: 25 to 30 minutes

Calories per serving: 285
Saturated fat: 3 g
Cholesterol: 100 mg

Total fat: 10 g
Polyunsaturated fat: 4 g
Sodium: 115 mg

Variation: Fresh shrimp may be substituted for chicken, but cook for only 7–10 minutes in all. Overcooking will toughen shrimp.

Note: To make a more authentic Thai curry, use about 1 cup coconut cream (p. xxviii) in step 1. Then add ½ cup coconut milk in step 3. Keep in mind that there are approximately 277 calories and 25 mg of saturated fat in one cup of coconut milk.

Chicken in Yellow Curry Paste
(*Kaeng Kari Kai*)

The use of turmeric, cinnamon, and nutmeg links this dish closely with Indian curries. Be sure to read the paragraph under the curry on page 255.

1 tablespoon safflower oil
2 large cloves garlic, minced
½ cup onions, finely chopped
1½ cups plain low-fat yogurt or
    milk
3–4 tablespoons Yellow Curry
    Paste (p. 152)

3 chicken legs and 3 half
  breasts, cut into small serving pieces
½ cup or more unsalted
  chicken stock (p. 10)
½ teaspoon nutmeg, freshly
  grated
2-inch piece cinnamon stick
2 lemon or citrus leaves (bai
  makrut), or bay leaves

1 small potato, peeled and cut
  into ½-inch cubes
1 fresh or dried chili pepper,
  seeded and finely chopped,
  or cayenne pepper, to taste
  (optional)

1. In a heavy saucepan, heat oil and saute garlic and onion. Add ½ cup yogurt and curry paste and stir constantly 3–4 minutes.
2. Add chicken, turning pieces to coat with sauce. Cook on both sides over medium heat until chicken changes color.
3. Add the rest of the yogurt and remaining ingredients. Stir well, turn heat down to lowest setting and simmer uncovered for 15–20 minutes or until chicken is tender. Add more yogurt or stock if mixture seems dry. Serve with rice and 2 or 3 accompaniments to curry (p. 000).

Yield: 6 servings

Cooking time: 25–30 minutes

Calories per serving: 290
Saturated fat: 3 g
Cholesterol: 100 mg

Total fat: 10 g
Polyunsaturated fat: 4 g
Sodium: 120 mg

Variation: Beef or shrimp may be substituted for the chicken.

Note: For more authentic taste, substitute ½ cup coconut cream (p. xxviii) for the yogurt in step 1 and coconut milk for the yogurt in step 3.

Beef Curry
(*Kaeng Phet Nua*)

Be sure to read the paragaph under the curry on p. 255.

1 teaspoon safflower oil
2 large cloves garlic, minced
3–4 tablespoons Red Curry
    Paste (p. 254)
1½ cups plain low-fat yogurt or
    milk
1½ pounds very lean round
    steak, or other lean tender
    beef, cut into 1-inch cubes

2 lemon or citrus leaves (bai
    makrut), or bay leaves
1–2 fresh or dried red chili
    peppers, seeded and
    chopped, or cayenne pep-
    per, to taste (optional)
Fresh basil or coriander
    leaves, chopped, for gar-
    nish

1.   In a large saucepan, heat oil and saute garlic. Add curry paste and ½ cup yogurt, stirring constantly 3–4 minutes.

2.   Add beef, turning pieces to coat with sauce. Cook over medium heat until meat changes color.

3.   Add the rest of the yogurt and remaining ingredients. Stir well, lower heat, and simmer 15–20 minutes uncovered, or until meat is tender. There should be enough sauce to spoon on rice. Add a little more yogurt or stock if curry seems dry. Serve with boiled white rice and at least 3 condiments for curry (pp. 309–10).

Yield: 6 servings

Cooking time: 25–30 minutes

Calories per serving: 310
Saturated fat: 6 g
Cholesterol: 110 mg

Total fat: 12 g
Polyunsaturated fat: 4.5 g
Sodium: 105 mg

Note: For more authentic taste, substitute coconut cream for the yogurt in step 1, and coconut milk for the yogurt in step 3.

Seafood and Chicken
(Pla and Kai)

Fish Fillets in Garlic and Tamarind Sauce
(Pla Chien)

Tamarind (*mak kam*) has a fruity, acidic flavor that is perfect for low-salt cooking. Though the flavor is quite different, lemon peel and juice may be substituted for it with fairly good results. The fish sauce is left out of this recipe.

1 pound firm fish fillets	1–3 fresh or dried chili peppers,
1 tablespoon safflower oil	seeded and chopped
2 large cloves garlic, minced	¼ cup tamarind water (p. xxx-
1 tablespoon fresh ginger	ii),
root, minced	or grated rind of 1 lemon
1 teaspoon low-sodium soy	and ¼ cup lemon or lime
sauce	juice
1 tablespoon palm or brown	2 scallions, cut into 1-inch
sugar	pieces
½–1 teaspoon black pepper	Fresh coriander leaves,
	chopped for garnish

1.   In a nonstick pan, heat oil and gently saute fish for 1–2 minutes on each side until just done. Do not overcook. Remove to a heated serving dish and keep warm.
2.   Add garlic and ginger to the pan and stir-fry until lightly browned. Add soy sauce, sugar, peppers, and tamarind water and stir until sugar dissolves. If mixture seems dry, add 2 or 3 tablespoons water.
3.   Add scallions and cook 1 to 2 minutes longer.
4.   Spoon the sauce over the fish and serve garnished with coriander leaves.

Yield: 4–6 servings

Cooking time: 7–8 minutes

Calories per serving: 165
Saturated fat: 0.5 g
Cholesterol: 60 mg

Total fat: 5 g
Polyunsaturated fat: 3.5 g
Sodium: 125 mg

Shrimp Ginger Stir-Fry
(*Kung Phat Khing*)

This ginger stir-fry may be made with shrimp, chicken, beef, pork, or squid, and most of these choices are usually available on Thai restaurant menus, just as they are for sweet-and-sour dishes. I can't think of a simpler, more delicious way to prepare shrimp or meat. No salt is needed here, just the pungent taste of ginger and garlic spiked with pepper. The following recipe is written for both shrimp and chicken. Have the rice and all other parts of the meal ready to serve before you start cooking.

1 ⅓ *pounds shrimp (yields
    about 1 pound without
    shells), or 1 pound
    chicken breast meat, cut
    into ½-inch cubes*
1 *tablespoon safflower oil*
4 *tablespoons fresh ginger
    root, minced*
4 *large cloves garlic, minced*
4 *scallions, cut into ½-inch
    pieces*
1–4 *fresh or dried chili pep-
    pers, seeded and chop-
    ped, or cayenne pepper to
    taste*
½–1 *teaspoon sugar, dissolved
    in 3 tablespoons water*

1.   Shell, devein, and rinse shrimp without removing tails. Dry.
2.   Heat a wok or nonstick skillet over high heat. Add oil. Stir-fry ginger, garlic, scallions, and pepper 1–2 minutes.
3.   Add shrimp (or chicken) and stir-fry for 1–2 minutes or until shrimp are pink and firm. (Cook chicken pieces longer if necessary.)

4. Mix in sugar and water. Cook a minute or so longer, stirring constantly to blend well, and serve at once.

Yield: 4–6 servings   Cooking time: 5–7 minutes

Nutritional analysis for shrimp:
  Calories per serving: 200   Total fat: 5 g
  Saturated fat: 0.5 g   Polyunsaturated fat: 3.5 g
  Cholesterol: 120 mg   Sodium: 165 mg

Nutritional analysis for chicken:
  Calories per serving: 265   Total fat: 10 g
  Saturated fat: 2 g   Polyunsaturated fat: 4.5 g
  Cholesterol: 90 mg   Sodium: 75 mg

Stir-Fried Chicken with Fresh Basil Leaves
(*Kai Phat Horapa*)

Dried basil leaves may *not* be substituted in this dish. Only fresh basil should be used. *Horapa* is a variety of the sweet basils grown in the West. In Thailand, this perennial favorite is often made with the native basil-like balsam leaves (*bai kaprao*), and is known as *Kai Phat Bai Kaprao*.

1 tablespoon safflower oil
1 small onion, thinly sliced
1–4 fresh or dried chili peppers,
   seeded and cut into thin
   slices, or cayenne pepper,
   to taste
2 large cloves garlic, minced
1 tablespoon fresh ginger
   root, minced
1 pound boneless chicken, all
   skin and fat removed, cut
   into bite-sized pieces

½ cup fresh basil leaves,
   chopped (bai kaprao, if
   available)
½–1 teaspoon fish sauce (nam
   pla), or Vietnamese fish
   sauce (nuoc mam), or
   low-sodium soy sauce
½ teaspoon sugar
½ teaspoon vinegar

1. Heat a nonstick skillet or wok over high heat. Add oil, and just before it begins to smoke, stir-fry the onion, chili peppers, garlic, and ginger for 1–2 minutes or until onions are transparent.

2. Add chicken pieces and stir-fry briskly 1–2 minutes or until chicken changes color.

3. Add remaining ingredients and mix well. Add a tablespoon or two of water, cover, and cook 1–2 minutes. Do not overcook. Serve with rice.

Yield: 4–6 servings   Cooking time: 6–8 minutes

Calories per serving: 255   Total fat: 10 g
Saturated fat: 2.5 g   Polyunsaturated fat: 4.5 g
Cholesterol: 100 mg   Sodium: 130 mg

Variation: Fish may be substituted for chicken.

Grilled Chicken with Garlic
(Kai Yang kap Gratium)

This may seem like a lot of garlic and pepper, but it isn't. If grilling is inconvenient, cook the chicken in a lightly greased baking dish. The result is just as good.

1 whole chicken breast and 2
   chicken legs, skinned and
   cut into serving pieces
6–8 large cloves garlic, finely
   minced
3 tablespoons coarsely
   ground black pepper

½–1 teaspoon fish sauce (nam
   pla), or Vietnamese fish
   sauce (nuoc mam), or
   low-sodium soy sauce
¼ cup lemon or lime juice
2 tablespoons safflower oil
¼ cup fresh coriander leaves,
   finely chopped

1. Combine ingredients and rub into chicken pieces. Marinate for an hour or more. If you are not going to grill the chicken, marinate the pieces in a lightly greased baking dish.

2. Grill over a charcoal fire, under an oven broiler, or bake in a 350° oven, turning to brown both sides.

3. Serve with cucumber salad (Yam Daengua; p. 271) and dipping sauce (Nuoc Cham; p. 168), if desired.

Yield: 4–6 servings   Cooking time: 25 to 35 minutes

Nutrient analysis does not include dipping sauce or salad.

Calories per serving: 300
Saturated fat: 2.5 g
Cholesterol: 100 mg

Total fat: 13.5 g
Polyunsaturated fat: 7.5 g
Sodium: 130 mg

Sweet-and-Sour Chicken Stir-Fry
(Kai Phat Priu Wan)

Phat means stir-fry and *priu wan* means sour-sweet. A sweet-and-sour stir-fry is everyday fare in Thailand. It derives from Chinese cookery, but the Thais have made it their own with the addition of cucumbers, chilies, and fish sauce. Tomato is often added, which gives the sauce a pink cast, and some cooks use fresh ginger root. In Thai restaurants, there are usually three or four choices of meat for a *phat priu wan*, so diners may have the dish prepared with either pork, beef, chicken, or shrimp. A whole fish with sweet-and-sour sauce is also commonly eaten in Thailand, as well as in Vietnam, and I have included a recipe for this dish in the Vietnamese chapter (p. 179). Chicken is used in the following recipe, although pork is the meat of choice in Thailand.

1–1½ tablespoons safflower oil
½ cup onion, coarsely chopped
2 large cloves garlic, minced
1 pound boned chicken meat, all skin and fat removed, cut into ½-inch cubes
2 medium green peppers, deribbed and cut into 1-inch squares
1–4 fresh chili peppers, seeded and sliced into thin strips, or crushed dried chilies, or cayenne pepper, to taste
1 cucumber, peeled lengthwise, leaving green strips for color, then quartered lengthwise and sliced into ¼-inch slices
2 small tomatoes, peeled and chopped into small pieces
3 tablespoons vinegar
3 tablespoons sugar, dissolved in a little water
1 teaspoon fish sauce (nam pla), or Vietnamese fish sauce (nuoc mam), or low-sodium soy sauce
1 teaspoon cornstarch, dissolved in 2 tablespoons water
2 tablespoons fresh coriander leaves, chopped for garnish

1.   Heat a wok or nonstick skillet over high heat. Add half the oil and, just before it begins to smoke, stir-fry onions and garlic until translucent.
2.   Add chicken pieces and stir-fry over high heat 1–2 minutes or until they change color. Remove from pan.
3.   Heat remaining oil and stir-fry green pepper 1 minute. Add chilies, cucumbers, and tomatoes and stir-fry 2–3 more minutes.

4. Mix vinegar, sugar, and fish sauce together. Add and stir until well blended. Return chicken and stir-fry 1 to 2 minutes or until heated through. Add 2 or 3 tablespoons of water if mixture becomes dry. Do not overcook.

5. Add cornstarch mixture and cook until sauce thickens slightly. Garnish with coriander leaves.

Yield: 4–6 servings

Cooking time: 5–8 minutes

Calories per serving: 320
Saturated fat: 2.5 g
Cholesterol: 100 mg

Total fat: 10 g
Polyunsaturated fat: 4.5 g
Sodium: 135 mg

Variations:

1. One pound pork, shrimp, or beef may be substituted for the chicken.

2. Or use a combination of one-half pound each of chicken and shrimp, or pork and shrimp. Stir-fry pork long enough before adding shrimp to be sure pork is sufficiently cooked through.

Salads and Vegetables
(*Yam* and *Phak*)

Salads
(*Yam*)

Thai salads, called *yam*, usually consist of cooked meat, fish, or shellfish decoratively arranged on a bed of raw vegetables. Most of these salads are easy to prepare and lend themselves to improvisation. The dressings vary, but they are usually hot, sour, and spicy. They may contain garlic, ginger root, onion, lemon juice, tamarind, bits of minced pork, fish sauce, and chilies. The garnishes may be chopped peanuts, fried onion or garlic flakes, as well as mint and coriander leaves. A *yam* is always eaten with rice, along with the other dishes in a meal. Some *yams* make excellent appetizers, and, if prepared in large enough quantities, they are substantial enough to be main dishes. They are very low in fat and cholesterol, and, if you use fish sauce and soy sauce sparingly, in sodium as well.

Shrimp Salad
(*Yam Kung*)

One and one-third pounds of shrimp will yield approximately 1 pound of edible meat. The shrimps will have more flavor if they are boiled in their shells. To avoid toughening they should be cooked only as long as it takes to make them turn pink. *Yam Kung* also makes a good appetizer.

1 ⅓ pounds green shrimp
2 slices of fresh ginger root
    (for stock)
2 portions of scallion, cut
    into 2-inch lengths (for
    stock)
 A bunch of watercress
    leaves, or lettuce leaves

1 small red onion, thinly sliced
    (optional)
3 scallions, cut into 2-inch
    lengths
Lime or lemon wedges

Dressing:

½ cup lime or lemon juice
1–2 teaspoons safflower oil
½–1 teaspoon fish sauce (nam
    pla), or Vietnamese fish
    sauce (nuoc mam), or
    low-sodium soy sauce
4 large cloves garlic, minced

1–4 fresh or dried red chili pep-
    pers, seeded and chopped,
    or cayenne pepper, to
    taste
3 tablespoons fresh coriander
    leaves, finely chopped

1. Bring a quart of water to a boil with a slice or two of fresh ginger and a chopped scallion. Add shrimp and cook 2–5 minutes, depending on their size, or until shrimp are pink. Cool, shell, and devein. Some cooks leave the tails on.

2. Combine dressing ingredients and mix with shrimp. Arrange on a bed of watercress (or lettuce), garnish with remaining vegetables, and serve with cucumber salad (*Yam Daengua*; p. 271).

Yield: 4–6 servings

Calories per serving: 180
Saturated fat: 0.5 g
Cholesterol: 120 mg

Cooking time: 5 minutes

Total fat: 2 g
Polyunsaturated fat: 1 g
Sodium: 210 mg

Squid Salad
(*Yam Pla Muk*)

The squid must be very fresh. You can tell by the color of the meat under the spotted skin, which ought to be an ivory white. Yellowing means the squid is old. Please read about squid in the ingredients section on p. xxv.

1 pound fresh squid (Yields about ⅔ pound edible meat)
1 tablespoon safflower oil
1 teaspoon fish sauce (nam pla), or Vietnamese fish sauce (nuoc mam), or low-sodium sauce

2 tablespoons rice wine, or pale dry sherry
1 small red onion, thinly sliced
Lettuce leaves
1 cucumber, thinly sliced
Coriander or mint leaves, for garnish

Dressing:

1 tablespoon ginger root, finely minced
3 large cloves garlic, finely minced
⅓ cup lime or lemon juice
1 teaspoon chili oil (p. 96)

3 tablespoons fresh coriander leaves, finely chopped
1–4 fresh or dried red chili peppers, seeded and chopped, or cayenne pepper, to taste

1.   Clean squid, discarding head, transparent quill, and everything inside body cavity. Rub off spotted skin. Reserve tentacles. Wash, drain, and cut into rings.

2.   Marinate squid rings for about five minutes (no longer) in fish sauce or soy sauce mixed with rice wine or pale dry sherry.

3.   Heat oil in a nonstick skillet or wok and saute squid for no longer than 2 or 3 minutes, as overcooking toughens it.

4.   Combine dressing ingredients and pour over squid. Mix well.

5.   In a shallow serving bowl, arrange cucumber and onion slices on lettuce leaves. Place squid mixture on top and garnish with coriander or mint sprigs.

Yield: 4–6 servings

Cooking time: 3 minutes

Calories per serving: 145
Saturated fat: 0.5 g
Cholesterol: 200 mg

Total fat: 6 g
Polyunsaturated fat: 4 g
Sodium: 145 mg

Chicken Salad with Lime and Ginger Dressing
(Yam Kai)

1 pound cooked chicken, boned
   and skinned with all fat removed, cut into small serving pieces
1 cucumber, sliced into thin
   rounds

2 tomatoes, quartered
1 onion, thinly sliced
   Lettuce leaves
   Coriander and mint leaves,
     for garnish

Lime and Ginger Dressing:

2 large cloves garlic,
   minced
2 tablespoons fresh ginger
   root, minced
1-4 fresh or dried chili peppers, seeded and finely
   chopped, or cayenne pepper, to taste
1/4–1/2 teaspoon freshly
   ground pepper
1/2–1 teaspoon sugar, dissolved
   in 2 tablespoons water

1/3 cup lime or lemon juice
1/2–1 teaspoon fish sauce (nam
   pla), or Vietnamese fish
   sauce (nuoc mam), or
   low-sodium soy sauce
1–2 teaspoons chili oil (p. 96)
3 tablespoons fresh coriander
   or mint leaves, finely
   chopped

1.   In a shallow serving bowl, place chicken pieces on top of lettuce, coriander, and mint leaves. Surround with cucumber and tomato slices.

2.   Combine dressing ingredients and pour over chicken. Garnish with chopped coriander or mint leaves.

Yield: 4 to 6 servings

Preparation time: 10 minutes

Calories per serving: 260
Saturated fat: 2 g
Cholesterol: 100 mg

Total fat: 7 g
Polyunsaturated fat: 1.5 g
Sodium: 135 mg

Variations:

1.   *Yam Nua* (Beef Salad): Substitute very lean roast beef sliced into thin 2-inch strips.

2.   *Yam Yai* means a large mixed salad. Arrange a combination of cooked chicken, beef, and shrimps on a platter and double the quantity of

dressing. Cooked snow peas, string beans, or other green vegetables may be included.

Galloping Horses
(Ma Ho)

A savory mixture of minced chicken and peanuts is piled on top of fresh orange segments. Serve this unusual dish as an appetizer or side dish. Chicken replaces pork in this recipe.

4 oranges, mandarin or navel,
    or tangerines, or fresh pine-
    apple
2 teaspoons safflower oil
1 large clove garlic, minced
2 tablespoons shallots or onions,
    finely chopped
2 ounces ground chicken, all
    skin and fat removed
2 tablespoons unsalted peanuts,
    finely chopped

½ teaspoon sugar
¼–½ teaspoon black pepper
¼ teaspoon fish sauce (nam
    pla), or Vietnamese fish
    sauce (nuoc mam), or
    low-sodium soy sauce
1–2 fresh red chili peppers,
    seeded and finely
    chopped, or cayenne
    pepper, to taste
Coriander or mint leaves,
    for garnish

1.   Peel and section oranges. Remove white pith and arrange segments decoratively on lettuce leaves. If using pineapple, cut into small serving slices.
2.   Heat oil and brown garlic and shallots.
3.   Add chicken, and stir-fry until well done.
4.   Stir in peanuts, sugar, pepper, fish sauce, and chili peppers and cook until well blended.
5.   Spread on top of orange sections and garnish with coriander leaves.

Yield: 4–6 servings

Cooking time: 5–10 minutes

Calories per serving: 150
Saturated fat: 1 g
Cholesterol: 15 mg

Total fat: 5.5 g
Polyunsaturated fat: 2.5 g
Sodium: 35 mg

Cucumber Salad
(*Yam Daengkwa*)

This salad is always served with curries because it provides a fresh crisp contrast to highly spiced dishes. Thin Japanese or English cucumbers are best, since they need not be peeled.

1 medium cucumber, cut in half lengthwise and very thinly sliced

½ small onion, cut in quarters and sliced in paper-thin slices

Dressing:

¼ cup lime or lemon juice, or white vinegar
¼ teaspoon fish sauce (nam pla), *or Vietnamese fish sauce* (nuoc mam), *or low-sodium soy sauce*

1 teaspoon sugar, or to taste
1–2 fresh or dried red chili peppers, seeded and chopped, or cayenne pepper, to taste

Combine the dressing ingredients and pour over cucumbers and onions. Toss and serve chilled.

Yield: 4–6 servings

Preparation time: 5 minutes

Calories per serving: 25
Saturated fat: 0 g
Cholesterol: 0 mg

Total fat: 0 g
Polyunsaturated fat: 0 g
Sodium: 25 mg

Cucumber Boats
(*Yam Nua Lae Daengkwa*)

This dish is suitable both as an appetizer and a side dish.

2 medium cucumbers,
     preferably English or
     Japanese
2 teaspoons safflower oil
1 cup onions, finely chopped
3 large cloves garlic, minced

2 ounces cooked chicken or roast
     beef, cut or shredded into
     thin strips
Lettuce leaves
Coriander or mint leaves,
     for garnish

Dressing:

3 tablespoons fresh mint leaves,
     finely chopped, or 1 table-
     spoon dried mint leaves
1/4 teaspoon fish sauce (nam pla),
     or Vietnamese fish sauce
     (nuoc mam), or low-sodium
     soy sauce
2 tablespoons lime or lemon
     juice, or to taste

1/4 teaspoon sugar
1/4–1/2 teaspoon black pepper
1–2 fresh or dried red chili
     peppers, seeded and
     chopped, or cayenne
     pepper, to taste

1.   Peel cucumbers lengthwise, leaving strips of green skin for color.
Cut in half crosswise and lengthwise. Scoop out seeds and pulp, forming
eight boats.
2.   Heat oil over high heat and brown onion and garlic until crisp.
Drain on paper towels.
3.   Combine dressing ingredients and stir until sugar dissolves. Add the
chicken, onion, and garlic and mix well.
4.   Fill the cucumber boats and arrange them on lettuce leaves. Garnish with coriander or mint leaves. Filled boats may be cut in half to make
16 appetizers.

Yield: 4–6 servings

Preparation time: 10 minutes

Calories per serving: 85
Saturated fat: 0.5 g
Cholesterol: 15 mg

Total fat: 3.5 g
Polyunsaturated fat: 2.5 g
Sodium: 40 mg

Vegetables
(*Phak*)

Thai cooks stir-fry vegetables in much the same way as Chinese cooks do. Please refer to pages 140–47 in the Chinese section for vegetable recipes to serve with Thai dishes and also to pages xxxiii–xxxiv for tips on stir-frying.

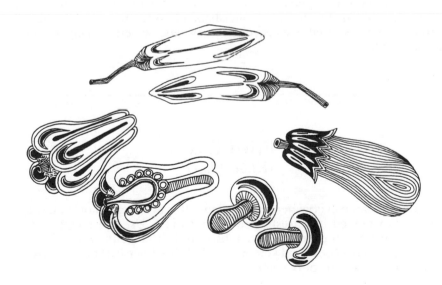

Rice and Noodles
(*Khao* and *Kuay-tiao*)

Boiled Rice
(*Khao*)

Thais prefer long grain rice and cook it without salt by the absorption method. The recipe in the Chinese section on page 148 is recommended. In the northeast, glutinous rice (sticky rice) is preferred. It is soaked for several hours and steamed in a cone-shaped basket. In central Thailand, glutinous rice is used exclusively for sweets, which usually contain coconut milk.

Fried Rice
(*Khao Phat*)

Fried rice is eaten everywhere in Thailand. It is even served on trains, appetizingly wrapped in a fresh green banana leaf. Use the recipe in the Chinese section on page 150 and substitute fish sauce (*nam pla*) for soy sauce. Some Thai cooks add ketchup to their fried rice (strange, but true), which gives it a faint pink color.

Stir-Fried Noodles
(*Phat Thai*)

Narrow, flat rice noodles are stir-fried with pork and shrimp, sometimes also with egg and soybean curd, and served with condiments for each diner to season to his own taste. An authentic *Phat Thai* would also contain a pickled, salted vegetable and salted dried shrimps; in addition, a bottle of fish sauce (*nam pla*) would be placed on the table as one of the garnishes. For the purposes of this book, all these are omitted, but it is still a very tasty dish.

8 ounces narrow (about ¼-inch wide) dried flat rice noodles, or 10 ounces fresh noodles

1 tablespoon safflower oil

3 large cloves garlic, minced

1–3 fresh or dried chili peppers, seeded and chopped

3 ounces chicken or very lean pork, cut into matchstick strips

3 ounces small fresh shrimp, shelled and deveined

1 teaspoon fish sauce (nam pla), or Vietnamese fish sauce (nuoc mam), or low-sodium soy sauce

1 teaspoon sugar

1 teaspoon rice vinegar

4 scallions, cut into 1-inch lengths

Condiments and garnishes:

2 limes, cut into wedges

2–4 tablespoons peanuts, chopped

1 cup fresh bean sprouts

Dried chili pepper flakes, or fresh shredded chili peppers

Fresh coriander leaves, chopped

1. Place condiments in separate small bowls and set aside

2. Soak dried noodles in warm water to soften 15 minutes and drain. Noodles should be almost tender and need only to be heated. For best results, be sure to consult cooking instructions on noodle package.

3. Heat a nonstick skillet or wok over high heat. Add oil and just before it begins to smoke stir-fry garlic, chilies and chicken for 1 minute. Add the shrimp and stir-fry ½ minute.

4. Mix in the fish sauce, sugar, and vinegar, and turn heat down to medium.

5. Add the noodles and stir-fry gently 1 minute or until heated through, keeping the noodles intact.

6. Stir in scallions. If noodles are not tender, add 2–3 tablespoons of water, cover and steam another minute or until done. Serve immediately on a large platter surrounded by the condiments.

Yield: 4 servings   Cooking time: 5 minutes

Nutrient analysis does not include condiments and garnishes.

Calories per serving: 182   Total fat: 6 g
Saturated fat: 1 g   Polyunsaturated fat: 4 g
Cholesterol: 45 mg   Sodium: 135 mg

India and Pakistan

◇      ◇

The Indian and Pakistani Kitchens

The small but distinctly separate minority of Indians and Pakistanis who have settled in Indonesia, Malaysia, Singapore, and Thailand have brought with them a rich and varied cuisine, some of which is made to order for a low-salt, low-fat diet. Most Westerners, when asked what food they associate with the Indian subcontinent, will say "curry," but will have little knowledge of the incredible variety of Indian foods and cooking styles. Not only does climate and geography determine this variety, but different religions impose food taboos that are strictly observed.

The majority of Indians are Hindu and therefore vegetarian. However, that does not always mean that all meat is forbidden. In India, being a vegetarian is endlessly variable. Some Hindus on the southwest coast eat fish, while Kashmiri Hindus exclude poultry and eggs but will partake of lamb and goat. The strictest vegetarian will eat no meat, but will also exclude eggs, onions, and garlic. Others will even exclude blood-colored vegetables such as tomatoes and beets.

Even root vegetables are forbidden to some, because the process of pulling them from the ground might cause the death of worms and grubs that live in the soil. Even with these seeming inconsistencies, if we think of vegetarianism as a cuisine that stresses the eating of vegetables, then it is from the south Indian states, which grow an abundance of vegetables and fruit, that an astonishing variety of vegetarian dishes has come. Perhaps the major contribution of religious vegetarianism is the evolution of the most imaginative and diverse vegetarian cuisine in the world, one that is guaranteed to convert the most dedicated meat eater. Unlike Chinese vegetarian cookery, which attempts to prepare a dish that will look, taste, and smell like meat, Indian vegetarian cooking concentrates on cooking vegetables so that they are appetizing and satisfying while manifestly retaining their identity.

A typical family vegetarian menu would include rice or bread, or both, *dal* (dried lentils or beans), two or more vegetable dishes, a yogurt salad (*raita*), and a chutney. A sweet dessert is optional, but fresh fruit is preferred. A non-vegetarian menu would substitute one or two meat, poultry, or fish dishes and include a rice dish. But there is no hard and fast rule, since one's economic circumstances and personal preferences must also be considered.

Each guest in an Indian meal is served on a separate round metal tray called a *thali*, on which are placed small metal bowls (*katori*) containing the various dishes for a meal. Rice or bread, which is the main part of the meal, is placed in the center of the tray. The dishes may also be served on a banana leaf, also referred to as a *thali*. The foods are placed directly on the leaf, making the use of small bowls unnecessary. Food is eaten with the fingers of the right hand only, not with those of the left, which is considered unclean. In cities, meals are served on plates and eaten with a dessert spoon and fork.

Adapting Indian and Pakistani Food to a Low-Sodium, Low-Cholesterol Diet

The following recipes have been chosen because they were most adaptable to the purposes of this book, while also being practical for Western cooks. The emphasis has been on vegetarian dishes that are not only exceptional in taste but also especially suitable for a diet low in fat and sodium. Deep-fried snacks, rich sweets, as well as elaborately rich meat and rice dishes have been left out. In every case, safflower oil and margarine have been substituted for coconut oil and ghee, a cooking medium similar to clarified butter.

All these dishes contain an enormous variety of seasonings and spices that should amply compensate for the omission of salt. Garlic, ginger root, and coriander leaves (Chinese parsley) are some of the fresh ingredients that give Indian foods their characteristic flavor. Spices are even more important and the section that follows tells in some detail about the various combinations used in curry powders and pastes. Some cooks will wish to experiment and use more or less of one seasoning or another or use a greater or lesser proportion of spices in any one dish. By all means do so, but I would caution against using too much turmeric. It adds more color than flavor and too much of it turns a dish into an unappetizingly intense yellow.

◊  ◊

Curry Powders and Pastes
(*Masalas*)

The importance and function of spices as preservative and seasoning agents, as well as for their purported medicinal properties, has been recognized from ancient times and is discussed in ancient Sanskrit writings. Spices have been used to combat various ailments from fevers and liver disorders to indigestion and halitosis. Today the emphasis is mostly on seasoning, although some legends remain about their benefits to health. Indians and Pakistanis use spices lavishly and cook with an amazing variety of them. The combinations—subtle or pungent, hot or mild—are limitless, and there is something to suit every palate.

North Indian and Pakistani cooks grind dry spices to make dry powders that can be stored for future use, whereas southern cooks use fresh spices and grind them with liquids such as lime juice, vinegar, or coconut milk to make "wet" *masalas* that cannot be stored. Sauces in northern dishes are allowed to cook away and the resulting dish is dry, whereas dishes from southern India are cooked with more liquid so there will be an abundance of sauce. This makes sense, since northern dishes are generally eaten with bread, while southern dishes are eaten mixed with rice.

As a result of the spice trade, over the centuries, Indian cooking styles, as well as culture and religions, found their way to Southeast Asia, and it is interesting to note that south Indian cookery has had the greatest impact on the cooking of the rice-eating countries of Indonesia, Malaysia, and Thailand. Indonesian and Malaysian cooks make "wet" *masalas* and Thais use curry pastes, but the ingredients and spice combinations have been so altered as to be quite distinct from their Indian sources.

Unfortunately, most Westerners are unaware of the enormous variety of spice combinations and mistakenly tend to lump them all under the term "curry," a word which comes from the Tamil *kari*, meaning "sauce." *Kari* implies a combination of seasonings in which meat or vegetables are cooked to produce a stew-like dish. In the West, and also in Japan, these seasonings have been reduced to a commerical product called "curry powder," which is usually mixed into a flour-thickened cream sauce that has no resemblance either in taste or fragrance to a fresh mixture of spices. No Indian cook would use such a mixture. Rather, individual spices are ground on a grinding stone and added to dishes in a variety of combinations and proportions depending on local custom and the inclination and artistry of the cook. These spices must be judiciously selected so that the final result is a smooth, subtle blend of tastes, neither raw nor strident.

Garam masala, which is a blend of spices, varies not only from region to region but also from cook to cook. Some use strong spices such as cumin and pepper; others use only fragrant spices such as cinnamon and cloves. Garam masala is usually added at the beginning of the cooking process, but a pinch is often sprinkled on the food in the final stage to add fresh aroma that may have been lost in long cooking. If spice cookery appeals to you, you owe it to yourself to create your own masalas. The few rules there are boil down to common sense. Strong spices such as cumin, turmeric, and coriander should not be used for sweets and should be cooked for a longer time to mellow any bitterness. Mild ones, such as cinnamon, nutmeg, and saffron, though used in sweets, may also be included in savory dishes. For those on a low-sodium diet, not enough can be said in praise of spices. Their aroma alone sparks the taste buds and the variety of combinations will be flavorful without the addition of a single grain of salt. The following masalas are just some possible combinations. Other combinations may stress a single spice with the addition of small quantities of others to complement it.

Ground Spice Mixture
(Garam Masala)

Roasting spices before grinding enhances their flavor. Preground spices may be used to save time, but they are not nearly as flavorful.

2 tablespoons coriander seeds	4 tablespoons cumin seeds
2 tablespoons whole cloves	2 3-inch cinnamon sticks
4 tablespoons cardamom pods	2 tablespoons whole black
(remove seeds from pods	peppercorns
after roasting)	1 whole nutmeg

In an oven preheated to 200°, roast spices (except the nutmeg) in a flat

pan for 20 to 30 minutes, stirring frequently. Remove and discard cardamom pods. Pulverize the mixture in a blender, pepper grinder, or mortar. Finely grate the nutmeg and mix in. Store in an air-tight container.

Note: The nutrient analysis is based on the estimate that most spices on the average contain 5 calories and 1 milligram of sodium per teaspoon.

Yield: About 1 cup

Calories per teaspoon: 5
Saturated fat: 0 g
Cholesterol: 0 mg

Preparation time: About 30 minutes

Total fat: 0 g
Polyunsaturated fat: 0 g
Sodium: 1 mg

Green Curry Paste
(*Dhania Masala*)

1 large clove garlic, minced
1 tablespoon fresh ginger root, minced
1 teaspoon ground coriander
½ teaspoon ground cloves
¼ teaspoon ground turmeric
¼ teaspoon black mustard seeds (optional)

¼ teaspoon cumin seeds
¼ cup firmly packed fresh coriander leaves
¼ cup firmly packed fresh mint leaves
½ teaspoon brown sugar
¼ cup lemon juice

Combine all the *masala* ingredients in an electric blender and pulverize into a paste. A teaspoon or two of water may be needed to keep the mass moving.

Yogurt Curry Paste
(*Dahi Masala*)

3 tablespoons hot water
⅔ cup plain low-fat yogurt
¼ cup lemon juice
1 cup onions, chopped
1 tablespoon fresh ginger root,
  minced
4 large cloves garlic, minced
1 teaspoon paprika

⅛–¼ teaspoon cayenne
  pepper (optional)
3 teaspoons garam masala
  (p. 282), or 1 teaspoon
  ground cumin and ½
  teaspoon each ground
  coriander, nutmeg, cin-
  namon, and cloves

Combine all the *masala* ingredients in an electric blender and pulverize into a paste. A teaspoon or two of water may be needed to keep the mass moving.

◊  ◊

Vegetarian Dishes
(*Shakahari*)

Indians like most of their vegetables cooked very soft in a spicy stew-like gravy. This means that by Chinese and Japanese standards, no matter how delicious the result, the vegetable is overcooked. I tend to prefer vegetables to retain their natural color for aesthetic and health reasons, and that can only be accomplished with short cooking. So in most of these dishes I have recommended no more than 5–10 minutes cooking time. Indian cooks would more likely simmer them up to 40 minutes to ensure that the spices completely penetrate the vegetable. Try it both ways and decide which is best for you.

Spiced Green Beans
(*Sem ki Phali*)

A quick, delicious way to cook string beans or long beans is to just stir-fry them in spices until they are tender but very crisp.

1 pound string beans
  (approximately 4 cups)
1 tablespoon safflower oil
¼ teaspoon ground turmeric

1–2 teaspoons garam masala
  (p. 282), or ⅓ teaspoon
  each *ground coriander,*
  cumin, and black pepper
1 tablespoon lemon juice

1.   Wash and dry beans. Then trim and cut them into 1½-inch lengths.
2.   Heat oil in a nonstick pan and add spices. Stir for 30 seconds.
3.   Add beans and stir-fry over high heat about 5 minutes or until they are tender. Add lemon juice. If necessary, cover pan for half a minute to steam, but stir-fry them again to regain crispness. Serve immediately.

Yield: 4–6 servings

Cooking time: 5–10 minutes

Calories per serving: 65
Saturated fat: 0.5 g
Cholesterol: 0 mg

Total fat: 4 g
Polyunsaturated fat: 3 g
Sodium: 5 mg

Cauliflower and Tomatoes
(*Phool Gobhi aur Tamatar*)

Almost any non-leafy vegetable can be cooked with a light spicing either alone or paired with another vegetable. The usual method is to fry the onions with the garlic and ginger, then add the spices and finally the vegetable. Tomatoes add flavor and necessary moisture to cook the vegetable to the desired tenderness. Some cooks add a little yogurt and lemon juice. Other vegetables that may be substituted for the combination in this recipe are green peas and mushrooms; zucchini, eggplant, and tomatoes; broccoli and cauliflower flowerets; and okra and tomatoes. Another favorite, though it is a bit drier in texture, is the northern dish called *Aloo Gobhi*, which is made of cauliflower and potatoes.

1 tablespoon safflower oil
½ cup onions, finely chopped
1 tablespoon fresh ginger
    root, minced
2 large cloves garlic, minced
½ teaspoon mustard seeds
¼ teaspoon turmeric
1–2 teaspoons garam masala
    (p. 282), or ⅓ teaspoon
    each ground cumin, cor-
    iander, and black pepper

1–2 fresh or dried chili peppers,
    seeded and chopped, or
    cayenne pepper, to taste
1 small head cauliflower,
    divided into small
    flowerets
1 large ripe tomato, coarsely
    chopped
1–2 tablespoons lemon juice
    Fresh coriander leaves,
    chopped, for garnish

1.   Heat oil in a large nonstick skillet and saute onions, ginger root, and garlic until soft.

2.   Add the spices and peppers and cook for 3 or 4 minutes, stirring constantly.

3.   Add the cauliflower and stir and turn the flowerets until they are evenly coated with the onion mixture.

4.   Stir in the tomato, reduce the heat, and cook 3 to 5 minutes or until the cauliflower is tender but not mushy. Add lemon juice.

5.   Garnish with chopped coriander leaves.

Yield: 4–6 servings

Cooking time: 10 minutes

Calories per serving: 80
Saturated fat: 0.5 g
Cholesterol: 0 mg

Total fat: 4 g
Polyunsaturated fat: 3 g
Sodium: 15 mg

Spiced Cabbage
(*Patta Gobhi*)

1 tablespoon safflower oil
1 large onion, thinly sliced
2 large cloves garlic, minced
1 tablespoon fresh ginger
    root, minced
1/2 teaspoon each ground
    cumin, coriander, and
    turmeric
1/8–1/2 teaspoon ground cayenne
    pepper (optional)
1 small head cabbage,
    coarsely shredded (about
    8 cups)
1–2 tablespoons lemon juice
    Pinch of garam masala (p. 282)

1.   Heat oil in a nonstick pan and saute the onions, garlic, and ginger until soft.

2.   Add the spices and cook for 3 or 4 minutes, stirring constantly.

3.   Add the cabbage, and stir and toss until cabbage is evenly coated with the spices. Cook, stirring frequently, for 4 or 5 minutes or until wilted. Add 1 or 2 tablespoons water if necessary to steam cabbage to desired tenderness. Add lemon juice.

4.   Sprinkle *garam masala* on top.

Yield: 4–6 servings　　　　　Cooking time: 10 minutes

Calories per serving: 70　　　Total fat: 2.5 g
Saturated fat: 0.5 g　　　　　Polyunsaturated fat: 2.5 g
Cholesterol: 0 mg　　　　　　Sodium: 25 mg

Variation:　A pound and a half of trimmed and washed spinach may be substituted for the cabbage if you wish to try the tasty *Palak Gobhi.*

Spiced Eggplant Puree
(*Baigan Bartha*)

This dish, which is absolutely delicious when eaten hot with freshly made *nan* (p. 315) or *chapathis* (p. 316), also makes a good appetizer served chilled with unsalted crackers or French bread.

1 large eggplant (about 1½ pounds)
1 teaspoon safflower oil
½ cup onions, finely chopped
1 large clove garlic, minced
1 tablespoon fresh ginger root, minced
½ teaspoon ground turmeric
2 teaspoons ground cumin
1 tablespoon ground coriander
1 teaspoon ground cinnamon (optional)

1–2 fresh or dried chili peppers, seeded and chopped, or cayenne pepper to taste (optional)
3 medium fresh ripe tomatoes, coarsely chopped
2–3 tablespoons lemon juice
½ cup plain low-fat yogurt
Lemon wedges
3 tablespoons fresh coriander leaves, finely chopped

1.　Wash eggplant and cut several ½-inch gashes in the skin. Place in a shallow baking dish and bake in a preheated oven (400°) for 45 minutes to 1 hour, or until eggplant is very soft and falling apart.
2.　With a spoon scrape the pulp away from the skin. Discard the skin and mash the pulp with a fork. Set aside.
3.　In a nonstick pan, heat oil and saute onions, garlic, and ginger root until soft. Add spices and cook over low heat for 4 or 5 minutes, stirring constantly.
4.　Stir in tomatoes and cook 5 minutes.
5.　Add the eggplant, lemon juice, yogurt, and half the fresh coriander leaves. Cook until the mixture thickens and most of the liquid evaporates.

6.   Serve hot, garnished with remaining coriander leaves and lemon wedges. May also be served chilled.

Yield: 4–6 servings

Cooking time: 1 hour

Calories per serving: 90
Saturated fat: 0.5 g
Cholesterol: 5 mg

Total fat: 2.5 g
Polyunsaturated fat: 1 g
Sodium: 20 mg

Spiced Potatoes and Peas
(*Aloo Mattar*)

The proportion of potatoes to green peas in this dish is variable, as I learned from an international potluck supper I attended in Berkeley. By coincidence this dish was brought by two different people from India. One was a potato dish with a few peas thrown in for color, while the other was mostly a pea dish with a few chunks of potatoes.

1 tablespoon safflower
    margarine, or oil
½ cup onions, finely chopped
1 large clove garlic, minced
1 tablespoon fresh ginger
    root, minced
½ teaspoon ground turmeric
⅛–¼ teaspoon cayenne
    pepper (optional)
1½ teaspoons garam masala
    (p. 282), or ½ teaspoon
    each ground coriander,
    cumin, and black pepper

2 ripe tomatoes, coarsely
    chopped
3 or 4 small new potatoes,
    peeled and cut into ½-
    inch cubes
¼–½ cup hot water
1 cup shelled fresh green
    peas; frozen peas may be
    substituted
3 tablespoons fresh
    coriander or mint
    leaves, chopped

1.   In a medium saucepan, heat margarine and saute the onions, garlic, and ginger root until soft and golden.
2.   Add the spices and cook for 2 or 3 minutes, stirring constantly.
3.   Add tomatoes and half the coriander leaves and cook 4 or 5 minutes.
4.   Add the potatoes and cook a minute or so, stirring constantly.

5. Add the water, cover, and cook over low heat for 10–15 minutes or until potatoes are tender.

6. Add the peas and cook 2 or 3 minutes. Some cooks prefer longer cooking to intensify flavor. Sprinkle with a pinch of garam masala, if desired, and garnish with remaining coriander leaves.

Yield: 4–6 servings

Cooking time: 30 minutes

Calories per serving: 135
Saturated fat: 0.5 g
Cholesterol: 0 mg

Total fat: 4 g
Polyunsaturated fat: 3 g
Sodium: 10 mg

Variation: Add ½ cup plain low-fat yogurt after step 5.

Mixed Spiced Vegetables
(*Sabji Bhaji*)

This appetizing, intriguingly spiced vegetable dish, when paired with Lentil and Rice Kedgeree (p. 295), is an excellent vegetarian meal, filling as well as nutritious. Served with yogurt, it provides all the nutrients necessary for a complete meal.

2 tablespoons safflower oil
3 large cloves garlic, minced
½ teaspoon each *black mustard seeds, cumin seeds, and coriander seeds*
¼ teaspoon each *fenugreek seeds and fennel seeds (If seeds are not available, substitute ground spices.)*
½ teaspoon ground turmeric
1–2 fresh or dried chili peppers, chopped, or to taste

1 cup onions, thinly sliced
¼ cup water
1 cup each carrots, turnips, green beans, and bell peppers cut into small bite-sized pieces (Other vegetables in season may also be added or substituted.)
2 tomatoes, coarsely chopped
Fresh coriander or mint leaves, chopped, for garnish

1. In a large nonstick pan or skillet, heat oil and cook the garlic, spices, and pepper together for a few seconds, stirring constantly.

2. Add the onions and saute lightly until soft. Stir in ¼ cup water.

3. Add the vegetables one by one, the longest cooking vegetable

first—in this case, the carrots—and turn them about until they are well coated with the mixture. Cover and cook to the desired tenderness, 10 to 15 minutes.

4.   Garnish with chopped coriander leaves and serve with Lentil and Rica Kedgeree (p. 295) if desired.

Yield: 6 servings

Cooking time: 25 minutes

Calories per serving: 90
Saturated fat: 0.5 g
Cholesterol: 0 g

Total fat: 5.5 g
Polyunsaturated fat: 4 g
Sodium: 25 mg

Spiced Stewed Tomatoes
(*Tamatar Cobhi*)

1 tablespoon safflower oil
2 large cloves garlic, minced
½ cup onions, thinly sliced
2 teaspoons ground coriander
½ teaspoon ground turmeric
2-inch stick cinnamon
   Pinch of cayenne pepper
   (optional)

8 medium tomatoes, cut into
   eighths
½ tablespoon sugar
1 tablespoon vinegar
   Fresh coriander or mint
   leaves, chopped, for garnish

1.   In a medium saucepan, heat oil and saute garlic and onion until soft.

2.   Add spices and cook 2 minutes, stirring constantly.

3.   Add tomatoes, sugar, and vinegar. Bring to a boil. Turn heat down and simmer 10 to 15 minutes. If mixture seems dry, add a tablespoon or two of water. Garnish with coriander leaves.

Yield: 4–6 servings

Cooking time: 20 minutes

Calories per serving: 120
Saturated fat: 0.5 g
Cholesterol: 0 mg

Total fat: 4.5 g
Polyunsaturated fat: 3 g
Sodium: 15 mg

◇  ◇

Legumes: Dried Peas, Beans, and Lentils
(Dal)

Dal is the Hindi name for all members of the legume or pulse family, which includes an astonishing variety of lentils, peas, and beans that are prepared into savory soup-like dishes. Most Indians are Hindus and cannot eat beef for religious reasons. Members of the higher castes are strict vegetarians who exclude meat, fish, and fowl, as well as eggs, and sometimes even dairy products, from their diet. For them, *dals* are the primary source of protein. Even in non-vegetarian families, a *dal* is eaten at most meals. All dried (though not fresh) peas, beans, and lentils are the richest source of vegetable protein and provide almost as complete a protein as animal foods do. Soybeans and foods made from soybeans such as bean curd (tofu) contain protein that most closely resembles animal protein, making them excellent substitutes for meat. It is important to note that the amino-acid balance of legumes can be improved by eating them with rice, corn, or any grain or cereal food. That's what Indians do, as well as Mexicans and other Latin Americans. Though some varieties of Indian legumes are obtainable only at Oriental food markets, most of the common dried peas, beans, and lentils available in any supermarket may be successfully substituted in these recipes. *Dals* are simple to prepare, although some beans must be soaked for several hours before cooking. Each region of India cooks *dal* in a different way—some with vegetables; some sweet-and-sour, with jaggery (a form of molasses) and tamarind; some very spicy; and others very mild. The usual procedure is to soak and cook the beans and then combine them with onions that have been previously sauteed with spices. Garlic and ginger root may also be added to the spices. The consistency varies, but it should be thicker than a thick pea soup.

Lentil Puree
(Dal)

Almost any kind of lentil may be cooked this way with minor variations. The common brown lentil, the salmon-colored lentil (*masur dal*), or the yellow mung bean (*mung dal*) are short-cooking legumes and require no soaking. Generally speaking, Indians from south India prefer *dals* to be thin because they eat them with rice, whereas Indians from north India like them thick, since they eat them with bread.

1 ½ cups lentils (about ½ pound)
4 cups water
1–2 bay leaves
2-inch cinnamon stick
½ teaspoon ground turmeric
⅛–¼ teaspoon cayenne pepper
1 teaspoon safflower oil

1 cup onions, thinly sliced
2 large cloves garlic, minced
1 tablespoon fresh ginger root, minced
1 teaspoon ground cumin
1 teaspoon lemon juice
2 tablespoons fresh coriander leaves, chopped, and lemon wedges, for garnish

1.   Wash the lentils, discarding those that float to the surface as well as any foreign matter.
2.   Add water, bay leaves, cinnamon stick, tumeric, and pepper, and bring to a boil over high heat. Turn heat down to low, and cook until lentils are tender but still intact, about 20–30 minutes. Taste for doneness after 20 minutes and add more water if necessary. When done, lentils should have a consistency thicker than a thick soup.
3.   In a nonstick skillet, heat oil and saute onions, garlic, ginger, and cumin, stirring constantly until the onions are soft and golden.
4.   When the lentils are done, add the onion mixture and lemon juice and simmer over low heat 2 or 3 minutes, stirring constantly. Taste for seasoning and add more pepper and lemon juice if desired.
5.   Garnish with chopped coriander leaves and lemon wedges and serve with rice or *chapathis*.

Yield: 4–6 servings

Cooking time: 45 minutes

Calories per serving: 240
Saturated fat: 0.5 g
Cholesterol: 0 mg

Total fat: 2 g
Polyunsaturated fat: 1 g
Sodium: 15 mg

Spiced Chickpeas
(Chana Masala)

Chickpeas (*chana dal*), red kidney beans (*rajma dal*), black-eyed peas (*lobhia dal*), or any other legume may be used for this dish. Dried beans should be soaked overnight before they are cooked, but the low-sodium canned beans save a lot of time and substitute very well. If the low-sodium brands are not available in your market, rinsing the beans in water for 3 minutes will eliminate much of the salt.

1 cup chickpeas, or other dried beans, or two 15-ounce cans cooked beans
1 tablespoon safflower oil
1 cup onions, finely chopped
2 large cloves garlic, minced
1 tablespoon fresh ginger root, minced
½ teaspoon turmeric
1½–2 teaspoons garam masala (p. 282), or ½ teaspoon each ground cumin, coriander, and black pepper

Fresh or dried chili pepper, chopped, or cayenne pepper, to taste
1 tomato, coarsely chopped
2–4 tablespoons lemon or lime juice
½ cup fresh coriander or mint leaves, chopped
Lemon wedges, for garnish

1.   If using dried beans, wash them thoroughly and soak overnight in 1 ½ quarts of water. Boil with enough water to cover and cook until tender. Add more water if necessary. Depending on the age of the beans, the time to cook them will vary from 30 minutes to 1 hour. When done, take off heat and drain, reserving liquor.

If using low-sodium canned beans, heat them in the water in which they are packed. Otherwise, drain and rinse beans in cold water for 3 minutes to rid them of salt.

2.   Heat oil in a large saucepan, and saute onions, garlic, and ginger root until soft and golden.

3.   Add spices and cook 2 or 3 minutes, stirring constantly. Add tomatoes and cook over moderate heat for 5 minutes. Stir to keep from sticking.

4.   Add some of the cooking liquid from the beans and half the coriander leaves, and simmer 10 minutes.

5.   Stir in the drained beans and lemon juice and cook until heated through. Taste for seasoning and add more pepper and lemon juice if desired. Mixture should be thick, but how thick depends on individual

preference. Some Indians prepare it so that it remains quite soupy; others prefer a dry dish in which the beans have soaked up most of the liquid. Serve in a soup bowl garnished with remaining coriander leaves and lemon wedges.

Yield: 6 servings

Cooking time: Dried beans,
1 hour
Canned beans,
20 minutes

Calories per serving: 215
Saturated fat: 0.5 g
Cholesterol: 0 mg

Total fat: 2 g
Polyunsaturated fat: 1 g
Sodium: 15 mg

Lentil and Rice Kedgeree
(*Khitcherie*)

What is a kedgeree? According to the Oxford English Dictionary, it is an Anglo-Indian word. "Kedgeree, kitchery, khicheri; a mess of rice cooked with butter and *dal* and flavoured with a little spice, shredded onion and the like; a common dish all over India." I believe lentils and rice are an ancient food combination; they are even thought to have been the dish referred to in the Bible as "Esau's pottage." It is certainly a well-known dish in the Middle East. Whatever you call it, the fact is that this hearty dish is very nutritious. It can be prepared with more liquid so that it has the consistency of a thick soup, or with just enough liquid to produce a dry, fluffy result to be paired with spicy, vegetable dishes in a vegetarian meal.

3/4 cup red, yellow, or brown,
  short-cooking lentils
3/4 cup long grain rice
2 tablespoons safflower oil, or
  unsalted margarine
3 cups onions, finely chopped
2 teaspoons garam masala
  (p. 282), or 1/2 teaspoon
  each coriander, cumin, and
  black pepper
2-inch cinnamon stick

4 whole cloves
2 cardamom pods
1/2 teaspoon cumin seeds
6 whole peppercorns
2 or 3 bay leaves
1/2–1 teaspoon turmeric
  Cayenne pepper, to taste
2 1/2–4 cups hot water
  Fresh mint or coriander
  leaves, chopped, for
  garnish

1.   Wash lentils, discarding those that float to the surface as well as any foreign matter.

2.   In a soup kettle, heat oil and saute onions until soft and golden brown. Remove half the onions and reserve for garnish.

3.   Stir in spices and cook for a minute or so.

4.   Add rice and lentils to pan and cook for 4 or 5 minutes, stirring constantly.

5.   Add hot water and bring to a boil. Cover and simmer over low heat for 20 to 25 minutes, or until rice and lentils are tender. Be careful not to let mixture stick to the pan.

6.   Serve garnished with reserved browned onions and chopped mint leaves. Good served with plain yogurt or a *raita*.

Yield: 4–6 servings

Cooking time: 35–45 minutes

Calories per serving: 360
Saturated fat: 1 g
Cholesterol: 0 mg

Total fat: 7.5 g
Polyunsaturated fat: 6 g
Sodium: 20 mg

Split Pea and Vegetable Soup
(*Sambhar*)

This is a lemony, spicy, south Indian vegetarian dish somewhere between a soup and stew. The protein-rich dried peas and the variety of fresh vegetables make this a complete meal.

1½ *cup yellow split peas (about*
   ½ *pound)*
2 *or 3 bay leaves*
⅓ *cup tamarind water (p. xxxii),*
   or lemon juice
2 *tablespoons safflower oil*
½ *small eggplant*
1 *green pepper*
1 *carrot*
1 *cup green beans*
1 *small onion*
1 *large tomato*
6 *whole cloves*

½ *teaspoon black mustard*
   seeds
2 *tablespoons ground*
   coriander
2 *teaspoons ground cumin*
½ *teaspoon turmeric*
1 *teaspoon black pepper*
1–2 *fresh or dried chili peppers,*
   chopped, or cayenne pep-
   per, to taste
½ *cup fresh coriander or mint*
   leaves, chopped, and
   lemon wedges, for garnish

1.   Wash dried peas thoroughly, removing any foreign matter and, if possible, soak them for an hour before cooking in 8 cups water.

2.   Add tamarind water and bring to a boil. (If tamarind pulp is not available, leave it out and add lemon juice at end.) Reduce heat and cook until peas are tender but not mushy, 30 minutes to 1 hour, depending on age of peas.

3.   Chop eggplant, green pepper, carrot, green beans, and onion into small pieces and set aside. Chop tomato and keep separate.

4.   In a nonstick pan, heat oil and saute spices for a minute or so.

5.   Add vegetables and saute until well coated with spices. Add tomato and continue to stir for 1 or 2 minutes.

6.   Add vegetable-and-spice mixture to peas. Simmer uncovered for 10–15 minutes, or until vegetables are tender. Add lemon juice to taste. Garnish with coriander leaves and lemon wedges. Serve with *nan* (p. 315) or *chapathis* (p. 316), if desired.

Yield: 4–6 servings

Cooking time: 1 hour 15
                     minutes

Calories per serving: 340
Saturated fat: 0.5 g
Cholesterol: 0 g

Total fat: 5.5 g
Polyunsaturated fat: 4 g
Sodium: 25 mg

◊  ◊

Yogurt Dishes
(Raita)

Raita, which is a chilled combination of yogurt and chopped vegetables or fruit, may be served as an accompaniment to every Indian meal. Like a salad, it provides a refreshingly cool contrast to highly seasoned dishes. In general, south Indian cooks tend to season *raitas* more than north Indian or Pakistani cooks. The seasonings may include garlic, toasted black mustard seeds, fenugreek seeds, fresh ginger, and chilies. A fruit *raita* usually has grated coconut added to it, especially if it is meant to be eaten in lieu of dessert.

Yogurt with Cucumbers
(Kheera ka Raita)

1 *medium cucumber*	2 *cups plain low-fat yogurt*
1 *teaspoon ground cumin or*	2 *tablespoons fresh coriander or*
cumin seeds	*mint leaves, finely chopped*
1 *large clove garlic, minced*	*Cayenne pepper to taste*

1. Peel and seed cucumber. Cut lengthwise into ¼-inch strips, then into thin slices crosswise, and set aside for a few minutes. Drain off moisture.

2. Toast cumin seeds for a few seconds in a dry frying pan.

3. Stir yogurt briskly until it is smooth and mix it with cumin, garlic,

coriander leaves, and pepper. Combine mixture with cucumbers and chill before serving.

Yield: 4–6 servings

Preparation time: 5 minutes

Calories per serving: 75
Saturated fat: 1.5 g
Cholesterol: 10 mg

Total fat: 2 g
Polyunsaturated fat: 0.5 g
Sodium: 55 mg

Variation:

1. A tomato cut into small pieces may be included with the cucumbers.
2. My own variation, which makes a delicious soup or side dish, is to thin the yogurt with a little milk, then add minced garlic, sliced cucumber, fresh seedless grapes, and walnuts. Garnish with fresh mint leaves and serve chilled.

Yogurt with Eggplant
(Baigan ka Raita)

1 large eggplant, about 1 ½
   pounds
1 teaspoon safflower oil
1 large clove garlic, minced
¼ cup onions, finely
   chopped
1 tablespoon fresh ginger
   root, chopped
½–1 teaspoon ground cumin
1 ½–2 teaspoons ground
   coriander

¼ teaspoon ground turmeric
⅛–¼ teaspoon cayenne
   pepper (optional)
2 tablespoons fresh
   coriander or mint
   leaves, finely chopped
1 ½ cups plain low-fat yogurt
1 tablespoon lemon juice

1. Wash eggplant and cut several ½-inch gashes in the skin. Place in a shallow baking dish and bake in a pre-heated oven (400°) for 45 minutes to 1 hour or until it is soft and falling apart. Scrape pulp away from skin and mash with a fork.
2. Heat oil and saute garlic, onions, and ginger root until soft and lightly browned. Add spices and cook for 5 minutes.

3.   In a large bowl combine eggplant, onion mixture, coriander leaves, yogurt, and lemon juice and mix thoroughly. Chill before serving.

Yield: 4–6 servings   Cooking time: 1 hour

Calories per serving: 90   Total fat: 2.5 g
Saturated fat: 1 g   Polyunsaturated fat: 1 g
Cholesterol: 5 mg   Sodium: 45 mg

Yogurt with Spinach
(Palak ka Raita)

1 pound (about 6 cups) fresh
    spinach, washed, trimmed,
    and finely chopped
1 teaspoon cumin seeds
1 teaspoon safflower oil
½ cup onions, finely chopped
1 large clove garlic, minced
¼ teaspoon black mustard seeds
    (optional)

¼ teaspoon freshly ground
    black pepper
Dash of cayenne pepper
1½ cups plain low-fat yogurt
2 tablespoons lemon juice

1.   Toast cumin seeds in a dry frying pan until brown.
2.   In a large saucepan, heat oil and cook onions and garlic until soft. Add spices and cook a minute or so, stirring constantly.
3.   Add chopped spinach and toss and turn until spinach wilts. Cover for a few seconds to steam. Spinach should be fully cooked but remain a bright green color. Remove from heat and cool.
4.   Combine yogurt and lemon juice and mix with cooled spinach. Chill before serving.

Yield: 4–6 servings   Cooking time: 10 minutes

Calories per serving: 100   Total fat: 3 g
Saturated fat: 1 g   Polyunsaturated fat: 1 g
Cholesterol: 5 mg   Sodium: 80 mg

Yogurt with Bananas
(*Kelay ka Raita*)

2 ripe but firm bananas
1½ cups plain low-fat yogurt
2 tablespoons lemon juice
2 tablespoons freshly grated or packaged coconut (optional)

½ teaspoon cumin seeds
¼ teaspoon black mustard seeds (optional)
1 tablespoon fresh mint leaves, chopped

1. Peel bananas and slice into ¼ inch rounds.
2. In a serving bowl combine yogurt, lemon juice, and coconut. Add sliced bananas.
3. Heat a small skillet and toast cumin and mustard seeds lightly for 2 or 3 minutes. Mix into banana and yogurt mixture.
4. Garnish with mint leaves.

Yield: 4 servings

Cooking time: 3 minutes

Calories per serving: 120
Saturated fat: 2 g
Cholesterol: 5 mg

Total fat: 2.5 g
Polyunsaturated fat: 0.5 g
Sodium: 45 mg

Variation: Sliced peaches, pears, or orange sections may be substituted for the bananas. Sliced mangoes and papayas are more authentic and are scrumptious.

◊  ◊

Non-Vegetarian Dishes
(Masahari)

Baked Fish Fillets with Green Masala
(Machli Dhania Patta)

The fresh-tasting, zesty spice mixture of green *masala* is lovely on fish. Though it contains a large number of ingredients, it's not difficult to put together even for an everyday meal.

1 pound firm fish fillets
1 tablespoon safflower oil
1 cup onions, finely chopped
1 recipe of green masala *(p. 283)*

1 small tomato, finely chopped
Fresh coriander or mint
* leaves, and lemon wedges,*
* for garnish*

1.   Heat oil and saute onions until soft and golden. Add *masala* and cook for 8 to 10 minutes, stirring constantly. Add tomato and cook for 1 more minute.

2.   In a lightly greased baking dish, spread spice mixture on fish fillets and bake in a 350°F oven for 15 to 20 minutes, or until fish is tender. Fish may also be cooked on top of the stove in a skillet with a tight lid. Do not overcook.

3.   Garnish with fresh coriander or mint leaves and lemon wedges.

Yield: 4 servings

Cooking time: 30 minutes

Calories per serving: 175
Saturated fat: 0.5 g
Cholesterol: 60 mg

Total fat: 5 g
Polyunsaturated fat: 3.5 g
Sodium: 85 mg

Variation: You may also prepare a whole fish by stuffing it with half the *masala* and then spreading the remaining half on top of it. Place in a lightly greased baking dish and bake 20 to 30 minutes or until tender.

Barbecued Chicken with Yogurt Masala
(*Tandoori Murg*)

Tandoori chicken, which takes its name from the clay oven in which it is cooked, may be successfully duplicated in an ordinary outdoor barbecue or kitchen oven. The chicken is marinated in a lemony mixture of spices and yogurt and then roasted until it is brown and crispy. The recipe is simplicity itself and can't fail to delight.

2½–3 pound chicken cut into
  serving pieces, skin and
  fat removed

Onion, tomato, and lemon
  slices for garnish
1 recipe yogurt masala (*p. 284*)

1. Make small deep cuts into the chicken to ensure penetration of the marinade.
2. Coat chicken evenly with the *masala* and marinate for at least 2 hours, or overnight if stronger flavor is desired. Remove the chicken from the refrigerator an hour before cooking.
3. Cook the pieces on both sides on a moderately hot charcoal fire, under the broiler, or in a lightly oiled baking dish in the oven, until they are evenly browned and crispy.
4. Arrange the chicken on a bed of thinly sliced onions, tomatoes, and lemons and serve with rice and a *raita*.

Yield: 4–6 servings

Cooking time: 40 minutes

Calories per serving: 270
Saturated fat: 2.5 g
Cholesterol: 100 mg

Total fat: 7 g
Polyunsaturated fat: 1.5 g
Sodium: 110 mg

Variation: Cubes of lean lamb, preferably from the leg, or firm-fleshed fish, either whole or in cubes, may be marinated and cooked as above. If desired, cubes may be placed on skewers.

Chicken with Spices
(Murg Masala)

For stronger flavor, marinate the chicken for 2 or 3 hours.

One 2½–3 pound chicken,
  cut into serving pieces,
  skin and fat removed
1 tablespoon safflower oil
½ cup onions, finely chopped
2 large cloves garlic, minced
1 tablespoon fresh ginger
  root, minced
3–4 teaspoons garam masala,
  (p. 282), or 1 teaspoon
  ground cumin and ½ teaspoon each ground cor-
  iander, cardamon, cin-
  namon, and black pepper

2 bay leaves
1 or 2 chopped fresh or dried
  chili peppers, or cayenne
  pepper, to taste
½ teaspoon turmeric
2 medium tomatoes, coarsely
  chopped
½ cup plain low-fat yogurt
2 tablespoons raisins (optional)
2 tablespoons lemon or lime
  juice

1.   In a heavy nonstick saucepan, heat oil and saute onion, garlic, and ginger root until soft.
2.   Add *garam masala*, bay leaves, chili peppers, and tumeric, and stir gently over medium heat for 2 or 3 minutes.
3.   Stir in tomatoes and cook another 2 or 3 minutes.
4.   Add chicken and cook 4 or 5 minutes, turning in pan to coat evenly with spice mixture.
5.   Stir in yogurt and raisins. Bring to a simmer and turn heat down to low. Cover and cook about 30 minutes or until chicken is tender. Stir in lemon juice. Turn chicken from time to time so it cooks on both sides. Serve with a *raita* and two or more accompaniments to curry (pp. 309–10).

Yield: 4–6 servings

Cooking time: 45 minutes

Calories per serving: 310
Saturated fat: 3 g
Cholesterol: 100 mg

Total fat: 10 g
Polyunsaturated fat: 4.5 g
Sodium: 110 mg

Maharaja Chicken Biryani
(*Murg Moghlai Biryani*)

This recipe is a sort of cross between a *biryani* and a *pulao*. A *biryani* is the most elaborate of the rice dishes. It is usually a rich, high-caloried preparation of Moghul origin made with chicken or lamb. Besides spiced meat, vegetables, nuts, and two *masalas*, it is made with large amounts of *ghee* (clarified butter) and saffron, garnished with fresh mint and coriander leaves, and then decorated with silver leaf. There are many different versions and a great variety of combinations of ingredients, and an elaborate *biryani* is usually served only on special occasions. The recipe that follows is not nearly as rich or as highly seasoned as an authentic *biryani* would be. It was given to me by Ms. Naheed Aftab of Pakistan, who brought the dish to an international pot-luck supper in Berkeley. Besides using salt, the difference between her recipe and mine is that she used nearly twice as much rice and a lot more oil, and she did not remove the skin and fat from the chicken before cooking it. To help compensate for the omission of salt, I have increased the amount of garlic and ginger root. I used *basmati* rice and washed it as she instructed. Other long-grain rice need not be washed.

> One *2½–3 pound chicken,*
> *cut into small serving*
> *pieces, all skin and fat*
> *removed*

Seasonings for the stock:

1 onion, quartered	2 cardamom pods (optional)
1 tablespoon coriander seeds	1 tablespoon fennel seeds
1 tablespoon cumin seeds	2 2-inch cinnamon sticks
1 teaspoon black peppercorns	

To make broth:

1.   Tie seasonings securely in a cloth.
2.   Place chicken, seasonings, and 5 cups water in a large soup kettle. Bring to a boil, reduce heat, and simmer 15–20 minutes. Remove breasts when no longer pink. Continue to simmer until the dark meat of the chicken is done.
3.   Remove chicken pieces and set aside. You may bone the chicken if desired to reduce the bulk in the final cooking. Discard spices and strain the stock.

To cook rice:

2½ *cups* basmati *rice, or other long-grain rice*
1 *tablespoon safflower oil*
1 *large onion, sliced into thin rings*
4 *tablespoons fresh ginger root, minced*
4 *cloves garlic, minced*
2 *tablespoons golden sultana raisins, or dark raisins (optional)*
½ *cup plain low-fat yogurt*
1 *teaspoon saffron threads*

Garnish:

Chopped fresh coriander or mint leaves

1.   Preheat oven to 250°.
2.   If using *basmati* rice, wash in 2–3 changes of cold water and drain thoroughly.
3.   Combine saffron threads with 3 tablespoons boiling water and soak 10 minutes.
4.   In an oven-proof casserole, heat oil and brown onion until golden. Add ginger, garlic, and raisins and cook a few seconds longer.
5.   Mix in yogurt and cook until heated through.
6.   Add chicken pieces and cook 4–5 minutes, turning frequently to coat well with yogurt mixture.
7.   Add rice and 4 cups broth. Mix well and bring to a boil. Cover and cook for about 10 minutes, or until rice has absorbed most of the water.
8.   Place the casserole in a preheated oven and cook for 45 minutes. Uncover and drizzle saffron water and threads over top to streak with yellow color. Taste a few grains to be sure rice is tender. Cover casserole again and return to oven for 10–15 minutes more.
9.   Fluff rice and serve directly from casserole or on a large heated platter. Garnish with coriander leaves and serve with yogurt to be spooned over rice if desired.

Yield: 6–8 servings

Cooking time: 1½ hours

Calories per serving: 565
Saturated fat: 2.5 g
Cholesterol: 100 mg

Total fat: 10 g
Polyunsaturated fat: 3.5 g
Sodium: 110 mg

Lamb and Yogurt Curry
(*Roghan Josh*)

Pakistanis and Muslims from northern India are avid meat eaters. Since pork is forbidden and the cow is sacred, it is not surprising that lamb is the favored meat. There is a large repertory of inspired lamb dishes to choose from, but since this book's emphasis is away from red meat, only one is included for infrequent indulgence as a change of pace. Like every other Indian dish, there are many versions. I like this one with tomato added, because it gives the dish a nice tang.

1 ½–2 pounds lean lamb, preferably from the leg, cut into 1-inch cubes, all fat removed
1 ½ cups plain low-fat yogurt
3 large cloves garlic, minced
1 tablespoon fresh ginger root, minced
1 tablespoon ground coriander
1 teaspoon ground cumin
¼ teaspoon each ground mace, nutmeg, cardamom, and fennel
½ teaspoon ground turmeric

⅛–½ teaspoon cayenne pepper, or to taste
1 tablespoon safflower oil, or unsalted margarine
½ cup onions, finely chopped
2 large very ripe tomatoes, peeled and coarsely chopped
¼ teaspoon garam masala (p. 282)
¼ teaspoon freshly grated nutmeg
Fresh coriander leaves, chopped, for garnish

1.   In a large bowl, combine yogurt, garlic, ginger root, and spices. Add lamb, mix thoroughly to coat all pieces, cover, and marinate at least one hour.

2.   In a heavy saucepan, heat oil and saute onions until they are golden.

3.   Add tomatoes and cook 4 or 5 minutes.

4.   Add lamb and its marinade and bring to a boil, stirring constantly. Cover, and simmer over low heat about 45 minutes. Add a little more yogurt or water if mixture becomes dry, and cook 10 to 15 minutes longer. Taste for seasoning.

5.   Sprinkle with *garam masala*, nutmeg, and coriander leaves, and serve with *nan* (p. 315) or *chapathi* (p. 316), plain rice, and two or more accompaniments to curry (pp. 309–10).

Yield: 6–8 servings   Cooking time: 1 hour

Calories per serving: 295   Total fat: 12 g
Saturated fat: 7 g   Polyunsaturated fat: 4 g
Cholesterol: 175 mg   Sodium: 135 mg

◊  ◊

Accompaniments to Curry
(Chatni)

A curry would not be complete if it were not accompanied by a dab of chutney. But contrary to popular belief, Indian chutneys are not preserved relishes; rather, they are simple, fresh preparations made daily from a variety of fruits, vegetables, and seasonings. That is not to say that the preserved Major Grey type of chutney is unsuitable. It is just not originally Indian, though it is popular precisely because it goes very well with Indian foods. Chutneys are easy to prepare and provide much room for improvisation. Most fresh ones are salted heavily to make the ingredients wilt, while the cooked ones are prepared with vinegar.

Other side dishes to serve as a foil to curry are sliced bananas, tart apples sprinkled with lemon juice, unripe mangoes sliced paper thin and sprinkled with cayenne pepper, fresh pineapple, and unsalted peanuts. Chilled *raitas* are also suitable, especially cucumber *raita* (p. 298). Two or more of these accompaniments will enhance your enjoyment of any curry-based meal.

Fresh Mint Chutney
(Podina Chatni)

1–2 tablespoons lemon or lime
    juice
1 scallion chopped
1 large clove garlic, chopped

½ teaspoon ground cumin
1–2 fresh chili peppers,
    chopped, or cayenne
    pepper, to taste

½ teaspoon sugar
1 cup firmly packed mint
  leaves
1 cup plain low-fat yogurt

Place all ingredients except the yogurt in an electric blender and pulverize until the mixture is reduced to a puree. To keep the mass going, it may be necessary to add a little of the yogurt. Transfer to a bowl and add remaining yogurt. Taste for seasoning and add more lemon juice, pepper, and sugar, if desired.

Yield: About 1 cup   Preparation time: 5 minutes

Calories per tablespoon: 13   Total fat: 0.2 g
Saturated fat: 0.1 g   Polyunsaturated fat: 0 g
Cholesterol: 1 mg   Sodium: 7 mg

Variation: Substitute coriander leaves to make fresh coriander chutney.

Mango Chutney
(Am Chatni)

3–4 large unripe mangoes   *¾ cup sugar*
1–2 fresh or dried chili peppers,   *¾ cup mild vinegar*
  finely chopped, or cay-   *¼ teaspoon each ground*
  enne pepper, to taste   *coriander and cumin*
2 large cloves garlic, minced   *1-inch cinnamon stick*
2 tablespoons fresh ginger   *¼ cup raisins or sultanas*
  root, minced

1.   Peel and seed mangoes and cut them into thick slices.
2.   In a stainless steel or enameled saucepan combine chilies, garlic, ginger root, sugar, vinegar, and spices and bring to a boil. Simmer 15 to 20 minutes.
3.   Add mangoes and raisins and cook until mango is tender and syrup is thick. Taste for seasoning. Add more sugar or pepper if desired. If mixture seems dry, add more vinegar or a little water.

Yield: About 2½ cups   Cooking time: 30 minutes

Calories per tablespoon: 28   Total fat: 0 g
Saturated fat: 0 g   Polyunsaturated fat: 0 g
Cholesterol: 0 mg   Sodium: 1 mg

Variation: Firm peaches, apricots, or pears may be substituted for the mangoes. A combination of fruits is also good.

◊  ◊

Rice and Breads
(*Pulao, Nan,* and *Chapathi*)

Rice
(*Pulao*)

Rice is the most important staple food in Indian cookery, and, as in other countries in the Far East, it has a deep religious and cultural significance. There are many varieties of Indian rice, each used for particular dishes, prepared according to regional differences. For Indian vegetarians, rice is the very soul of every meal. Like *dal*, rice plays an important role in the Indian vegetarian diet, *dal* supplying the protein and rice the bulk. The number of rice dishes in Indian cuisine is staggering—some plain and some spiced; some cooked with lentils; some with various combinations of vegetables, meat, or chicken; some cooked sour, with lime juice; and still others cooked sweet, with coconut, raisins, and nuts. Perhaps the most prized variety is the long-grain *basmati* rice, used for making *pulao* (pilaf) and *biryani*, rice dishes for which Indian cookery is deservedly famous. The difference between the two is often a puzzle. But, as I understand it, unlike a *pulao*, in which the rice takes precedence over the meat and vegetables it may contain, a *biryani* is essentially a meat-rice preparation in which the rice is often cooked separately and used as a bed upon which to place succulent pieces of meat in their sauce. Some *biryanis* and *pulaos* can be rich, elaborate dishes containing meat, vegetables, nuts, and raisins. Others are less so. But they are usually a meal in themselves and require no accompaniment beyond a refreshing salad or *raita*.

Saffron Rice
(Kesar Chaval)

This *pulao* can be as simple or elaborate as one desires. First, the onions, vegetables, and spices are sauteed; then the rice, and finally the liquid is added.

1 ⅓ cups basmati *rice, or other long-grain rice*
⅔ teaspoon *saffron threads*
2 ⅓ cups *boiling water, or unsalted chicken stock (p. 10)*

2 tablespoons *unsalted safflower margarine*
½ cup *onions, finely chopped*
2-inch *piece cinnamon*
4 whole *cloves*
4 whole *peppercorns*

1.   Combine saffron threads with 3–4 tablespoons boiling water and soak for 10 minutes.
2.   Heat margarine in a heavy saucepan and gently saute the onions, cinnamon, cloves, and peppercorns for 2 or 3 minutes.
3.   Add the rice and continue stirring over low heat for 8–10 minutes, or until rice grains turn milky white. Do not allow to brown.
4.   Add water; stir gently and bring mixture to a boil. Sprinkle the surface of the rice with the saffron water and threads. Reduce the heat to low, cover tightly, and cook 20–25 minutes without lifting lid or stirring. Turn off heat and let rice stand covered 5–10 minutes.
5.   Fluff rice with fork and serve.

Yield: 4 cups (4–6 servings)

Calories per cup: 305
Saturated fat: 1 g
Cholesterol: 0 mg

Cooking time: 40 minutes

Total fat: 7.5 g
Polyunsaturated fat: 6 g
Sodium: 10 mg

Variation: One medium carrot cut into thin matchstick strips and two tablespoons sultanas or dark raisins may be sauteed with the onions in step 2. Two or three tablespoons of sugar may also be added in step 4 for a sweeter rice.

Sweet Saffron Rice with Lime Juice
(Kesar Pulao)

²/₃ teaspoon saffron threads
2 tablespoons unsalted margarine
4 cardamom pods, bruised
6 whole cloves
1-inch stick cinnamon
1 cup basmati *or longgrain rice*

2 or 3 tablespoons unsalted
  cashews or slivered almonds
2 or 3 tablespoons raisins
1 tablespoon sugar
¼ cup fresh lime juice
1½ cups boiling water

1.   Preheat oven to 350°.
2.   Combine saffron threads with 2 tablespoons boiling water and soak for 10 minutes.
3.   In a heavy casserole dish, heat margarine and cook cardamom, cloves, and cinnamon for 3–4 minutes.
4.   Add the rice and fry over low heat, stirring constantly, 5 to 7 minutes, or until rice grains turn a milky color.
5.   Add the nuts and raisins and stir 2 or 3 minutes longer.
6.   Add the sugar, lemon juice, boiling water, and saffron water and threads and stir briefly until well mixed. Cover with a tight lid and cook in a preheated oven for 25 minutes, or until rice is tender and has absorbed all the liquid in the casserole. If the cover is not tight, place a sheet of aluminum foil under lid.
7.   Fluff rice gently with fork and serve directly from casserole.

Yield: 4 servings

Cooking time: 40 minutes

Calories per serving: 285
Saturated fat: 1.5 g
Cholesterol: 0 mg

Total fat: 9 g
Polyunsaturated fat: 6 g
Sodium: 7 mg

Note: This recipe may be cooked on top of the stove just as well. Turn the heat down to low and cook 25 minutes without lifting lid. Then turn heat off and let stand 5–10 minutes.

Breads
(Nan and Chapathi)

Indian and Pakistani people who live in the north in the Punjab and Kashmir areas like to eat thicker curries than their southern countrymen.

Consequently, they are fonder of breads than of rice. The two most popular of the many types are *nan* and *chapathi*. *Nan* are wonderful breads made of leavened dough. The dough is allowed to rise, is worked and stretched much like pizza dough, and is then thrown up against the inner side of a *tandoor*, a country-style Indian oven that has a wood fire in its center. It usually comes out looking like a lopsided pizza with no topping, but it tastes very good. Indians like to brush it with butter when it comes out of the oven, but perhaps we can do without the extra fat. *Chapathi* are little unleavened breads about the size and thickness of crepes that are wonderful for soaking up sauce. Indians use them in lieu of utensils in helping them to eat.

Flat Leavened Bread
(Nan)

Stephen Comee suggested this Indian bread as a perfect accompaniment to wet curries. It is very popular in Pakistan and northern India.

1 ¼ cup nonfat milk	1 tablespoon safflower oil
2 tablespoons active dry yeast	2 cups whole-wheat flour
1 teaspoon honey	1 ½ cups all-purpose white flour

1.   Heat milk until lukewarm and pour into a large bowl. Sprinkle in the yeast, add the honey, stir, and cover. Set aside for 5–7 minutes, until the yeast has become frothy and doubled in volume. (If this doesn't happen, start again.)

2.   To the yeast mixture, gradually add the whole-wheat flour; then add enough of the white flour to form a non-sticky dough. Turn dough out on a well-floured board and knead about 15 minutes, or until dough is smooth and comes away from the sides of the bowl. Keep dusting with extra white flour to keep dough from sticking. The more you knead, the lighter the bread will be.

3.   Place the dough in a large, oiled bowl, turning it to cover all sides with oil. Cover with a sheet of plastic wrap or a damp towel, and set aside in a warm place. Allow the dough to double in volume (about 1 ½ hours).

4.   Punch down, and divide dough into four portions. Knead each portion for a minute, then flatten to the desired shape (if round, about 6 inches each), making sure the board is well floured to prevent sticking. Cover with plastic wrap and allow to rise 15 minutes, while you preheat the oven to 450°F.

5.   Roll each bread (if round) into a 10-inch circle. Place on baking sheets, and bake one at a time, about 5–7 minutes, or until the crust gets a golden color. When done, serve at once.

Yield: 4 10-inch breads

Cooking time: 2 hours

Calories per bread: 150
Saturated fat: 0.5 g
Cholesterol: 0 mg

Total fat: 1.5 g
Polyunsaturated fat: 1 g
Sodium: 5 mg

Whole-Wheat Flat Bread
(*Chapathi*)

This southern Indian bread is easier to prepare than most, because it contains no yeast and therefore needs no rising time. *Chapathis* are perfect for those on a low-fat diet because they are made with whole-wheat flour and contain no fat. They have a chewy texture and a very good flavor.

1 cup whole wheat flour, or ½ cup whole wheat flour mixed with ½ cup all-purpose white flour

¼–½ cup lukewarm water

1. Place flour in a large bowl and make a well in the center. Add up to ½ cup of water a little at a time. Use only enough water to form a dough that can be gathered into a compact ball.

2. On a well-floured board, knead at least 10 minutes, or until dough is smooth and leaves the bowl clean. Keep dusting with flour to keep dough from sticking. The more you knead, the lighter the bread will be. Cover with a sheet of plastic wrap or damp towel, and let the dough rest at least 1 hour.

3. Divide the dough into 8 small balls. Roll out each ball to the thickness of a thin pancake. Be sure the board is well floured to prevent sticking.

4. Heat a heavy griddle or nonstick frying pan until a drop of water sizzles on contact. Without adding any fat, cook each *chapathi* one minute or less on each side, or until it is lightly browned. Transfer to a serving plate and keep warm while you cook the remaining breads.

Yield: 4 servings (8 breads)

Cooking time: About 25 minutes

Calories per bread: 50
Saturated fat: Trace
Cholesterol: 0 mg

Total fat: 0.5 g
Polyunsaturated fat: 0.5 g
Sodium: 5 mg

Desserts

Japan: Fruit Sorbet
(*Furutsu Shabetto*)

The finale to most Asian meals is fresh fruit, but, as a change, a fruit ice for dessert will add no fat or sodium and is a refreshing low-calorie way to end a meal. This recipe contains no milk or egg whites, as some sherbets and sorbets do, and is very simple to make.

2 cups fresh or frozen
   strawberries or raspberries,
   or 2 large fresh ripe pears
   or peaches, peeled
   and chopped

⅓ cup sugar
½ cup white wine

1. In a small saucepan, bring fruit, sugar, and wine to a boil and cook until tender, about 5 minutes. Puree in an electric blender until smooth, or put through a sieve. Freeze until solid.
2. Remove from freezer. Return to the electric blender and blend into a slush. If a blender is not available, use an electric mixer. Place into a storage container and freeze again. Serve as needed.

Yield: 4 servings

Cooking time: 5 minutes

Calories per serving: 95
Saturated fat: 0 g
Cholesterol: 0 mg

Total fat: 0 g
Polyunsaturated fat: 0 g
Sodium: 5 mg

Korea: Steamed Rice Delight
(*Yak-Shik*)

The Korean name of this delicious pudding translates as "medicine food." I am certain that it was given such a name not only because the word *yak* is often used in the name of desserts sweetened with honey, since honey is taken with medicine by Koreans, but also because it tastes so good it *must* be good for you. This recipe was suggested by Stephen Comee.

1 ¾ cups glutinous rice
½ pound chestnuts (in shells)
2 ½ ounces dates

2 ½ ounces raisins
1 tablespoon pine nuts, or
    chopped unsalted walnuts
    (optional)

Seasoning mixture:

2 teaspoons low-sodium soy
    sauce
¼ cup dark brown sugar
½ cup honey

2 tablespoons sesame oil
½ teaspoon cinnamon
¼ teaspoon powdered ginger

1. Wash glutinous rice and soak in water overnight. (If you do not have enough time to do so, soak it for at least three hours before steaming it.)
2. Shell the chestnuts and cut into halves. Place in cold water and let soak for 30 minutes.
3. Pit the dates and chop roughly.
4. Drain rice, place in a steamer, and steam over high heat until cooked, about 30 minutes.
5. Transfer rice to a large bowl. Add seasoning mixture to hot rice and mix thoroughly. Then stir in chestnuts, dates, raisins, and pine nuts (or walnuts).
6. Place the bowl of pudding in the steamer and steam for about 5 minutes, until the chestnuts are soft and the pudding looks set. Add more water if necessary. Pour one teaspoon of honey over each serving and garnish with extra pine nuts (or walnuts).

Note: The hot pudding mixture can be placed in a round bundt pan or similar mold, and unmolded for serving attractively on a platter.

Yield: 6 servings

Calories per serving: 315
Saturated fat: 0.1 g
Cholesterol: 0 mg

Cooking time: 45 minutes

Total fat: 5 g
Polyunsaturated fat: 4 g
Sodium: 65 mg

China: Almond Diamonds
(*Xingren Doufu*)

A sweet dish might be served between courses in a Chinese banquet as a change of pace, or as a snack between meals, but an authentic Chinese meal does not end with a dessert but with fresh fruit. Of course, everybody loves Peking glazed apples, a truly exquisite sweet, but it is tricky to make and involves deep frying, making it off-limits for this book. Happily, there is one dish that is eminently suitable for dessert that is low in calories and fat. Almond Diamonds is simple to make and keeps for several days in the refrigerator. This is a highly adapted recipe using gelatin as a jelling agent instead of agar-agar (a form of seaweed), and almond extract instead of almond liquid.

2 tablespoons unflavored gelatin	2½ cups nonfat or low-fat milk
1 cup cold water	1 teaspoon almond extract
⅓ cup sugar	

Garnish: Mandarin oranges are the usual garnish, but fresh or frozen berries, pineapple, peaches, or plums with juices, or litchi nuts or longans with juices may be substituted.

1. Sprinkle gelatin over ½ cup cold water in a saucepan to soften. Add the remaining water and sugar. Bring to a boil and stir until gelatin dissolves and water clears.
2. Remove from heat and let cool. Stir in milk and almond extract and mix well. Pour into a shallow rectangular dish about 7 × 12 inches. Refrigerate until set, preferably overnight. If desired, pour into individual serving dishes.
3. Cut jelled mixture on the diagonal into diamond shapes. Place in shallow bowls. Add fruit with juices.

Yield: 6 servings   Cooking time: 15 minutes

Nutrient count does not include fruit.

Calories: 80	Total fat: 0.5 g
Saturated fat: 0.5 g	Polyunsaturated fat: 0 g
Cholesterol: 5 mg	Sodium: 55 mg

The Philippines: Baked Lime Caramel Custard
(*Leche Flan*)

The Filipinos usually have fresh fruit after a meal but they also like sweets made of condensed milk and sugar. Even the flan (caramelized custard) that they learned to make from the Spanish is also made with evaporated milk and a large quantity of sugar. In this recipe, low-fat milk is used instead and the amount of sugar is reduced. I recommend no sugar in the custard because the caramel adds enough sweetness.

Caramel:

½ cup sugar
2 tablespoons water

1. Have ready 4 individual cups, preferably of heavy ceramic glaze. It helps in spreading the caramel if they have been warmed slightly.
2. In a heavy skillet, bring sugar and water to a boil over high heat, stirring constantly until the sugar is completely dissolved. Reduce the heat to medium and continue to stir, tipping the pan back and forth until the sugar mixture is the color of maple syrup. This will take about 10 minutes.
3. Now you must work very fast while the syrup is hot. Quickly spoon about a tablespoon of syrup into the first cup and swirl it around to cover the bottom of the cup. Do the same with each of the remaining cups.

Custard:

2 cups nonfat or low-fat milk   *0–2 tablespoons sugar*
2 teaspoons finely grated fresh   *2 whole eggs, beaten*
   lime rind

1. Preheat oven to 300° F.
2. Beat eggs in a separate bowl and set aside.
3. Blend together milk, lime rind, and sugar. Add eggs and beat well.
4. Pour into custard cups. Place the cups in a large shallow baking pan, and pour in enough hot (not boiling) water to come halfwey up the sides of the cups. Bake at low heat for 45 minutes to 1 hour. Do not allow the water to boil or the custard will be spoiled. Test for doneness by inserting a silver knife near the edge of the cup. If the blade comes out clean, the custard will be solid in the middle by the time it has cooled. Do not overcook.

5.   Remove from the water and chill thoroughly, 3–4 hours. To unmold, run a sharp knife around the edge and dip the bottom of the cup briefly in hot water. Place a plate on top of the cup and quickly turn upside down. The flan should slide out easily.

Yield: 4 to 6 servings   Cooking time: 5 minutes to
                                                        1 hour

Calories: 153   Total fat: 1.5 g
Saturated fat: 0.5 g   Polyunsaturated fat: 1 g
Cholesterol: 0 mg   Sodium: 2 mg

Vietnam: Fresh Orange Treats
(Mat Ong Vo Cam Ron)

This light dessert, another contribution by Stephen Comee, is a nice way to end a meal that might have been a little too salty or oily for the Western palate. It is as refreshing to look at as it is to eat.

4 navel oranges   *1 cup honey*
1 teaspoon alum (optional)

1.   Without taking off the whole peel, shave away the outermost layer of skin, leaving some orange color behind. Then make six deep slits lengthwise in the oranges.
2.   Place the oranges in a large pot and cover with water. Bring to a boil and boil 30 minutes. Drain and allow to cool.
3.   Gently press the top of each orange until the slits widen and pull out the excess pulp and pith that appears. Continue until the oranges are only about 1½ inches high, but leave some of the pulp inside.
4.   Place the oranges in the pot once more, with water to cover, adding the alum (which helps keep the rind firm). Bring to a boil over high heat and boil for another 30 minutes. Drain and cool. When cool, press firmly to drain excess water.
5.   Place the oranges once again in the pot, pour the honey over them, and add ¾ cup water. Bring to a boil quickly over high heat, then reduce to low. Simmer until the syrup has almost disappeared. Turn the oranges occasionally, being very careful not to let them crumble.
6.   Remove from pot and cool. Serve cool, sliced or whole, depending upon one's diet or desire.

Note: These oranges will keep for 2–3 months in a tightly sealed container if refrigerated; if frozen, they will keep about 6 months.

Yield: 4–6 servings	Cooking time: 1½ hours
Calories per serving: 320	Total fat: 1.0 g
Saturated fat: 0.5 g	Polyunsaturated fat: 0.5 g
Cholesterol: 0 mg	Sodium: 5 mg

Indonesia, Malaysia, and Singapore:
Fruit Salad with Spicy-Sweet Sauce
(*Rujak*)

The shrimp paste and soy sauce have been left out of this recipe not only because they add too much sodium but because they are not necessary. The fruits are so delicious on their own that lemon, sugar, and a dash of chili is really all they need. Other fruits in season may be substituted.

2 navel or mandarin oranges
½ grapefruit or ½ small
  pomelo
2 tart apples
1 firm banana
¼ small fresh pineapple
3–4 tablespoons palm or brown
  sugar

3–4 tablespoons lime or
  lemon juice
1 teaspoon Sambal Ulek
  (p. 232), or 1–2 fresh or
  dried chili peppers, seeded
  and chopped, or cayenne
  pepper, to taste

1. Peel and section citrus fruits, removing membranes.
2. Peel and cut apples and pineapple into bite-sized pieces. Slice banana.
3. Mix sugar, lime juice, and *sambal ulek* or pepper. Add to fruit and mix well.

Yield: 6–8 servings	Preparation time: 10 minutes
Calories per serving: 115	Total fat: 0.5 g
Saturated fat: 0 g	Polyunsaturated fat: 0.2 g
Cholesterol: 0 mg	Sodium: 3 mg

Thailand: Fried Bananas
(*Kluai Thot*)

Although the Thais more often have fresh fruit or sweets made of condensed milk and sugar, fried bananas offer a nice change of pace. Popular in Thailand they are loved and served all over Southeast Asia. Although fried, this banana dessert is very satisfying, and is actually rather low in fat. Best of all, it's simple to make.

4 fresh very firm bananas
1 teaspoon unsalted safflower margarine or oil

2 teaspoons brown sugar, or palm sugar, if available
Lime or lemon wedges

1.   Peel and slice bananas lengthwise, then cut lengths in half.
2.   In a nonstick pan, heat margarine and gently brown bananas on both sides. Try to keep them intact.
3.   Sprinkle sugar over tops and serve warm with lime wedges.

Yield: 4 to 6 servings

Cooking time: 5 minutes

Calories per serving: 125
Saturated fat: 0.5 g
Cholesterol: 0 mg

Total fat: 1.5 g
Polyunsaturated fat: 1 g
Sodium: 2 mg

India: Rice and Milk Pudding
with Cardamom and Nuts
(*Kheer*)

Indians make a wide variety of sweets, and most of them are rich and delicious and high in calories. *Kheer* is an exception. It is a simple and nutritious rice pudding that is usually served cold, but I find it very comforting when eaten warm. A nonstick or very heavy saucepan is crucial here, because the milk tends to stick to the bottom.

1 quart nonfat or low-fat milk
2 tablespoons long-grain rice
2 tablespoons sugar (less or more depending on taste)
1/4 cup slivered unsalted blanched almonds or pistachio nuts

3 cardamom pods bruised, or 1/4 teaspoon ground cardamon
1/2 teaspoon rose water (leave out if not available)

1. In a heavy, nonstick saucepan, bring milk to a boil with the cardamom and rice, stirring constantly to keep from sticking.

2. Reduce heat and continue to cook until rice is very soft, stirring frequently.

3. Add sugar and ½ the nuts and continue to cook, stirring constantly, until milk has reduced to half its original volume and the pudding is thick enough to coat the spoon heavily. The process may take an hour or more, so be prepared to ease the wait by listening to music, reading a book, or cooking the dinner to be eaten before the dessert.

4. Discard the cardamom pods and stir in the rose water. Pour into a shallow serving bowl and decorate with remaining nuts.

5. Stir in the rose water and serve warm or chilled, sprinkled with freshly grated nutmeg.

Yield: About 6 servings

Cooking time: 1 hour

Calories per serving: 160
Saturated fat: 0.5 g
Cholesterol: 3 mg

Total fat: 2.5 g
Polyunsaturated fat: 0.7 g
Sodium: 85 mg

Appendixes

Appendixes

Fat-Cholesterol-Sodium Tables

Meat, poultry, fish, dairy products, fats, and oils provide the major sources of fats in the diet. The following tables (pp. 332–36) were compiled from the data used to calculate the nutrient analyses given at the end of the recipes in this book. All the figures have been rounded *up* to the nearest 5 or 10 mg, and to the nearest 0.5 g. In reading these figures, you will find a difference between the total fat and the sum of the values listed for individual fats. This is because there are other fatty acids that have not been included in the analysis. All of these nutrient values should be regarded fundamentally as estimates.

Also included is data on the sodium content of some Asian condiments, which have been based largely on the work of Teresa Chew. Most brands tested showed sizeable disparities from sample to sample, although sauces manufactured under Japanese brand names proved to be highly standardized. To my knowledge, no data is yet available on Southeast Asian pastes and fish sauces.

Disparities notwithstanding, these figures should prove useful as a tool in comparing one food with another, thereby showing in a relative sense which foods are low and which are high in fat, cholesterol, and sodium.

Table 1

Meat, Poultry, Fish, Tofu (uncooked, boneless, no skin or fat)	Unit	Calories	Total Fat (g)
Chicken, white meat	1 oz	51	1.4
Chicken, dark meat	1 oz	52	1.8
Chicken liver, cooked	1 whole	41	1.1
Beef, lean	1 oz	59	2.7
Lamb, lean	1 oz	53	2.0
Pork, lean	1 oz	62	3.9
Fish, lean	1 oz	26	0.3
Fish, fatty (e.g. salmon)	1 oz	48	1.6
Shrimp	1 oz	34	0.35
Soybean curd (tofu)	1 oz	21	1.25
Dairy Products			
Milk, whole	1 cup	150	8.2
Milk, low-fat	1 cup	105	2.6
Milk, nonfat (skimmed)	1 cup	90	0.4
Yogurt, plain, low-fat	1 cup	145	3.5
Buttermilk, low-fat	1 cup	100	2.2
Egg, whole: fresh, medium	1	80	5.6
Egg white	1	15	Trace
Egg yolk	1	65	5.6
Butter	1 Tbsp	110	12.3
Fats and Oils			
Polyunsaturated oils			
Corn oil	1 Tbsp	120	13.6
Safflower oil	1 Tbsp	120	13.6
Sesame oil	1 Tbsp	120	13.6
Soybean oil	1 Tbsp	120	13.6
Monounsaturated oils			
Olive oil	1 Tbsp	119	13.5
Peanut oil	1 Tbsp	119	13.5
Saturated oils			
Coconut oil	1 Tbsp	120	13.6
Nuts and Seeds			
Coconut, shredded	1 cup	280	28.2
Sesame seeds: dry, hulled	1 Tbsp	47	4.4

A dash (—) indicates data not available.
Abbreviations used in this table are: oz=ounce; Tbsp=tablespoon; tsp=teaspoon.
Sources for this information listed on page 335.

Fat-Cholesterol-Sodium Table

Saturated Fat (g)	Monounsaturated Fat (g)	Polyunsaturated Fat (g)	Cholesterol (mg)	Sodium (mg)
0.4	0.7	0.3	22	18
0.5	0.6	0.4	26	24
0.4	0.3	0.2	158	13
1.23	1.1	0.1	26	19
0.9	0.8	0.1	28	15
1.6	2.1	0.5	25	20
0.02	0.01	0.06	14	19
0.5	0.8	0.1	10	33
0.05	0.05	0.15	46	41
0.2	0.25	0.65	0	2
5.1	2.4	0.3	33	120
1.6	0.8	0.1	10	125
0.3	0.1	0	4	130
2.3	1.0	0.1	14	160
1.3	0.6	0.1	9	257
1.7	2.2	0.7	274	60
0	0	0	0	50
1.7	2.2	0.7	274	10
7.5	3.6	0.6	36	150
1.7	3.4	7.9	0	0
1.3	1.7	11.6	0	0
2.1	5.5	5.7	0	0
2.0	3.1	7.8	0	0
1.9	9.8	1.2	0	0
2.6	6.2	4.1	0	0
11.7	0.8	0.2	0	0
25.0	1.7	0.5	0	0
0.6	1.6	1.8	0	—

Table 2

Approximate Sodium Content
of Some Condiments Used in Asian Cookery

	Unit	Calories	Sodium (mg)
Brown bean sauce	1 tsp	—	425
Hot bean sauce	1 tsp	—	300
Sweet bean sauce	1 tsp	—	160
Fermented black beans			
Rinsed	1 tsp	—	100
Unrinsed	1 tsp	—	125
Hoisin sauce	1 tsp	—	160
Miso paste	1 tsp	60	285
Nori (seaweed)	1 sheet	—	115
Oyster sauce	1 tsp	—	260
Shrimp sauce	1 tsp	—	415
Soy sauce, Kikkoman's			
All Purpose	1 tsp	4	320
Soy sauce, Kikkoman's			
Low-Sodium	1 tsp	4	170
Monosodium glutamate	1 tsp	0	495
Salt	1 tsp	0	2,000

Note: Southeast Asian fish sauces and fish pastes not included because no data available.
A dash (—) indicates data not available.

Abbreviations used in this table are: oz=ounce; Tbsp=tablespoon; tsp=teaspoon.

Sources for this information listed on page.

Major Sources for the Nutrient Content of the Recipes

This list gives the major sources used in obtaining the data used in the computer analysis of the nutrient content of the recipes given in this book. Although the figures are approximate, since sources often vary considerably in the amount of a certain element or compound contained in a given food, the values given at the end of each recipe represent, to the best of my knowledge, the most recent values available.

Bowes & Church's Food Values of Portions Commonly Used, Pennington and Church, 13th Edition, Harper & Row and J. B. Lippincott Co.
Composition of Foods, Agriculture Handbook No. 8, U.S. Department of Agriculture.
Computer Program: *Nutriplan*, Version 2.1, Micromedx.
Nutrient Analysis of Common Foods, in *The Living Heart Diet*, Simon and Schuster, Inc., New York, 1984.
Nutritive Value of American Foods, Agriculture Handbook No. 456, U. S. Department of Agriculture.
Sodium Content of Food, No. 233, U. S. Department of Agriculture.
Sodium Values of Chinese Condiments and Their Use in Sodium-Restricted Diets, Teresa Chew, R.D.
Standard Tables of Food Composition in Japan, 4th Revised Edition, 1982, Resources Council, Science and Technology Agency, Government of Japan.

Bibliography

Alejandro, Reynaldo. *The Philippine Cookbook*. New York: The Putnam Publishing Group, 1985.

Amatyakul, Charlie. *The Best of Thai Cooking*. Hong Kong: Travel Publishing Asia, Ltd., 1987.

American Heart Association. *American Heart Association Cookbook*. New York: David McKay Company, Inc., 1979.

———. *The American Heart Association Diet: An Eating Plan for Healthy Americans*. 1985.

———. *Cholesterol and Your Heart*, 1985.

———. *Facts About Potassium: How to Meet Your Potassium Requirements*, 1986.

———. *Nutrition for the Fitness Challenge*, 1986.

———. *Cooking Without Your Saltshaker*, 1978.

Andoh, Elizabeth. *At Home with Japanese Cooking*. New York: Alfred A. Knopf, 1980.

Anwar, Zarinah. *With an Eastern Flavour*. New York: Barron's Educational Series, Inc., 1979.

Benedictine Sisters of Peking. *The Art of Chinese Cooking*. Rutland, Vermont, and Tokyo: Charles E. Tuttle Co., 1956.

Beranbaum, Rose Levy. "New Japanese Desserts: Tiny, Delicious." *New York Times,* January 18, 1984.

Boffey, Philip M. "U.S. Seeks to Curb Reliance on Drugs for Blood Pressure," The 1984 Report of the Joint National Committee on Detection, Evaluation, and Treatment of High Blood Pressure. *New York Times,* April 30, 1984.

Brennan, Jennifer. *One-Dish Meals of Asia*. New York: Times Books (a division of Random House, Inc.), 1985.

———. *The Original Thai Cookbook*. New York: Coward, McCann and Geoghegan, 1981.

336

Brissenden, Rosemary. *South East Asian Food*. Harmondsworth: Penguin Books, 1970.

Brody, Jane E. "Garlic May be Good Against a Variety of Ills." *New York Times*, 1984.

———. *Jane Brody's Nutrition Book*. New York: W. W. Norton & Co., Inc., 1981.

———. "Rx on Diet: Low Fat and High Fiber," Report on findings of Dr. B. S. Reddy, Nutritional Biochemist at the American Health Foundation in Valhalla, New York. *New York Times*, July 1985.

———. "Salt and Hypertension: The Link Still Appears to be Strong." *New York Times*, August 23, 1984.

Burros, Marian. "Answering the Call for Low-Fat Diets." *New York Times*, January 23, 1985.

———. "High-Fat Fish: Healthful and Tasty." *New York Times*, September 4, 1985.

———. "High-Fiber Diet: Taste is Hidden Attraction." *New York Times*, June 22, 1983.

———. "Meat Getting Trimmer for a Comeback Fight." *New York Times*, October 8, 1986.

Carr, Carol. *See* Committee on Diet, Nutrition, and Cancer.

Chakravarti, Aravinda and Morizot, Donald C. *Not Everything We Eat is Curry: A Bengali Guide to Indian Cuisine*. Houston: Harold House, Publishers, 1978.

Chang, K. C., ed. *Food in Chinese Culture: Anthropological and Historical Perspectives*. New Haven: Yale University Press, 1977.

Chang, Wonona W., et al. *An Encyclopedia of Chinese Food and Cooking*. New York: Crown Publishers, Inc., 1970.

Chen, Pearl Kong, et al. *Everything You Wanted to Know About Chinese Cooking*. New York: Barron's Educational Series, Inc., 1983.

Chew, Teresa, R.D. "Sodium Values of Chinese Condiments and Their Use in Sodium-Restricted Diets." *Journal of the American Dietetic Association* 82(4): April 1983.

Choi, E. Soon and Lee, Ki Yull. *Practical Korean Recipes*. Seoul: Yonsei University Press, 1977.

Committee on Diet, Nutrition, and Cancer. "Nutrition and Cancer," Washington, D.C., NAS/NRS, 1982.

Connor, L. Sonja, M.S., R.D., and Connor, William E., M.D. *The New American Diet*. New York: Simon and Schuster, 1986.

Connor, William E., M.D., and Lin, Don S., M.D. " The Effect of Shellfish in the Diet Upon the Plasma Lipid Levels in Humans." *Metabolism: Clinical and Experimental* 31(10): October 1982.

Cronin, Isaac. *The International Squid Cookbook*. Berkeley: Aris Books, Harris Publishing Co., 1981.

DeBakey, Michael E., M.D., et al. *The Living Heart Diet*. New York: Simon and Schuster, Inc., 1984.

deKeijzer, Arne J. and Kaplan, Frederic M. *The China Guidebook*. New York: Eurasia Press, 1980.

DeWit, Antoinette and Borghese, Anita. *The Complete Book of Indonesian Cooking.* Indianapolis and New York: The Bobbs-Merrill Company, Inc., 1973.

"Dietary Guidelines for Healthy Adult Americans." A statement directed to physicians, released to the media August 26, 1986, at a news conference in Washington D.C. Published in *Circulation,* an American Heart Association journal, December 1986.

Duong, Thi Thanh Lien. *Vietnamese Dishes.* Printed in Taiwan, Republic of China (no publisher or date).

Gilroy Garlic Festival Association, Inc. *The Garlic Lover's Cookbook.* Gilroy, California: Celestial Arts, 1982.

Gin, Margaret and Castle, Alfred E. *Regional Cooking of China.* San Francisco: 101 Productions, 1975.

Glomset, John A., M.D. "Fish, Fatty Acids, and Human Health." An editorial in the *New England Journal of Medicine* 312(19): May 9, 1985.

Griffin, Stuart. *Japanese Food and Cooking.* Rutland, Vermont, and Tokyo: Charles E. Tuttle Co., 1956.

Gupta, Pranati Sen. *The Art of Indian Cuisine.* New York: Hawthorn Books, Inc., 1974.

Hahn, Emily. *The Cooking of China.* New York: Time-Life Books, 1968.

Harris, Lloyd J. *The Book of Garlic.* Los Angeles: Panjandrum / Aris Books, 1974.

Haydock, Yukiko and Robert. *Food in a Japanese Mood.* New York: Kodansha International, Ltd., 1984.

Howe, Robin. *Far Eastern Cookery.* New York: Drake Publishers, Ltd., 1971.

Hom, Ken, with Steiman, Harvey. *Chinese Technique.* New York: Simon and Schuster, 1981.

Horsting, Maudie, et al. *Flavors of Southeast Asia.* San Francisco: 101 Productions (dist. 1979).

Hyun, Judy. *The Korean Cookbook.* Elizabeth, N.J. and Seoul: Hollym International Corp., 1984.

Jaffrey, Madhur. *An Invitation to Indian Cooking.* New York: Alfred A. Knopf, 1973.

Jameson, Sam. " 'Internationalizing' Japan: New Waves Lap at Insularity." *Los Angeles Times,* December 25, 1986.

Johns, Yohanni. *Dishes from Indonesia.* Australia: Thomas Nelson, Ltd., 1971.

"Japan, U.S.A., Japan in America." *Business Week,* July 14, 1986.

Jervey, Phyllis. *Rice and Spice: Rice Recipes from East to West.* London: Arco Publishers, Ltd., 1957.

Kagawa, Dr. Aya. *Japanese Cookbook.* Tokyo: Japan Travel Bureau, 1967.

Kagawa, Yasuo. "Impact of Westernization on the Nutrition of Japanese: Changes in Physique, Cancer, Longevity and Centenarians." *Preventive Medicine* 7(2): June 1978.

Kamroff, Manuel, ed. *The Travels of Marco Polo (The Venetian)*, revised from Marsden's translation. New York: Liveright Publishing Corp., 1930.

Konishi, Kiyoko. *Japanese Cooking for Health and Fitness*. New York: Barron's Educational Series, Inc., 1984.

Kreitzman, Sue. *Garlic*. New York: Harmony Books, 1984.

Kromhart, Daan, Ph.D. M.P.H., et al. "The Inverse Relation Between Fish Consumption and 20-year Mortality from Coronary Heart Disease." *New England Journal of Medicine* 312(19): May 9, 1985.

Kuper, Jessica, ed. *The Anthropologists' Cookbook*. London: Routledge and K. Paul, 1977.

Leaf, Alexander, M.D. "Fish Story." *Harvard Medical School Health Letter* 11(4): February 1986.

Lee, Calvin B. T. and Lee, Audrey Evans. *The Gourmet Chinese Regional Cookbook*. New York: Putnam Publishing Group, 1976.

Lee, Sek-Hiang. *Indonesian Cooking*. New York: Crown Publishers, Inc., 1963.

Lee, Tak H., et al. "Effect of Dietary Enrichment with Eicosapentaenoic and Docosahexaenoic Acids on in Vitro Neutrophil and Monocyte Leukotriene Generation and Neutrophil Function." *New England Journal of Medicine* 312(19): May 9, 1985.

Leong, Yee Soo. *Singaporean Cooking*. Singapore: Eastern Universities Press (no date).

Ma, Nancy Chih. *Mrs. Ma's Chinese Cookbook*. Rutland, Vermont, and Tokyo: Charles E. Tuttle Co., 1960.

Ma, Nancy Chih, et al. *The Ma Family Cookbook*. New York and Tokyo: Kodansha International, 1973.

Martin, Peter, and Martin, Joan. *Japanese Cooking*. Harmondsworth: Penguin Books, 1972.

Miller, Gloria Bley. *The Thousand Recipe Chinese Cookbook*. New York: Grosset and Dunlap, 1970.

Miller, Jill Nhu Huong. *Vietnamese Cookery*. Rutland, Vermont, and Tokyo: Charles E. Tuttle Co., 1968.

Minear, Ralph E., M.D. *The Joy of Living Salt-Free*. New York: Macmillan Publishing Company, 1984.

Mitchell, Kenneth. *The Flavour of Singapore*. Hong Kong: Four Corners Publishing Co. (Far East) Ltd., 1973.

Morris, Harriet. *The Art of Korean Cooking*. Rutland, Vermont, and Tokyo: Charles E. Tuttle Co., 1979.

National High Blood Pressure Education Program, National Heart, Lung, and Blood Institute. The 1984 Report of the Joint National Committee on Detection, Evaluation, and Treatment of High Blood Pressure. *Archives of Internal Medicine* 144: May 1984.

Ngo, Bach, and Zimmerman, Gloria. *The Classic Cuisine of Vietnam*. New York: Barron's Educational Series, 1979.

Ok, Cho-Joong. *Home Style Korean Cooking in Pictures.* Tokyo: Shufutonomo Co., Ltd., 1981.

Omae, Kinjiro, and Tachibana, Yuzuru. *The Book of Sushi.* New York and Tokyo: Kodansha International, 1981.

Ortiz, Elisabeth Lambert, with Endo, Mitsuko. *The Complete Book of Japanese Cooking.* New York: M. Evans and Co., Inc., 1976.

Phillipson, Beverley E., M.D., et al. "Reduction of Plasma Lipids, Lipoproteins, and Apoproteins by Dietary Fish Oils in Patients with Hypertriglyceridemia." *New England Journal of Medicine* 312(19): May 9, 1985.

Rau, Santha Rama. *The Cooking of India.* New York: Time-Life Books, 1970.

Ross, Irma Walker. *Recipes from the East.* Rutland, Vermont, and Tokyo: Charles E. Tuttle Co., 1955.

Rutt, Joan, and Mattielli, Sandra, eds. *Lee Wade's Korean Cookbook.* Seoul: Pomso Publishers, 1974.

Sandler, Sandy Takako. *The American Book of Japanese Cooking.* Harrisburg, Pa.: Stackpole Books, 1974.

Sasaki, Naosuke, M.D. "The Relationship of Salt Intake to Hypertension in the Japanese." *Geriatrics* 19(10): October 1964.

Schumann, Dolly and Jack. *Low Carbohydrate Cookery.* Rutland, Vermont, and Tokyo: Charles E. Tuttle Co., 1966.

Solomon, Charmaine. *The Complete Asian Cookbook.* New York: McGraw Hill Book Co., 1976.

Sonakul, Sibpan. *Everyday Siamese Dishes.* Bangkok: The Chatra Press, 1952.

Spunt, Georges. *The Step-By-Step Chinese Cookbook.* New York: Thomas Y. Crowell Co., 1973.

Steinberg, Rafael. *The Cooking of Japan.* New York: Time-Life Books, 1967.

―――. *Pacific and Southeast Asian Cooking.* New York: Time-Life Books, 1974.

Thailand into the 80s. Office of the Prime Minister, Royal Thai Government, 1979.

Tropp, Barbara. *The Modern Art of Chinese Cooking.* New York: William Morrow and Co., 1982.

Tseng, Rose. *Chinese Cooking Made Easy.* Rutland, Vermont, and Tokyo: Charles E. Tuttle Co., 1963.

Tsuda, Nobuko. *Sushi Made Easy.* New York and Tokyo: John Weatherhill, Inc., 1982.

Tsuji, Shizuo. *Japanese Cooking: A Simple Art.* New York and Tokyo: Kodansha International, 1980.

Ueshima, Hirotsuga, et. al. "Dietary Intake and Serum Total Cholesterol Level: Their Relationship to Different Lifestyles in Several Japanese Populations." *Circulation* 66(3): September 1982.

Vermeulen, Rita T., R.D., et al. "Effect of Water Rinsing on Sodium Content of Selected Foods." *Journal of the American Dietetic Association* 82(4): April 1983.

Villaneuva, Eva S. and Poethig, Eunice B. *Filipino Family Cookbook.* Quezon City: New Day Publishers, 1972.

Wilson, Marie M. *Siamese Cookery.* Rutland, Vermont, and Tokyo: Charles E. Tuttle Co., 1965.

Recipe Index, by Country

JAPAN   3

Recipe Index, by Food Category

350

Soups

Meats

Yogurt Dishes

INDIA & PAKISTAN

Doughs and Batters

CHINA

INDONESIA, MALAYSIA & SINGAPORE

JAPAN

KOREA

Desserts

CHINA

INDIA & PAKISTAN

INDONESIA, MALAYSIA & SINGAPORE

JAPAN

KOREA

THE PHILIPPINES

THAILAND

VIETNAM